WHO IS THIS KING OF GLORY?

WHO IS THIS KING OF GLORY?

Experiencing The Fullness of Christ's Work in Our Lives

TONY EVANS

MOODY PRESS

CHICAGO

All Scripture quotations are taken from the *New American Standard
Bible,* © 1960, 1962, 1963, 1968, 1971, 1972, 1973, 1975, and 1977 by The
Lockman Foundation, La Habra, Calif. Used by permission.

ISBN: 0-8024-3922-5

Printed in the United States of America

*This book is lovingly dedicated
to my sisters-in-law,
Elizabeth Cannings
and Ruth Ann Cannings,
whose flames for Christ continue
to burn brightly*

CONTENTS

PART THREE
THE PURSUIT OF CHRIST

WITH GRATITUDE

I want to say a special word of thanks to my friend and editor, Philip Rawley, for his excellent help in the preparation of this manuscript; and to Greg Thornton, Bill Thrasher, and Cheryl Dunlop and the rest of the team at Moody Press for their encouragement and quality work on this project.

INTRODUCTION

We live in a day of celebrity worship. The advertising industry on Madison Avenue has done an extraordinary job of creating heroes and stars, people who have reached a recognized status in life because of their accomplishments, their wealth, or some other notable reason.

Celebrities grab our attention. People want to get close to them, to get an autograph or even a glimpse of the famous person. Sometimes people crowd around just to see the car or limousine carrying a celebrity. People watch the films or television programs of Hollywood celebrities. They go to the ball games of their sports heroes. They read about their favorites in the newspapers.

But one problem with human celebrities is that their status is always temporary. As time goes on, their significance inevitably dims. Youth and beauty fade as someone younger and more beautiful comes along to replace yesterday's star. Or athletic skills erode, followed by the tearful retirement announcement.

Even if a professional athlete winds up in his sport's Hall of Fame, he's still an ex-ballplayer. The next generation of young people will barely recognize his name, if they hear it at all.

During my day, for example, the top celebrity spot in professional basketball was accorded to Julius Erving, "Dr. J." We thought we would never see anyone do on a basketball court the things Dr. J. did. But one day he was supplanted by a young man named Michael Jordan. It doesn't matter what arena of human activity or what person you can name, human celebrities dim and pass from the scene.

But one celebrity has glory that will never dim, and His fame will never decrease. He is, in fact, the only truly worthy celebrity in the universe. As time passes, He attracts more followers and His recognition increases.

This celebrity was born apart from the laws of nature, raised in poverty in an obscure little town by parents with no status or "name recognition." Yet in infancy, this celebrity startled a king. In childhood, He confounded the most learned men of His day. And in adulthood, He ruled the course of nature—even though He only once crossed the borders of the land in which He was born.

This celebrity could walk on water and heal broken bodies, even though He never took a course in medicine. He could also heal broken hearts and raise the dead.

Jesus Christ is the only authentic Celebrity in the universe. He never wrote a song, yet more songs have been written about Him than about any other person in history. He never wrote a book, yet entire chains of bookstores cannot hold the volumes written about Him.

Time itself is divided into two segments by the birth of Jesus Christ, and there is hardly a person in the world who has not heard of Him. In fact, thousands of people risk their lives traveling to the ends of the earth to tell others about the glory of this Celebrity.

Without a doubt, Jesus Christ is the ultimate Celebrity. Join me as we examine together the wonder of history's only authentic Celebrity and answer the question, "Who is this King of Glory?"

PART ONE

THE UNIQUENESS OF CHRIST

CHAPTER ONE

THE UNIQUENESS OF THE PERSON OF CHRIST

Jesus Christ is *the* unique, one-of-a-kind person in all of history.

Jesus has undoubtedly been the subject of more devotion, more study, more books, and more songs than anyone else who has ever lived. His appearance on earth was so monumental that history divided around His life, B.C. and A.D. Time only has meaning to us as it is defined by the presence of Jesus Christ in history.

On one occasion Jesus' disciples voiced the question that people have been asking about Him for two thousand years. Having witnessed His miraculous calming of the sea, the Twelve looked at one another and asked in amazement, "What kind of a man is this?" (Matthew 8:27). The Gospels and the rest of the New Testament were written to answer that most important of all questions and explain its implications for our lives.

The person and work of Jesus Christ is a subject so big that we will spend all eternity learning about Him. In these pages we want to explore this greatest of all subjects, considering the uniqueness and authority of Jesus, and then tackling the question of what it means to pursue Jesus Christ by giving Him the worship and devotion of our lives.

I want to begin this study by considering what the Bible teaches about the person of Jesus Christ. We can make a number of opening statements here.

For instance, Jesus is unique because He is the only person who existed before He was born and who is today what

He has always been. He is the only person whose conception had no relationship to His origin, yet He was not a man before His incarnation. By virtue of His birth as a man, Jesus Christ is now both Son of God and Son of Man. He is Deity, and He is humanity. Jesus is the God-man.

JESUS CHRIST'S DEITY

Let's begin with the deity of Jesus Christ, His nature as "very God of very God," to use a phrase theologians use to try to declare Christ's divine nature.

A lot of people respect Jesus Christ as a great person, an inspiring teacher, and a great leader, but reject His deity. This is heresy. You cannot hold Jesus in high regard while denying He is the eternal God, a point Jesus Himself made quite clear to the rich young man (Mark 10:17–18).

Jesus Christ clearly and directly claimed to be God when He said "I and the Father are one" (John 10:30). This statement is significant because the word *one* is neuter in form meaning that He and the Father were one, perfect in nature and unified in essence. This was a personal claim of total equality with the Father. Those who heard this statement clearly understood it is to be a claim to deity, for they immediately tried to stone Him for blasphemy because He made Himself equal to God (v. 33).

Christ's Pre-existence

We could use a number of lines of argument to demonstrate Jesus' deity. I want to consider four points, beginning with His pre-existence.

We have already said that Christ existed before His birth. The prophet stated Christ's pre-existence this way: "As for you, Bethlehem Ephrathah, too little to be among the clans of Judah, from you One will go forth for Me to be ruler in Israel. His goings forth are from long ago, from the days of eternity" (Micah 5:2).

This is a significant verse for several reasons, not the least of which is Micah's accuracy in prophesying Jesus' birthplace. I have been to Bethlehem, and even today it's a small town. It was even smaller and more insignificant in Jesus' day, so for Micah to predict Bethlehem as Messiah's birthplace was, humanly speaking, like finding a needle in a haystack.

But notice what the prophet said about this One who would be born in Bethlehem. He had no beginning; His existence reaches back into eternity past.

Isaiah gave Jesus Christ the title "Eternal Father" (Isaiah 9:6), or "Father of eternity," in his prophecy of Jesus' first and second comings. Since Jesus is the Father of eternity, He is also the Father or initiator of time.

But the only way Jesus could be the initiator of time is if He existed before time. This verse speaks of His pre-existence and tells us that Christ is of a different nature than anyone else who has ever lived.

The prophets were not the only ones who taught Jesus' pre-existence. Jesus declared it Himself in an exchange that stunned and infuriated His Jewish detractors.

They had accused Jesus of having a demon (John 8:52) because He claimed that anyone who believed in Him would not see death. They reviled Him and asked this question: "Whom do You make Yourself out to be?" (v. 53).

That's a great question, but they didn't like Jesus' answer, especially when He said, "Your father Abraham rejoiced to see My day" (v. 56). The Jews replied, "You are not yet fifty years old, and have You seen Abraham?" (v. 57). They were getting upset because Jesus was making claims no man had ever made before.

Then Jesus made this crucial statement: "Truly, truly, I say to you, before Abraham was born, I am" (v. 58).

Don't miss the importance of the verb tenses Jesus used here. He was making an incredibly important claim. He did not say, "Before Abraham was born, I *was*," but "I am."

This is significant because "I AM" is the name God gave Himself when He sent Moses to redeem Israel from Egypt. "God said to Moses . . . 'Thus you shall say to the sons of Israel, "I AM has sent me to you" ' " (Exodus 3:14).

This is the name we transliterate as *Yahweh*, the self-existing God. This name describes God's personal self-sufficient and eternal nature. The eternal God has no past, so He cannot say "I was." He has no future, so cannot say "I will be." God exists in an eternal now. Time is only meaningful to us because we are not independently self-sufficient and eternal.

When Jesus told the Jews that He predated Abraham, He was claiming not only pre-existence, but Deity.

Jesus' Equality with God the Father

There is another important claim in what Jesus told His Jewish opponents in John 8. By taking to Himself the most personal and hallowed name of God, Jesus was making Himself equal with God.

His hearers understood this perfectly, because they picked up stones to stone Jesus for blasphemy (John 8:59).

Jesus' claim is even stronger in John 5:17–18. "'My Father is working until now, and I Myself am working.' For this cause therefore the Jews were seeking all the more to kill Him, because He not only was breaking the Sabbath, but also was calling God His own Father, making Himself equal with God."

These people understood Jesus to mean that He was placing Himself on equal standing with God because He was claiming to be of the same essence as God.

The Bible elsewhere equates Jesus with God. Genesis 1:1 says that God created the world. But Colossians 1:16 says that by Jesus Christ, "All things were created." Either we have two Creators, or the God of Genesis 1 is the God of Colossians 1.

John made the identical claim for Jesus when he began his gospel by declaring, "In the beginning was the Word, and the Word was with God, and the Word *was* God" (John 1:1, italics added). So the Word is distinct from God, yet the Word is equal with God.

John doesn't leave us in doubt about the identity of the Word. "And the Word became flesh, and dwelt among us, and we beheld His glory, glory as of the only begotten from the Father, full of grace and truth" (John 1:14).

Then verse 18 adds, "No man has seen God at any time; the only begotten God, who is in the bosom of the Father, He has explained Him."

When you put these three verses together, you get quite a picture of Jesus Christ. He is distinct from God, yet equal with God. He took on human flesh for the purpose of making the invisible God visible to human beings.

The writer of Hebrews said that Jesus "is the radiance of

[God's] glory and the exact representation of His nature, and upholds all things by the word of His power" (Hebrews 1:3). So don't let anyone tell you that Jesus is just a great Man or merely *a* son of God. He is God the Son.

There is even stronger language in Hebrews 1:8, because here God Himself is the speaker. "Of the Son He says, 'Thy throne, O God, is forever and ever.'" God the Father is calling His Son "God."

Nothing could be clearer or more direct than that. No wonder Paul wrote that in Jesus, "All the fulness of Deity dwells in bodily form" (Colossians 2:9). This cannot be said about anyone else. Jesus claimed equality with God, and the writers of Scripture consistently support that claim.

Jesus' Acceptance of Worship

Another strong argument for Jesus' deity is the fact that He readily accepted the worship of His disciples and others. For a mere human being to do that would be blasphemy. But Jesus' disciples came to recognize Him as God, and after Jesus' resurrection and ascension they had no hesitation in making that known.

One example of this worship is that great scene in John 20 when Jesus appeared to the disciples after His resurrection. Thomas had been absent during an earlier visit, and he said he would not believe unless he saw with his own eyes (v. 25).

So Jesus came to the disciples and invited Thomas to touch His hands and side and to believe (v. 27). Thomas responded, "My Lord and my God!" (v. 28).

Not only did Jesus accept Thomas's declaration of worship, but He said that all those who believe in Him are "blessed" (v. 29). Notice that when Thomas said, "My Lord and my God," Jesus said in effect, "Yes, I am He." He accepted the worship that is due to Deity alone.

We can see worship being offered to Jesus throughout the Gospels. Earlier in Jesus' ministry, the disciples worshiped Him after He calmed a storm (Matthew 14:33). Even demons acknowledged His deity, although Jesus silenced them (Mark 1:23–25).

But Jesus Himself offered the strongest proof of His deity. He answered Satan's temptation with the statement,

"Begone, Satan! For it is written, 'You shall worship the Lord your God, and serve Him only'" (Matthew 4:10). Jesus said worship belongs to God alone, yet He received that worship. Only God could say what Jesus said.

Christ's Membership in the Trinity

Titus 2:13 tells us that Jesus Christ is "our great God and Savior." The Bible teaches that Jesus Christ is the Son of God, and yet He is fully God. It also teaches that God the Father is God. The question the early church grappled with was how Jesus could be God, but also be distinct from the Father as the Son.

A child at our church in Dallas once asked me, "Pastor, if Jesus is God, then who was He talking to on the cross when He said, 'My God, My God, why hast Thou forsaken Me?' Was He talking to Himself?"

That's a very perceptive question. Jesus was not talking to Himself on the cross, but to the Father. We can say this with confidence because the Bible teaches that the Godhead is composed of three distinct, yet coequal persons who share the same divine substance: Father, Son, and Holy Spirit. The term *trinity* is used for this foundational truth.

So when we talk about God, we could be talking about either the Godhead corporately or about any one of the three persons who make up the Godhead. God's Word teaches Jesus' deity because it presents Him as a member of the Godhead, the divine Trinity.

Jesus identified Himself as distinct from the Father when He called Himself "the Son of God" (John 10:36). Yet, just a few minutes before He said that, He also said, "I and the Father are one" (v. 30).

The unity of the Trinity, and yet the distinction of its three members, is evident in Jesus' commission to His disciples. He told us to baptize people "in the name of the Father and the Son and the Holy Spirit" (Matthew 28:19). Normally we would expect to read the word *names* (plural) here, because Jesus mentioned three names. But He used the singular, *name*. So we must conclude either that Jesus was mistaken, or that He used the singular on purpose because the three members of the Godhead make up one entity. There's no question which of these conclusions is correct.

The name of God is singular because the triune God is one God. This is the consistent teaching of Scripture. Paul closed one of his letters with this benediction: "The grace of the Lord Jesus Christ, and the love of God, and the fellowship of the Holy Spirit, be with you all" (2 Corinthians 13:14). Paul integrated the three persons of the Godhead because they are one.

The Trinity is not an easy concept to grasp because there is nothing like it in the universe. Without the Bible we would have no knowledge of this kind of existence. It is outside our realm of understanding to think of one God existing in three equal persons who are distinct personalities while sharing the same essence.

There have been a number of illustrations suggested for the Trinity, but they all fall short of the mark because the Trinity is unique.

For example, someone has suggested the illustration of water, ice, and steam. All are made up of the same essence, yet they are distinct forms of that essence.

The problem with this is that if we apply it to the Godhead, it makes it appear that God appears sometimes as Father, sometimes as Son, and sometimes as Spirit. But that is a heresy because the fullness of the Godhead is always present in each member of the Trinity.

Another common illustration of the Trinity is the egg. An egg has three parts—the shell, the yolk, and the white. The problem with this illustration is that none of these three parts by itself can be defined as an egg. They are just part of the egg. But the fullness of Deity resides in each individual member of the Godhead. Jesus Christ isn't part God; He is fully God. The same can be said of the Father and the Holy Spirit.

The best illustration I have come up with for the Trinity is a pretzel. A typical pretzel has three circles or holes formed by the dough.

These holes are distinct from one another, and each hole is complete within itself. Yet the three holes are interconnected because they belong to the same piece of dough. They have the same character. There is only one pretzel, not three.

This is not a perfect illustration, but I think it gets closer to the point. The biblical doctrine of the Trinity establishes the full deity of Jesus Christ. He is God.

JESUS CHRIST'S HUMANITY

Jesus is also man. He partakes of the nature of Deity because He is the Son of God. He also partakes of the nature of humanity because He is the "Son of Man." In fact, this was Jesus' favorite title for Himself.

In this section we want to talk about Jesus' humanity, because it is this union of Deity and humanity that makes Jesus unique in history. Jesus left heaven to take on human flesh, which is what we mean by the term *incarnation*. Jesus became flesh and blood, an event that was prophesied in Scripture hundreds of years before Jesus was ever born.

The Distinctives of His Human Nature

We need to look at two prophecies from the book of Isaiah and their fulfillment in the New Testament, because putting these passages together gives us a picture of Jesus' human nature. He was fully human, but He was distinct in several important ways.

The most important distinctive of Jesus' human nature is that He was born of a virgin. In Isaiah 7:14 the prophet wrote, "The Lord Himself will give you a sign: Behold, a virgin will be with child and bear a son, and she will call His name Immanuel."

Then in a verse we have already noted, Isaiah 9:6, we read: "A child will be born to us, a son will be given to us." Notice how careful the Holy Spirit is with the language here.

The Son is "given," not born. Why? Because as the Son of God, Jesus already existed. But the child is "born," a reference to Jesus' birth in Bethlehem. God the Father gave the Son to us through a supernaturally wrought conception in human flesh through the process of a human birth.

Paul brought these prophecies from Isaiah together when he wrote, "When the fulness of the time came, God sent forth His Son, born of a woman, born under the Law" (Galatians 4:4).

God "sent forth" the Son because the Son is given (Isaiah 9:6). Jesus was "born of a woman" because a child was to be born. This is the incarnation of Jesus Christ.

The story of Jesus' birth confirms His distinctiveness as God in the flesh. Matthew says that the events of Jesus' birth happened "that what was spoken by the Lord through the prophet [that is, Isaiah] might be fulfilled." Then Matthew quoted Isaiah 7:14 to explain the angel's appearance to Joseph (Matthew 1:21–23). Immanuel means "God with us," a description of the baby who was to be born.

Back in Matthew 1:16 there is another testimony to the distinctiveness of Jesus' human nature. As Matthew listed the Lord's genealogy, he said, "To Jacob was born Joseph the husband of Mary, by whom was born Jesus, who is called Christ."

The phrase "by whom" is critical here, because it is a feminine singular relative pronoun. That is very important because the Bible is saying that Jesus was conceived through Mary, but not by Joseph. This, in other words, is a careful witness to His virgin birth.

Joseph is important in Jesus' genealogy, because Matthew is showing that Joseph was descended from David. Since Joseph was Jesus' legal—though not biological— father, Jesus had a rightful claim to the throne of David.

Jesus was conceived by the Holy Spirit (Luke 1:35), and not by Joseph, in order that His human nature might be sinless. This is why He would be called "the Son of God" at His birth. Jesus' humanity had both a heavenly origin through the power of the Holy Spirit and an earthly origin through Mary.

The fact that Jesus' nature is different from ours in terms of being sinless and virgin born has led some people in church history to deny that His humanity was real. They believed He just appeared to be human. But that is another heresy that denies the reality of His life and His death for sin.

Make no mistake; Jesus was fully human. The Gospels demonstrate this again and again. He was the God who made everything, the God who never becomes weary or needs to sleep. Yet in His humanity He could be tired and thirsty (John 4:6–7). We know Jesus had human emotions because He wept at Lazarus's grave (John 11:35) and felt compassion for people (Matthew 9:36). He also loved us with an everlasting love. And He had a human soul and spirit (Matthew 26:38; Luke 23:46), which all human beings have.

The Perfections of His Human Nature

Some people have a problem with Jesus' human nature because they assume if He was human, He had to be sinful. Not when the Holy Spirit oversees the birth process. We have already noted that Jesus was conceived by the Holy Spirit, bypassing the sinful human nature of Joseph as the father.

The same objection is raised about the Bible. If the Bible was written by human beings, the argument goes, it must have errors in it. That might be true except for one thing: The Holy Spirit oversaw the writing of Scripture to preserve it from error (2 Peter 1:21).

What the Spirit did with the written Word of God, He did with the incarnate Word of God, Jesus Christ. The Spirit superintended the conception of both the written and the incarnate Word so that there was no human contamination in either.

Lest you think all of this is just the musings of theologians, you need to realize that everything Jesus did, and is doing, for you and me is tied to His sinless humanity.

Paul said that God made Jesus, "who knew no sin," to become sin on our behalf so we might partake of God's righteousness (2 Corinthians 5:21). If Jesus were just a sinful human being, His death would have done nothing to save us.

According to Hebrews 4:15, Jesus' present ministry in heaven as our Great High Priest is also dependent upon His sinlessness. He could not help us in our weakness if He were as sinful and weak as we are.

THE PERFECT UNION OF
CHRIST'S TWO NATURES

The two natures of Jesus Christ form what theologians call the hypostatic union. This is a big term that simply means undiminished Deity and perfect humanity united forever in one person.

In other words, Jesus was no less God when He became a perfect Man. He was fully human, but without sin. It's important that we understand Jesus is one person, not two. He is the God-man, not sometimes God and sometimes man. He is one person with two natures.

Jesus has a perfect human and divine nature, which makes Him unique. Nobody else is God become a man—God in the flesh.

One passage puts all of this together: Philippians 2:5–11. We will deal with this phenomenal passage in greater detail in the chapter on Christ's humiliation, but here I want to hit the highlights to show you that this text teaches us how we should live in response to what Jesus did in taking on human nature.

Paul prefaced this passage by calling believers to be humble rather than prideful, to be concerned about the interests of others rather than just their own interests—which is the way Jesus lived when He came to earth.

A Picture of Jesus' Deity

Then Paul wrote, "Have this attitude in yourselves which was also in Christ Jesus, who, although He existed in the form of God, did not regard equality with God a thing to be grasped" (vv. 5–6).

This is a tremendous statement of Jesus' deity. He existed as God prior to His birth in Bethlehem. He was equal with the Father in divine essence. Here is a succinct statement of what the Bible says about Jesus' deity.

A Picture of Jesus' Humanity

But then we come to Jesus' humanity. He "emptied Himself, taking the form of a bond-servant, and being made in the likeness of men" (v. 7). Does this mean that Jesus emptied Himself of His deity?

Not at all. It was impossible that Jesus Christ could cease being God. This famous verse is not talking about what Jesus emptied Himself of, but what He emptied Himself into.

It's like pouring something from one pitcher into another. Jesus took all of His deity and poured it into another vessel, the "form of a bond-servant." He didn't stop being who He is, but He changed the form of who He is.

When He came to earth, Jesus moved from His preexistent, glorified form and poured the fullness of His deity into a human form.

Simply becoming a human being was enough of a step down for the Son of God. But Jesus became a "bond-servant," a slave, the lowest possible position on the social ladder in that day. We could say that He who is very God of very God became "very slave of very slave."

That's why most of the people in Jesus' day missed His birth. They were looking for a king, not a servant. They expected a king to be born in a palace to rich parents, not in a stable to the poorest of the poor. And a baby king is wrapped in fine clothes, not in grave clothes, which is what Mary used to wrap around Jesus.

Jesus came as a lowly servant, which is good news for us because that means there is no one with whom Jesus cannot identify. If you are not very high on the social ladder, Jesus understands because He has been there. And no matter how high you may be, Jesus has been higher because He is the Son of God.

When Jesus took on flesh, He was "made in the likeness of men" (Philippians 2:7). That simply means that even though Jesus was much more than just a man, those who saw Him would think He was just a man.

Jesus didn't go around with a halo around His head. He looked like a man. Luke 2:52 says Jesus grew in the same ways as other people: physically, spiritually, emotionally, and socially. Isaiah said Jesus had "no stately form or majesty" in His human appearance that would make people stop and look twice (Isaiah 53:2).

Jesus was not only born in humble circumstances, but "He humbled Himself by becoming obedient to the point of death, even death on a cross" (Philippians 2:8). In His sacrifice for our sins, Jesus humbly accepted the most painful, humiliating form of death the Romans could inflict.

In Jesus' crucifixion we get an idea of what is meant when the Bible says He emptied Himself. Jesus chose to lay aside the independent use of His divine attributes, submitting Himself completely to His Father's will.

How do we know this? Because when Peter attacked the high priest's servant, Jesus told Peter He could call more than twelve legions of angels to rescue Him if He desired (Matthew 26:53).

But Jesus did not do that because in order for His sacrifice to be effective for sin, He had to suffer and die and defeat Satan as a perfect Man. He could not simply call on His divine power to wipe out Satan, but had to submit Himself to death.

The Only Sensible Response

But Philippians 2 does not end with verse 8. Because Jesus was obedient to death, "God highly exalted Him, and bestowed on Him the name which is above every name, that at the name of Jesus every knee should bow . . . and that every tongue should confess that Jesus Christ is Lord, to the glory of God the Father" (vv. 9–11).

When we understand the uniqueness of Jesus Christ, only one response makes sense—to fall on our knees and confess Him as Savior and Lord.

There are two ways we can do this. We can either bow in humble submission today, confessing Jesus and receiving Him as our Savior, or we will be forced to bow to Him at the judgment. But every creature in heaven, on earth, and in hell is going to bow to Jesus Christ.

When you bow to Jesus in repentance and submission, He becomes Lord of your life. And when He becomes Lord of your life, He takes over. That means He deserves all of your respect, honor, and obedience because of who He is and what He has done for you.

We spend a lot of time paying respect to people in authority in this world. That's OK, because the Bible tells us to honor those in positions of authority over us. In some cases, we have to respect people's positions even if the people themselves are not worthy of respect.

But let me tell you the difference between the honor we give to other people and the honor Jesus alone deserves. The honor we give to a judge or a police officer, for example, is called *ascribed* honor.

That is, we ascribe or assign honor to these people because of the robe or the uniform they wear. Apart from the robe or the uniform, though, they are just ordinary men and women.

But the honor Jesus Christ commands is *intrinsic* honor, not just ascribed honor. He is worthy of honor because of who He is. Honor and glory are intrinsic to His nature. They are not simply a matter of His position. They don't depend on a piece of clothing or a symbol of authority like a badge.

Jesus is King of the universe and Lord of our lives. He is the unique God-man to whom every knee will someday bow. The wisest thing you and I can do is bow to Him today!

CHAPTER TWO

THE UNIQUENESS OF CHRIST IN PROPHECY AND TYPOLOGY

Since Jesus Christ is unique in all of history, the focal point of everything God is doing in the world, we would expect Jesus to occupy a unique place in Bible prophecy and typology. And He does.

Biblical prophecy and typology are related in the sense that both of them present us with pictures of Christ before He came to earth. Prophecy foretells the coming of Christ the first time to be the Savior from sin and the second time to rule as King.

Prophecy is found in both the Old and New Testaments. Typology is also a study for which we need both testaments. That's because the pictures or types are the means by which the Old Testament foreshadows the person and work of Christ. A type is an Old Testament picture that reveals and points forward to a New Testament truth. The New Testament is the fulfillment of the type, the reality behind the shadow.

I want to deal with prophecy first, and then turn to typology and the ways in which the Old Testament portrays Christ.

The central truth of prophecy as it relates to Jesus Christ is the fact that He is both the prophesied Messiah of the Old Testament and the prophesied King who will rule not only over Israel, but over the world.

John the Baptist hit the issue of prophecy squarely on the head when he sent some disciples from his prison cell to ask Jesus, "Are You the Expected One, or do we look for someone else?" (Luke 7:19).

John was asking Jesus if He was the prophesied Messiah. If not, John and his disciples needed to be doing something else and looking elsewhere for God's redemption. John wavered in doubt for a minute, and Jesus reassured him. But the point I want you to see is that prophecy is critical to our understanding of who Jesus Christ is.

My purpose here is not to deal with every prophecy in Scripture related to Jesus. That would take a book in itself. My purpose is to show you that Jesus is the focus of Bible prophecy and is therefore unique.

THE SUBJECT OF PROPHECY

I want to do that by going to a familiar passage of Scripture in which the risen Christ Himself teaches about His central place in prophecy. Jesus does this in Luke 24, during a walk with two of His disciples to the village of Emmaus the very evening of resurrection day. Later that night Jesus appeared to the eleven remaining apostles and other disciples and taught further truth concerning Himself.

The two men on the Emmaus road were talking about the recent uproar in Jerusalem over this Man named Jesus. This was not just another ordinary weekend. The whole town was in pandemonium over Jesus, who was called "King of the Jews" and who claimed to be the Son of God, but who had been crucified a few days earlier. Now it was reported that He was alive again. His grave was empty.

No wonder there was no place a person could go in Jerusalem where people were not discussing Jesus. Everybody was talking about the events that had just happened. So it was natural that these two disciples would be discussing this incredible weekend on their way home.

The Things About Jesus

The Bible says that as they walked, "Jesus Himself approached, and began traveling with them. But their eyes were prevented from recognizing Him" (Luke 24:15–16).

Jesus asked them, "What are these words that you are exchanging with one another?" (v. 17). Cleopas (v. 18) and the other disciple must have been having quite a discussion, because the word *exchanging* means a heated debate. They couldn't believe Jesus did not know about what had happened in Jerusalem.

So they said, "The things about Jesus the Nazarene, who was a prophet mighty in deed and word in the sight of God and all the people, and how the chief priests and our rulers delivered Him up to the sentence of death, and crucified Him. But we were hoping that it was He who was going to redeem Israel" (vv. 19–21).

The men went on to tell Jesus how some women had gone to the tomb early that morning and found it empty, and how some other disciples had gone to verify the story (vv. 21–24).

This is the setting for Jesus' teaching. The thing you need to note is the disappointment in these disciples' voices (v. 21). Evidently, they didn't think the reports of Jesus' resurrection were really true.

The Prophetic Teacher

The problem is these disciples were uninformed about the truth of the events they had just experienced. Their lack of faith had caused them either to forget, or misunderstand, the prophetic word concerning the Messiah. So Jesus began to enlighten them:

"O foolish men and slow of heart to believe in all that the prophets have spoken! Was it not necessary for the Christ to suffer these things and to enter into His glory?" And beginning with Moses and with all the prophets, He explained to them the things concerning Himself in all the Scriptures. (vv. 25–27)

You can't get a better situation than this. Here are people who are thoroughly confused and discouraged because things didn't work out the way they should have, and it seems as if God's prophetic plan has backfired. But Jesus Himself comes along to clarify the situation.

Luke says Jesus enlightened these men by using the Old Testament to explain His coming and His ministry—"the things concerning Himself in all the Scriptures."

As they walked, Jesus walked these men through the Scriptures to bring them to an understanding of who He was, what was happening, and how they were to perceive the events they had just experienced.

In other words, Jesus taught from the Scriptures that

prophesied about Him. Even though we do not know exactly what He said to them, we know that everything Jesus taught was about Himself. He is the subject of prophecy. Revelation 19:10 says "the testimony of Jesus is the spirit of prophecy." Studying prophecy is like boarding a spacecraft and orbiting above the earth. You can see things more clearly because you see them at a distance. You get the big picture. Prophecy allows us to see things from a distance of many miles and many years.

The Wise Men are a good example. They saw Jesus' star from a great distance, closed in on it, and found Jesus. In order for the prophetic Word of God to become real to you, you have to be willing to take the trip. You must be willing to pursue that which God has spoken, because in your pursuit you are exercising faith that what God has said is true.

The two disciples from Emmaus had the greatest Teacher teaching from the greatest Book about the greatest person— Himself. And there were only two in the congregation.

The problem here was that the men were slow to believe. Later, Jesus said to the group of followers, "Why are you troubled, and why do doubts arise in your hearts?" (Luke 24:38). If you are going to understand the prophetic Word, you must be willing to give God your heart, not only your head.

THE CONTENT OF PROPHECY

After Jesus revealed Himself to the pair in Emmaus and then vanished, they hurried back to Jerusalem that same night. There they found the apostles and others, and as they were telling their story, Jesus came into the room and conversed with them (Luke 24:28–43). It was time for more teaching.

Let's look at the content of prophecy as it relates to Jesus. He summarized it for them, but first He said, "All things which are written about Me in the Law of Moses and the Prophets and the Psalms must be fulfilled" (v. 44). Here Jesus declared that the entire Old Testament spoke prophetically of Him.

Jesus' summary of these prophecies included these facts: "Thus it is written, that the Christ should suffer and rise again from the dead on the third day; and that repentance for forgiveness of sins should be proclaimed in His name to all the nations, beginning from Jerusalem" (vv. 46–47).

The Prophecies Announced

The death and resurrection of "the Christ," the Messiah, for the forgiveness of sin is the summary and the heart of prophecy. The entire Old Testament can be summed up as looking forward to the coming of the Messiah. This prophecy was first given at the very beginning, when God told Satan that the Seed would come which would crush Satan's head (Genesis 3:15).

The patriarch Israel said this Seed would come from the tribe of Judah (Genesis 49:10). And God told David that his throne would endure forever (2 Samuel 7:16) because David would have a greater Son, the Messiah, who would rule and reign. So the Old Testament prophecies concerning Messiah were very specific.

Prophecies of Christ's Birth

Now let's "fast-forward" to the opening chapter of the New Testament, Matthew 1:1–17, the genealogy of Jesus Christ. This is the part most people skip over so they can get to the Christmas story.

Big mistake! This record and the genealogy in Luke are critical to the unfolding of the prophetic story concerning Jesus. They demonstrate that Jesus' claim to be Messiah and King, the ruler from the line of David, was legitimate, because He was the Son of David both legally and biologically.

In other words, the Gospels' genealogies are marvelous testimonies to the subject we have been talking about in this chapter, the fact that Jesus is the unique focus and culmination of prophecy.

These written records were especially important for the Jews who would come along after Jesus. This is because in A.D. 70 all of Israel's genealogical records were lost when the Roman army under Titus sacked Jerusalem and burned the temple, where the records were stored.

Someone who was claiming to be Messiah, the rightful ruler from the line of David, needed to be able to trace his lineage back to David (2 Samuel 7:12–16; Isaiah 11:1–10). Therefore, God preserved the genealogical record of Jesus even though everyone else's records were destroyed. As I said, Jesus is the focus of prophecy.

Before we move on to consider the genealogy in Luke, let me point out a problem in Matthew 1:11, which mentions a man named Jeconiah. Remember, for Jesus to have proper claim to the title Messiah, it had to be proven that He was of the line of David.

But Jeconiah presents us with a problem, because God pronounced a curse on this faithless descendant of David (Jeremiah 22:28–30). This curse was that no child—that is, no physical descendant—of Jeconiah would ever succeed sitting on the throne of David.

The problem is Joseph was a physical descendant of Jeconiah. Had Jesus been Joseph's biological son, He would have been prevented from sitting on the throne of David by this curse.

However, Jesus was conceived not by Joseph, but by the Holy Spirit. Joseph was Jesus' legal father, but not His biological father. That's why Matthew 1:16 uses the feminine pronoun to refer to Jesus' birth, as I pointed out in the previous chapter.

Jesus bypassed the curse of Jeconiah and yet retained His legal right to the throne. Satan's attempt to corrupt the Messianic line had been thwarted.

But the Messiah still had to have a biological tie to David, because Old Testament prophecy specified Him as a Son of David. Luke's genealogy (3:23–38) deals with this need, since the lineage of Jesus is traced back to David through "Nathan, the son of David" (v. 31).

Luke takes Jesus' genealogy all the way back to Adam (v. 38). Why is it important that Jesus be connected to the Garden of Eden? Because of the prophecy of the righteous Seed that would come and crush Satan (Genesis 3:15). God is removing all doubt that Jesus is the fulfillment of prophecy.

Now about Nathan. He was a brother of Solomon, one of David's sons who never held the throne. Matthew traced the genealogy of Jesus through Solomon (Matthew 1:7), while Luke went through Nathan.

That's important because since Solomon *did* become king and Jesus is Solomon's legal descendant through Joseph, Jesus has a legitimate legal claim to the title of Messiah. But Jesus' biological tie to David was established through Nathan by Mary, since Nathan had a different line of descent than Solomon.

The point is that no matter how you trace this thing, Jesus was qualified to declare Himself Israel's Messiah. And any Jew who wanted to verify the record could do so because God preserved Jesus' lineage.

Prophecies of Christ's Death

Not only do the Old Testament prophecies deal with Christ's birth, they also deal with His death.

One classic prophecy that describes the Messiah's death for sin is Isaiah 53. I want to pick up a few key verses from this great passage and then see how they were fulfilled in Jesus. Of the Messiah, Isaiah wrote:

> He was despised and forsaken of men, a man of sorrows, and acquainted with grief. . . . Surely our griefs He Himself bore, and our sorrows He carried; yet we ourselves esteemed Him stricken, smitten of God, and afflicted. But He was pierced through for our transgressions, He was crushed for our iniquities; the chastening for our well-being fell upon Him, and by His scourging we are healed. (vv. 3–5)

What a tremendous prophecy of Jesus' crucifixion. The apostle Peter, who witnessed the Lord's death, wrote to believers urging them to bear up under unjust suffering the way Jesus did. Then Peter said:

> You have been called for this purpose, since Christ also suffered for you, leaving you an example for you to follow in His steps, who committed no sin, nor was any deceit found in His mouth; and while being reviled, He did not revile in return; while suffering, He uttered no threats, but kept entrusting Himself to Him who judges righteously; and He Himself bore our sins in His body on the cross, that we might die to sin and live to righteousness; for by His wounds you were healed. (1 Peter 2:21–24)

Compare these two passages, and you'll see the fulfillment of Isaiah 53 in Peter's letter. Peter even quoted Isaiah's reference to Jesus' wounds. Peter also noted that Jesus did not answer His accusers, which is what Isaiah prophesied (Isaiah 53:7).

Psalm 22 contains another great prophecy that the New Testament applies to Jesus Christ in His death on the cross. The psalm opens with the cry, "My God, my God, why hast Thou forsaken me?" (v. 1), the very cry Jesus uttered from the cross.

The psalmist also said, "I am a worm, and not a man, a reproach of men, and despised by the people. All who see me sneer at me; they separate with the lip, they wag the head, saying, 'Commit yourself to the Lord; let Him deliver him; let Him rescue him, because He delights in him'" (vv. 6–8).

Luke said that when Jesus was on the cross, "Even the rulers were sneering at Him, saying, 'He saved others; let Him save Himself if this is the Christ of God'" (Luke 23:35).

Look back at Psalm 22. "I am poured out like water, and all my bones are out of joint" (v. 14). "They pierced my hands and my feet" (v. 16). "They divide my garments among them, and for my clothing they cast lots" (v. 18).

When a person hung on a cross through crucifixion, the weight of his own body dislocated his joints. Psalm 22 speaks prophetically of the manner of Jesus' death. He was pierced through His hands and feet. The soldiers gambled for His clothing (Matthew 27:35). Jesus' death was clearly prophesied, and He fulfilled every prophecy to the detail.

Prophecies of Christ's Resurrection

The final point of prophecy I want to mention is prophecy concerning Jesus' resurrection.

The first thing we need to remember is that Jesus predicted His own resurrection on several occasions, both to His disciples (Matthew 17:23; 20:19) and to unbelieving Jews (John 2:18–21). John said that after Jesus was raised, the disciples remembered what He said, and they believed (v. 22).

In his Pentecost sermon, Peter drew on an Old Testament prophecy to prove that Jesus was the Messiah (Acts 2:25–28). The passage Peter quoted is Psalm 16:8–11, in which David wrote:

I have set the Lord continually before me; because He is at my right hand, I will not be shaken. Therefore my heart is glad, and my glory rejoices; my flesh also will dwell securely. For Thou wilt not abandon my soul to

Sheol; neither wilt Thou allow Thy Holy One to undergo decay. (vv. 8–10)

In Acts 2:29–32 Peter made it clear that the fulfillment of this passage was in the life of Jesus Christ. David looked ahead and spoke prophetically about the Christ, the Messiah. David wasn't the one resurrected; Jesus was. And, Peter said, "We are all witnesses" to the fact that God raised Christ from the dead.

This is the uniqueness of Christ in prophecy. When you see the many ways the prophetic Word about Christ was fulfilled in His first coming, you can have confidence in the prophecies about His second coming and glorious rule (Daniel 7:14; 1 Peter 1:10–11). If you believe Christ rose from the dead yesterday and is alive today, then you can know that your tomorrow is going to be OK.

THE SUBJECT OF TYPOLOGY

We could say that typology is the other side of the coin of prophecy. The two are related, because just as God gave us a prophetic map in Scripture that points to Jesus, He also gave us pictures in the Old Testament that point to Jesus and remind us of Him. Remember, Christ is the theme of the Old Testament (Matthew 5:17; Luke 24:27, 44; John 5:39).

That's what a type is, an Old Testament picture of a New Testament reality. Many of the Old Testament's ceremonies, regulations, and even people were types of Christ in that they illustrated various aspects of His person and work.

Here's an example. When John the Baptist pointed to Jesus and cried out, "Behold, the Lamb of God who takes away the sin of the world!" (John 1:29), John was using an Old Testament type and saying Jesus was the fulfillment of that type.

All those sacrificial lambs offered in Israel to cover sin temporarily were a picture of the Lamb who would come and offer His blood to take away sin forever. That's typology.

This is why we need the whole Bible, by the way. If you have an Old Testament without the New Testament, then you don't have the full picture because the Old is fulfilled in the New.

But if you have a New Testament without the Old, then you aren't going to understand a lot of what is written in the New, because a large part of the New Testament explains, applies, and fulfills what was written in the Old Testament. This is especially true about Jesus Christ.

Jesus on Typology

Jesus was intensely interested in the Old Testament's typology about Himself. We can see that in Luke 24, the passage we studied at the beginning of this chapter.

When Jesus took those two disciples through the Old Testament and explained what the Scriptures said about Himself (vv. 27, 44), He was talking about typology as well as prophecy. We can say that because He began with "the Law of Moses" (v. 44), the first five books of the Old Testament, which are full of types of Jesus Christ.

The tabernacle in the wilderness was a type of Christ, as was the entire sacrificial system, as we saw above. A lot of the events that happened in the books of Moses typified Jesus (John 3:14–15). Moses himself as the deliverer was a type of Christ.

The point is that Jesus explained His life and ministry using events that happened hundreds of years earlier. He could do this because these things pictured Him, anticipated Him, and pointed forward to Him.

That's why Jesus could make this astounding statement: "Do not think that I came to abolish the Law or the Prophets; I did not come to abolish, but to fulfill" (Matthew 5:17). Jesus came to bring the Old Testament to its God-intended consummation.

The Better Things of Christ

In Colossians 2:17 Paul said the things of the Old Testament were "a mere shadow of what is to come; but the substance belongs to Christ." Now tell me, would you rather hug a shadow or a person?

There's nothing like the real thing. To embrace the Old Testament alone is to embrace the shadow. To embrace Jesus Christ is to embrace the substance of the shadow, the reality behind the type.

I want to help you embrace the reality behind typology and show you the uniqueness of Christ, by turning to the book of Hebrews, a difficult book for many Christians to understand.

Hebrews is often tough to understand because the writer

assumes the reader understands the Old Testament. Hebrews is a book about typology—that is, about the fulfillment of the old covenant in Christ.

One of the author's favorite words in Hebrews was "better," which he uses thirteen times to show how the old covenant pointed ahead to something better in Christ.

For example, the writer said Jesus is "as much better than the angels, as He has inherited a more excellent name than they" (Hebrews 1:4). Angels are hot right now, but if you settle for the glory of angels you settle for second best. Jesus is better.

Hebrews 7:22 says, "Jesus has become the guarantee of a better covenant." The Old Testament law was a cumbersome way to live. It involved a complicated system of rituals and sacrifices. Jesus is a better way than the old covenant.

Besides, according to Hebrews 7:19, "the Law made nothing perfect." But Jesus introduced "a better hope," something we can hold on to and be confident in as we approach God.

The writer of Hebrews continued. Because the old covenant had become useless (see 7:18) in justifying sinners before God, it was necessary for a better sacrifice to be offered (9:23). This was the sacrifice Jesus made on the cross.

If you and I were living under the Old Testament, we'd have to bring to the temple a lamb or a goat or some other sacrifice, which would be killed and its blood offered to cover sin. But the good news of the gospel is that the final sacrifice for sin has already been made.

Thanks to what Christ has done for us, we can also look forward to "a better country, that is a heavenly one." God has prepared a city called heaven for us (Hebrews 11:16).

The promised land of Canaan was a type of heaven, but the Israelites' best day in Canaan cannot begin to compare with what Jesus has prepared for us (John 14:1–3). We have a better home.

Here's one more "better thing" in Hebrews. "God had provided something better for us, so that apart from us they should not be made perfect" (11:40). We have a better salvation. The "antetype," the New Testament fulfillment, is better than the type, the picture in the Old Testament.

TYPOLOGICAL PEOPLE

Now let's look at some of the biblical characters who became types of Christ. The fact that Jesus Christ was the only person whose life was foreshadowed in types tells us that He is unique in history.

We mentioned briefly above that Moses was a type of Christ in that Moses was the redeemer who liberated his people from slavery to Egypt, while Jesus liberated us from slavery to sin. I want to mention several other prominent types in the Old Testament.

Adam as a Type of Christ

Paul wrote in Romans 5:14, "Death reigned from Adam until Moses, even over those who had not sinned in the likeness of the offense of Adam, who is a type of Him who was to come."

Then the apostle said in 1 Corinthians 15:45, "'The first man, Adam, became a living soul.' The last Adam became a life-giving spirit."

In each case, Paul was comparing the two Adams, the Adam of creation and Christ. What is the relationship? Adam acted as the head of the human race when he sinned in Eden. He was our representative, so in the first Adam we all died when he died.

We got life through the first Adam, because it was through him that all of us are here. But we also inherited death from him.

However, the Last Adam, Jesus Christ, is the head of a new race. And He did not sin. He was obedient to God, so through His death we have eternal life. That's why Peter called the church a new race of people (1 Peter 2:9). Whereas we got our first life, physical life, from the first Adam, we get our spiritual life from the Last Adam.

So Adam is a type of Christ because both Adams give life. But the Last Adam is better than the first because although the first Adam gave us life, he also dealt us death when he sinned (Romans 6:23).

But while the first Adam was a death-dealer, the Last Adam is a life-giver. People who are related only to the first Adam will only see physical life. Their future is eternal death.

But people who are related to the Last Adam not only have the life of the first Adam physically, they have the life of the Last Adam eternally, which is a better life.

Aaron as a Type of Christ

A second person who served as a type of Christ was Moses' brother Aaron, the high priest of Israel. We'll deal more with Christ's priesthood in a later chapter when we talk about His present work of intercession, but I want to reference this type now because it is so foundational.

The writer of Hebrews said concerning the priesthood:

> For every high priest taken from among men is appointed on behalf of men in things pertaining to God, in order to offer both gifts and sacrifices for sins. . . . And no one takes the honor to himself, but receives it when he is called by God, even as Aaron was. So also Christ did not glorify Himself so as to become a high priest, but He who said to Him, "Thou art My Son, today I have begotten Thee"; just as He says also in another passage, "Thou art a priest forever according to the order of Melchizedek." (5:1, 4–6)

The writer mentioned two priesthoods and two types here, that of Aaron and Melchizedek. Let's start with Aaron and his priesthood, which came into being when the Law was given from Mt. Sinai. Aaron was called of God and anointed as high priest, and the tribe of Levi was chosen for priestly service. That's why the priesthood in Israel was often called the Levitical priesthood.

Aaron and the other priests served as mediators between God and the people, because sinful people could not come directly into the presence of a holy God. The priest acted as a mediator by offering sacrifices to cover sins, and the high priest offered the main sacrifice once a year on the Day of Atonement. This blood sacrifice addressed the people's sins for one year, but it had to be repeated every year.

In his ministry as mediator between God and man, Aaron served as a type of Christ. We have already seen that Jesus came to bring us something better, which includes His better sacrifice for sin. Jesus' blood did not merely cover sins for another year. His blood takes away our sin.

Jesus Christ was also a better mediator than Aaron. Why? Because Aaron had to offer a sacrifice for his own sins as well as for the people's sins (Hebrews 5:3). A priest could not approach God on behalf of others if his own sin was not atoned for.

But the Bible says that Jesus, our High Priest, was without sin (Hebrews 4:15). Therefore, He didn't have to offer a sacrifice for Himself. The full benefit of His death was applied to our sin account. Jesus perfectly fulfilled the type of high priest foreshadowed in Aaron and the Levitical priesthood.

There's another important way that the Old Testament type of the priest was completed in Christ. I quoted Hebrews 5:4–6 above, three verses that tell us no one could simply decide that he wanted to be a priest. A priest had to be appointed and anointed by God, the way Aaron was.

If you want to know how serious God is about this, read 2 Chronicles 26:16–21, which tells the story of how King Uzziah took it upon himself to act as the Lord's priest.

Uzziah entered the temple to burn incense on the altar, something only the priests could do. Azariah the chief priest and eighty other priests tried to stop Uzziah, but the king became enraged. However, God struck Uzziah with leprosy on the spot, and the king was a leper the rest of his life. He paid the consequences of trying to usurp the priesthood.

Jesus Christ fulfilled the type of the priesthood because He was a better priest serving in a better temple, the eternal temple in heaven (Hebrews 9:24). He offered His own blood, not the blood of animals (Hebrews 9:12). He entered the holy place to make His sacrifice once for all instead of just once a year (Hebrews 9:25–26).

In other words, a system of sacrifice that went on for more than a thousand years was wrapped up in one person. That makes Jesus Christ unique. He is the only One qualified to fulfill the type of Aaron's priesthood.

Melchizedek as a Type of Christ

The book of Hebrews also introduces us to Melchizedek, another priest with a very different priesthood. Melchizedek is the Bible's mystery man, mentioned only in Hebrews 5–7,

Genesis 14:18–20, and Psalm 110:4. He is also a type of Christ. The writer of Hebrews said this about Melchizedek:

> For this Melchizedek, king of Salem, priest of the Most High God, who met Abraham as he was returning from the slaughter of the kings and blessed him, to whom also Abraham apportioned a tenth part of all the spoils, was first of all, by the translation of his name, king of righteousness, and then also king of Salem, which is king of peace. Without father, without mother, without genealogy, having neither beginning of days nor end of life, but made like the Son of God, he abides a priest perpetually. (7:1–3)

We have a problem here. The Bible says Melchizedek was both a priest and a king. We just talked about Uzziah, the king who tried to act as a priest and was struck with leprosy. So what's the deal here?

The deal is that Melchizedek had nothing to do with the kings of Israel or Judah. He was of a different origin, so he could bring together in himself the offices of king and priest. Melchizedek was the only man in history, *other than Jesus Christ,* who could pull this off.

Genesis 14 shows us the greatness of Melchizedek because Abraham paid Melchizedek a tithe, a tenth, of the spoils he gained from his defeat of a confederation of Gentile kings. And Melchizedek pronounced a blessing on Abraham (Genesis 14:19–20).

Abraham's tithe showed that he recognized Melchizedek as his superior, because tithing required submitting to authority. Melchizedek's blessing also demonstrated his superiority.

Hebrews 7:7 says it plainly: "Without any dispute the lesser is blessed by the greater." Melchizedek was greater than Abraham, which is saying a lot. Who else is greater than Abraham? Jesus Christ, of whom Melchizedek was a type.

This king-priest also typified Jesus because as far as history is concerned, Melchizedek had no beginning or ending of life. Who does that sound like?

Of course, the Bible is not saying Melchizedek had no father or mother or genealogy. There was simply no record of his birth, death, or parentage. He was unique and the founder of a unique priesthood that did not depend on the Law of Moses for its existence or authority.

Melchizedek's priesthood is perpetual. So Jesus Christ was designated by God as a member of this eternal priesthood—not the temporary priesthood of Aaron.

Hebrews 7:11–17 gives us the payoff for all of this. Let me summarize it. First, if Jesus Christ had to qualify for His priesthood through the Law, He would be out. Why? Because Jesus was from the tribe of Judah, not Levi, and all priests under the Law had to be Levites (7:13–14). So Jesus could not be our Great High Priest by human descent.

Second, we need an eternal priest, not a temporary one. The Levitical priesthood was rendered obsolete when Jesus died on the cross to offer the once-for-all, final sacrifice for sin. So if Jesus were a Levitical priest, His ministry would be over.

But Christ is a priest in the order of Melchizedek. Therefore, His priesthood is eternal, based not on the Law but on "the power of an indestructible life" (7:16).

This has everything to do with us today, because if you are without a priest you are in trouble.

You may say, "But, Tony, I thought we didn't need a priest to offer sacrifices anymore now that Jesus has died."

That's true. You and I don't need a *human* priest to intercede with God for us anymore. We can come directly into God's presence. But, we definitely need the eternal priesthood of Jesus Christ in heaven. Here's why. Jesus is in heaven today at the right hand of the Father, applying His blood to our sins. This is why 1 John 1:7 says Christ's blood keeps on cleansing us from all sin. That's the meaning of the Greek verb "cleanses." Hebrews 7:25 says Christ "always lives to make intercession for [us]."

If a person under the Law did not bring a sacrifice for his sins, he had to bear the brunt of those sins himself. So when the Law was set aside and the Levitical priesthood ended, people would have been left without a priest were it not for Jesus Christ. And, you don't want to stand before a holy God without your Great High Priest.

But we don't have to do that, because Jesus is always on the job in heaven. We know that Satan is always there to accuse us, but whenever he tries to cut us off from God, Jesus steps in and says, "Father, those accusations are invalid. My blood has cleansed that person. He belongs to Me."

This is why you can't lose your salvation! Jesus never misses a day on the job as your High Priest. He never dies, like the Old Testament priests did. If He ever took a second off, you and I would be in deep trouble. But don't worry, Jesus is a "priest *forever* according to the order of Melchizedek."

Therefore, you need not fear that, just about the time you have settled into your heavenly mansion and are really enjoying yourself, some old sin is going to come up that gets you booted out of heaven! Heaven is yours, because Jesus Christ is the perfect fulfillment of the type of Melchizedek. And He alone could do that, because He is unique.

The Kinsman-Redeemer as a Type of Christ

There are other people we could study as types of Christ in the Old Testament, but that would be a major undertaking in itself. But there is one more human type of Christ I want to mention briefly before we move on. The kinsman-redeemer is a great picture of Christ's redemption.

The Law specified that it was a duty of the nearest kinsman or relative to buy back any of his family's property that may have been sold, or even to buy back a relative who had sold himself into servitude due to poverty (Leviticus 25:25, 47–49).

The best example of this Old Testament concept is in the story of Ruth and Boaz (Ruth 3–4). Boaz wanted to marry Ruth, the widow of his relative. But another relative was closer on the family tree to Ruth's deceased husband.

It was this man's responsibility to act as kinsman-redeemer to Ruth. But when he refused, Boaz was free to marry Ruth and redeem her from poverty, since Boaz was a wealthy man.

Boaz is a type of Jesus, our Kinsman-Redeemer, who stepped in and paid the price to redeem us from the slave market of sin. We need a relative like Jesus (Hebrews 2:14–15). You may have a godly mother, but she cannot redeem you. Our relatives need their own Redeemer.

Jesus put down the redemption price for us, not with gold or silver but with His "precious blood" (1 Peter 1:18–19).

In Romans 3:24, Paul used the same Greek word for redemption, but added a prefix that strengthens it. This new, stronger form of the word means to redeem or purchase something in such a way that the debt can never be brought up again. Jesus paid a final, *complete*, irrevocable payment to redeem us!

TYPOLOGICAL ITEMS AND EVENTS

Besides people, many other things in the Old Testament served as types of Christ and demonstrated His uniqueness. I want to highlight a few of these as we close this chapter.

Israel's Sacrifices

The Israelites offered five basic kinds of sacrifices under the Law. They were the burnt offering, the grain offering, the peace offering, the sin offering, and the trespass offering.

The first three offerings had to do with dedication to God, while the last two had to do with atonement. But Jesus Christ is pictured in all the sacrifices.

Jesus fulfilled the type represented by the first three sacrifices through His life of total submission and complete obedience to God the Father. Jesus' declaration on earth was, "Behold, I have come (in the roll of the book it is written of Me) to do Thy will, O God" (Hebrews 10:7).

If Jesus had disobeyed God even once, He would have been disqualified from being our Savior. But once again, He is unique among all people because He obeyed God perfectly.

The sin offering and trespass offering were fulfilled by Christ's death. We have already discussed the sacrificial nature of His death pretty thoroughly, so we just need to note it here.

The Tabernacle

The study of the tabernacle as a type of Christ is worth a book in itself. God specified in the book of Exodus how He wanted this place built, and every detail pointed ahead to Christ in some fashion.

Before the temple was built, the tabernacle was the dwelling place of God, the location of His *shekinah*, His glory. If you wanted to hang out with God, you had to hang out in the tabernacle.

Here are just a few of the ways Jesus fulfilled the type of the tabernacle. There was one door in the tabernacle. Jesus said He was the way (John 14:6). The tabernacle contained a brass altar for sacrifice. Jesus said in Mark 10:45 that He came to give His life as a ransom or sacrifice for many.

In the tabernacle was a laver where the priest washed his hands. Jesus told Peter, "If I do not wash you, you have no part with Me" (John 13:8). The tabernacle also contained a light, and we know that Jesus said, "I am the light of the world" (John 8:12).

Also in the tabernacle was a table on which sat some consecrated bread. Jesus called Himself "the bread of life" (John 6:48). The priest burned incense in the tabernacle to symbolize the prayers that went up to God. Jesus acted as our High Priest when He prayed for us (John 17:9).

Again, in the tabernacle there hung a veil that separated the outer chambers from the inner part, the Holy of Holies. It signified that full access to God was not yet achieved. But when Jesus died, the veil in the temple was torn in half (Matthew 27:51). The writer of Hebrews said the veil *was* Christ's body (Hebrews 10:20).

Finally, in the Holy of Holies was the ark of God with its covering called the mercy seat, where the blood of the sacrificial lamb was sprinkled to atone for sin. Jesus said in John 10:15, "I lay down My life."

Do you get the idea? The tabernacle, which was a tent, housed the presence and glory of God. When Jesus came, the Bible says, "The Word became flesh, and dwelt [literally, "tabernacled"] among us, and we beheld His glory" (John 1:14).

The word *dwelt* meant to pitch a tent, like the tabernacle. The connection between Christ and the tabernacle could not be clearer. The purpose of the tabernacle was to display God's glory, and when Jesus came people could see God's glory in Him. Jesus uniquely and perfectly fulfilled this type as well.

The Rock and the Manna

When Israel was wandering in the desert, the people got hungry and thirsty. So Moses struck a rock, and enough water gushed out to water the entire nation (Numbers 20:11).

That wasn't just a rock. It was a type of Christ. According to Paul, "[They] all drank the same spiritual drink, for they were drinking from a spiritual rock which followed them; and the rock was Christ" (1 Corinthians 10:4). That was the spiritual provision of God through the second person of the Trinity.

If Christ was sufficient for Israel in the wilderness, He can get you through your desert. He can give you water to drink and become your satisfaction.

The Israelites also needed manna to eat in the wilderness (Exodus 16:14–15). Jesus told the Jews, "I am the bread that came down out of heaven" (John 6:41). The manna was a picture, a type, that pointed forward to Jesus, the true Bread of Life that would come down from heaven and nourish us.

The Bronze Serpent

In John 3:14–15, Jesus said, "As Moses lifted up the serpent in the wilderness, even so must the Son of Man be lifted up; that whoever believes may in Him have eternal life."

Jesus was referring to a severe judgment God sent on Israel for disobedience, in which the people were being bitten by poisonous snakes (Numbers 21:4–9). God told Moses to make a bronze serpent and put it up on a pole, so that anyone who looked at the serpent on the pole would live.

Jesus said this figure was a type of the sacrifice He would make for sins. Being lifted up here does not mean lifting Jesus up in praise or adoration. It referred to His being lifted up on the cross—suspended on a pole, as it were.

Looking at the serpent required an act of faith, just as believing that Jesus' death on the cross will save you requires an act of faith. Some Israelites may have refused to look up at the serpent, looking around instead for a doctor. But whoever refused to look died!

Jesus says, "Look to Me and live." He is the Lamb of God prophesied to come. He is also the perfect fulfillment of every Old Testament type, the reality behind all the pictures.

Just as the twenty-six letters of the English alphabet are all we will ever need for any word in the English language, Jesus Christ is all we need for any situation or circumstance life may bring our way. He is our complete alphabet, our Alpha and Omega and every letter in between.

CHAPTER THREE

THE UNIQUENESS OF CHRIST IN HIS HUMILIATION

If I had to choose one passage of Scripture that best describes Jesus Christ and contains the core essentials of His person and ministry, without question I would turn to Philippians 2:5–11, which describes Jesus Christ in the uniqueness of His humiliation.

The term *humiliation* in this case is a theological term. It's used to describe the steps downward Jesus Christ took in leaving the highest position in heaven for the lowest position on earth. That required a level of self-humbling you and I will never fully understand.

The implications of Jesus' humiliation in coming to earth and dying on the cross are staggering, and we could fill theological libraries trying to grasp the fullness of what this means. In one short chapter, the best we can hope to do is get a basic understanding of this great passage in Philippians 2.

We did a cursory survey of verses 5–11 at the end of chapter 1, and you can review those pages. Paul went to the implications of Christ's humiliation right away when he urged us to live with the same attitude of self-humbling Jesus had (v. 5).

THE EXTENT OF CHRIST'S HUMILIATION

We can only begin to appreciate how far down Jesus was willing to come when we realize how exalted He is. Jesus "existed in the form of God" (v. 6).

Jesus' Full Deity

We have already seen how the Bible teaches Jesus' full deity. There never has been a time when Jesus did *not* exist as God. Verse 6 affirms His deity. The word *form* means inner essence or being.

Hebrews 13:8 says Jesus Christ is the same yesterday, today, and forever. Who Jesus is today, He always has been. Who Jesus was yesterday, He forever will be. And who Jesus forever will be, He is today. You can't get around His eternality as God.

That's good news for those of us who didn't get to walk with Jesus on earth the way Peter, James, and John did. We have the same Jesus they did, because Jesus never changes. The fullness of Deity resides in Him (Colossians 2:9).

But Philippians continues about this One who was and is fully God. "[Jesus] did not regard equality with God a thing to be grasped" (2:6). He did not hold on selfishly to all the glory and delights of heaven. Even though we will never understand completely what all this means, we need to come to grips with what Jesus did, because Paul commanded us to have the same attitude.

One thing we know is that Jesus was not insecure about letting go of the privileges of Deity. It's not as if someone else was going to usurp His place in heaven. Jesus had nothing to worry about there.

Jesus also did not need to hold on to His privileged position in heaven to maintain His position because none of His deity was diminished, compromised, or impaired in the slightest when He became a man. One thing we must understand is that whatever the humiliation and self-emptying of Jesus means, it does not mean He laid aside His deity.

The reason Jesus was willing to leave heaven and take on human form is because of the mind-set He had. He did not object to giving up His prerogatives for the greater good and glory of God.

If anybody had something worth keeping, it was Christ. All the benefits of Deity were His. But He knew that His Father was unfolding the plan of redemption and that this plan required the Son to take on human form. So Jesus was willing to forego many of the rights and privileges of Deity for the goal of obtaining salvation for the human race.

There's a lesson here for us. We live in a day when people

are adamant about claiming their rights. But whenever you cling to your rights to the extent that you miss out on the plan of God, you lose the very things you hold. Jesus Christ believed the plan of God was more important than His divine prerogatives.

Jesus could have said, "I don't want to be nailed to a tree to pay for the sins of those rebels." He could have said, "Send someone else."

But in eternity past, Jesus Christ made a decision to act on our behalf. No wonder John said, "We love, because He first loved us" (1 John 4:19).

Jesus' Self-Emptying

In verse 7 of Philippians 2, we get into the heart of what it meant for Christ to humble Himself. This is actually a somewhat controversial passage, because there are differences of opinion over what is included in Christ's emptying, or *kenosis* (the Greek term). Let's review the verse and then study it carefully.

The text says Christ "emptied Himself, taking the form of a bond-servant, and being made in the likeness of men." We need to compare verses 6–7 to see the extent of Christ's humiliation. He was "in the form of God," but took on "the form of a bond-servant," a slave.

Paul's use of this term is important. Why didn't he just say Jesus took on the form of a human being? That would be humiliation enough for God. There's a Greek word for humanity in general Paul could have used here, or he could have used the word that meant a male as opposed to a female.

But Paul used neither of these. Instead, he chose the more specific term *doulos*, which means slave. In other words, Jesus became a particular kind of man, a slave, the lowest position a person could become in the Roman world. He wasn't born in a mansion or a king's palace, but in a dirty stable among the animals. And He was wrapped in cheap death clothes. Jesus went as low as He could possibly go.

I point this out because it's good news for us. No matter what we go through, no matter how low we may get, we can never sink so far that Jesus cannot get under us and lift us up. He can identify with us in any situation, no matter how hard: poverty, loneliness, homelessness, rejection, you name it.

Jesus' Humanity

Philippians 2:7 goes on to say that Jesus was "made in the likeness of men." That means He looked like an ordinary man. He didn't go around with a halo around His head, floating above the ground. He looked like a servant, because that's what He was.

Jesus Himself said He came not to be served—which was His right and prerogative as God—but to serve, which is what a slave does (Mark 10:45). A slave doesn't have any rights. So when Jesus took on a human body, He also volunteered to accept the limitations of being human.

Jesus was still fully God while He was on earth. We need to keep this fact before us. But He lived as a man without using His deity for His personal comfort or benefit or to avoid having to face the hardships and temptations of normal everyday human life.

In other words, Jesus did not use His divine power to solve a problem for His humanity. One example of this is in His temptation, when He was hungry and the devil tempted Him to turn stones into bread (Matthew 4:3).

But the greatest example is in the Garden of Gethsemane, when Jesus rebuked Peter for drawing his sword, telling him that if He chose, He could call "more than twelve legions of angels" to deliver Him (Matthew 26:53).

Now don't misunderstand. Jesus did use His divine power on a number of occasions. We call them miracles. But they were always done for the benefit of the kingdom and the blessing of others, not to make Jesus' life easier.

The reason is that Jesus had to experience every pain and temptation we face (Hebrews 4:15), so He could reverse the first Adam's failure and win the spiritual battle Adam lost for mankind in Eden. Jesus lived out the will of God on earth, that He might be an acceptable substitute for man.

Hebrews 10:5 really underscores the nature of Christ's self-emptying. Speaking of Christ, the author said, "When He comes into the world, He says, 'Sacrifice and offering Thou hast not desired, but a body Thou hast prepared for Me.'"

When Jesus Christ emptied Himself, what He did was pour His deity into a container called a human body. This is what we call the Incarnation, Jesus taking on human flesh. The second person of the Trinity was encased in a body that God prepared for Him through the Virgin Birth, when the Holy Spirit conceived a baby in Mary's womb.

Notice again that Jesus did the emptying Himself. It was voluntary. He didn't have to do it, but He did it to save people like you and me, just because He loved us! We need to meditate on that regularly, because it will give us an attitude of gratitude, love, and humility—the attitude of Jesus!

Deity on Display

We'll go back to Philippians 2 in a little while, but we need to visit a biblical event that shows that Christ did not stop being God when He became a man.

The Transfiguration revealed the Deity that was veiled or hidden in Christ's humanity. Matthew 17:1 says Jesus took Peter, James, and John with Him to a mountain. Let's pick up the story:

> And He was transfigured before them; and His face shone like the sun, and His garments became as white as light. And behold, Moses and Elijah appeared to them, talking with Him. And Peter answered and said to Jesus, "Lord, it is good for us to be here; if You wish, I will make three tabernacles here, one for You, and one for Moses, and one for Elijah." While he was still speaking, behold, a bright cloud overshadowed them; and behold, a voice out of the cloud, saying, "This is My beloved Son, with whom I am well-pleased; listen to Him!" (vv. 2–5)

On this occasion, to put it into everyday language, Jesus Christ zipped down His humanity and revealed His deity. When He did so, Jesus' body blazed with a light so brilliant it was hard to describe (Mark struggled to find words to describe it—see Mark 9:3). This was nothing less than the glory of deity.

That was a tremendous witness of Jesus' deity to the disciples. But two other people showed up to testify, Moses and

Elijah. The selection of these men for this task was not accidental. They represented the Old Testament, often referred to as the Law and the Prophets, to declare that the Old Testament looked forward to Christ.

The New Testament was also represented by the presence of the three apostles. So in the Transfiguration we have the whole Bible coming together, with Jesus in the center. Both testaments witnessed to the fact that this ordinary-looking Man standing on a mountaintop is really God in all of His glory.

And to top off this testimony, the disciples heard the voice of God Himself, speaking from heaven to identify His Son. During His life on earth, Jesus' deity was veiled but never surrendered. And for a few minutes, He peeled back His humanity to give His disciples a view of His deity they never forgot (Matthew 17:1–8; 2 Peter 1:16–18).

Jesus' Power

Notice also that when this revelation was over, Moses and Elijah disappeared, the light faded, and the disciples were left with Jesus, who looked ordinary again (Matthew 17:7–8). Nothing like this happened again during Jesus' earthly ministry.

Remember I said earlier that Jesus did not use His deity to ease His way through life or make problems go away. But that does not mean He lived a powerless life. Not at all. He lived the most powerful, victorious life any person has ever lived.

If Jesus did not just draw on His own deity to live above the realm of the ordinary, how did He do it? The answer is given to us in an amazing sequence of events in Luke 4.

Luke 4:1 says that when Jesus went into the wilderness to be tempted by Satan, the most cataclysmic confrontation and spiritual battle any human being could ever face, He went "full of the Holy Spirit."

Then, when Jesus had decisively defeated Satan and was ready to commence His public ministry, the Bible says, "Jesus returned to Galilee in the power of the Spirit" (Luke 4:14). And the power in His ministry was apparent to all (v. 15).

But there's more. Jesus went to His hometown of Nazareth and attended the synagogue. When they handed Him the scroll of Isaiah to read from, the first words Jesus read were these:

> The Spirit of the Lord is upon Me, because He anointed Me to preach the gospel to the poor. He has sent Me to proclaim release to the captives, and recovery of sight to the blind, to set free those who are downtrodden, to proclaim the favorable year of the Lord. (vv. 18–19)

You can't miss the message. Jesus operated in total dependence on the power of the Holy Spirit to accomplish the will of God. He said Himself He was Spirit anointed and Spirit sent.

That's wonderful, but what does that have to do with us? We are to have the same attitude as Jesus—and guess what? We also have the capacity to live in total dependence on the power of the Holy Spirit. In fact, we are *commanded* to be filled with the Spirit. When you live this way, you get what Jesus got—the supernatural power of the Spirit operating in your life.

THE PURPOSE OF CHRIST'S EMPTYING

Now we can move on to Philippians 2:8, which tells us that Jesus took on human flesh and became a bond-servant for a very specific purpose: "And being found in appearance as a man, He humbled Himself by becoming obedient to the point of death, even death on a cross."

A Sacrifice for Sin

We have a later chapter on the death of Christ, so I don't want to steal any of that thunder here. But verse 8 mentions the Cross as the goal of Christ's humiliation, so we need to deal with it.

We can say right off that Christ did not go to the cross because His humanity wanted to go. Remember His prayer in Gethsemane? "My Father, if it is possible, let this cup pass from Me" (Matthew 26:39).

Have you ever prayed a prayer like that? So have I. Jesus

understands when you pray, "Lord, I don't want to take this route. It's too hard. Lord, if there is another way, please let me take it."

Jesus understands. But Philippians 2:8 also says He humbled Himself and obeyed His Father even to death. And because Jesus obeyed in a situation far harder than any you or I will ever be called to face, we can be obedient even in the hard times.

How difficult was it for Jesus to face the Cross? So difficult an angel had to strengthen Him in the Garden of Gethsemane as He bore the agony of it (Luke 22:43–44).

What was it about the Cross that caused Jesus such agony? Was it the physical torture and pain He would have to endure?

Crucifixion was a horrible way to die, for sure. The weight of the victim's body hanging from his wrists caused his joints to dislocate as he tried to push up on his feet to breathe and keep from suffocating. Eventually, the victim was no longer able to push himself up and finally suffocated.

Jesus endured that horrible trauma, not to mention the spikes through His wrists or the pain of the cross's rough wood scraping against His back, shredded from the beating He had received with a cat-o'-nine-tails.

Jesus suffered as no one else, but it wasn't the physical pain that caused Him the most suffering. Neither was it the taunting and humiliation He endured from His enemies as they watched Him die.

The true agony Jesus endured on the cross was the abandonment He suffered as God the Father turned His back on His Son. The Bible says when Jesus was on the cross, "About the ninth hour Jesus cried out with a loud voice, saying, 'Eli, Eli, lama sabachthani?' that is, 'My God, My God, why hast Thou forsaken Me?'" (Matthew 27:46).

This was the agony of the Cross for Jesus. This was the suffering He endured by becoming obedient to death. The Bible says that God made Jesus, who knew no sin, to be sin for us (2 Corinthians 5:21). The sins of the world were laid on Jesus on the cross, and God had to turn His back on the Son with whom He had enjoyed unbroken fellowship from all eternity.

To give you an idea of the depth of Jesus' suffering, being abandoned by God is the definition of hell. Hell is broken fellowship with God for all eternity. The suffering of hell is not first and foremost the fire, but the horrible reality of knowing that you are abandoned by God forever.

Jesus was abandoned by God on the cross, and in those hours He endured all the hell that all sinners will ever endure. Jesus had to go through this to bear your sin and mine. Jesus and His Father had enjoyed eternal fellowship. What happened on the cross had never happened before, not in all of eternity.

There had never been a disagreement, a moment of irritation or frustration, between Father and Son. But on the day of Jesus' crucifixion, He had to bear the sins of the world. And for an unbelievably agonizing few hours, God could not bear to look at His Son.

We don't completely understand what was being transacted on the cross between God the Father and Jesus, because it has eternal implications. But we know that Jesus was offering Himself as a sacrifice for our sins, and we know that God accepted that payment.

Jesus cried out just before His death, "It is finished!" (John 19:30). That is one word in Greek, meaning the debt was paid in full.

Jesus did not give up His spirit until He had said this, so there would be no doubt that the payment for sin was complete. Jesus died after making this announcement because His work on the cross was done.

You see, Jesus' physical death was not the real issue. He got a glorified body at His resurrection that was not limited by space and time. The issue on the cross was spiritual. Jesus endured spiritual death so that you and I would not have to endure it.

Jesus was obedient to death, "even death on a cross" (Philippians 2:8). In the Garden of Gethsemane, after asking that the Cross might be lifted from Him, Jesus prayed, "Yet not what I will, but what Thou wilt" (Mark 14:36).

We are to have the same attitude in ourselves. Remember, Jesus did not have to go to the Cross. But when He came to the greatest crisis of His life, He submitted Himself to God's will and was obedient to death because of His love for us.

Therefore, when you face the greatest crisis of your life,

you can be obedient to God and go through it by adopting the same attitude Jesus had.

A Mediator Between God and Man

Before we wrap up Philippians 2, I want to highlight another aspect of the purpose behind Jesus Christ's humiliation and self-emptying. It put Him in position to be exactly what we need, which is a mediator.

In 1 Timothy 2 Paul told us to pray for everyone. Then he said, "This is good and acceptable in the sight of God our Savior, who desires all men to be saved and to come to the knowledge of the truth. For there is one God, and one mediator also between God and men, the man Christ Jesus, who gave Himself as a ransom for all" (vv. 3–6).

A mediator is a go-between, someone who can stand between two parties who are at odds with each other and bring them together. On the cross, Jesus literally hung between two estranged parties, His Father and the human race, to bring us to God.

The concept of a mediator is an old one. In Job, the oldest book of the Bible, the patriarch sensed his need for a go-between with God so he could plead his case.

Job was struggling and hurting, as we know. He was desperate for help as his three friends accused him of sin. At one point, Job said, "How can a man be in the right before God? If one wished to dispute with Him, he could not answer Him once in a thousand times" (Job 9:2–3).

How can a human argue with God? That's what Job was asking. In verses 32–33 of the same chapter Job said of God, "He is not a man as I am that I may answer Him, that we may go to court together. There is no umpire between us, who may lay his hand upon us both."

Job wanted a go-between that the *New American Standard Version* translates as "umpire." This is the same principle as a mediator.

In order to be an effective mediator between a perfect, holy God and sinners, someone would have to know how God feels and thinks—someone like God, in other words. And this mediator would have to know how we think and feel—someone like us.

I need somebody to represent me before God. I need somebody who is God and man, somebody who doesn't compromise with sin, but who also knows what it is to feel the pain of living in a sinful world.

I need a God-man, and so do you. Jesus Christ uniquely fulfills that requirement. That's why the Bible says He is the *one* Mediator who can stand between God and us.

THE EXALTATION OF JESUS CHRIST

Now we're ready to talk about Philippians 2:9–11, where Paul wrote:

> Therefore also God highly exalted Him, and bestowed on Him the name which is above every name, that at the name of Jesus every knee should bow, of those who are in heaven, and on earth, and under the earth, and that every tongue should confess that Jesus Christ is Lord, to the glory of God the Father.

Jesus' humiliation is not the end of the story. God raised Jesus up from the grave of His humanity and exalted Him in heaven as the God-man.

Our Need to See the God-Man

When you and I meet Jesus in heaven, we will not see the preincarnate Jesus. We will see the resurrected Jesus, the God-man. I don't know if we will see God the Father in heaven, since He is pure spirit. But I can tell you, we will see what the martyr Stephen saw as he was being stoned. He looked intently into heaven and saw Jesus standing at the right hand of God (Acts 7:55). Jesus Christ is exalted above everyone and everything in the universe.

Our Need to Consider the God-Man

Let's talk about the implications of His exaltation for our lives. We've considered what His humiliation means for us, but His exaltation also has a lot to say about how we should live.

The Bible says we need to "keep seeking the things above,

where Christ is, seated at the right hand of God" (Colossians 3:1). So we aren't just supposed to see Jesus in heaven, we're supposed to center our lives on Him there.

Paul went on to say that Christ needs to be "our life" (v. 4), and our all in all (v. 11; see 1 Corinthians 15:28). This is the key. You will never know exaltation, you will never know power to endure your toughest crisis and do the will of God, you will never know the empowerment of the Holy Spirit if Christ is not your life and your all in all.

I'm afraid that for most Christians, Christ is an attachment. A nice attachment, an important attachment, but an attachment nonetheless. But the mind God wants us to have is the way of thinking that makes Christ the sum total of our lives.

In other words, Jesus must be the reason you wake up in the morning and the reason you go to bed at night. He must be everything in between, the whole show. You must define your life by Jesus Christ, "taking every thought captive to the obedience of Christ" (2 Corinthians 10:5).

When Christ is your life, you'll be able to handle the cross and still get up from the grave. You'll be able to face the difficult situations, the trials, the perplexities of life. We don't do that perfectly, but that is the goal.

How do you develop this kind of life, the kind of spiritual focus that makes Christ your all in all? Let us look at two verses from Hebrews that give two important clues.

The first is Hebrews 3:1, which says, "Therefore, holy brethren, partakers of a heavenly calling, *consider Jesus*, the Apostle and High Priest of our confession" (italics added). "Consider Jesus." Think about Him, reflect on Him, fix your mind on Him.

Hebrews 12:2–3 says the same thing. We are "fixing our eyes on Jesus, the author and perfecter of faith, who for the joy set before Him endured the cross, despising the shame, and has sat down at the right hand of the throne of God. For consider Him who has endured such hostility by sinners against Himself, so that you may not grow weary and lose heart."

This seems to me to be the summary of what we have been considering. When you're facing a trial and you want to throw in the towel because all you see ahead of you is a cross, consider Jesus. When people are abusing you, throwing stones at you, and trying to nail you, consider Jesus. When you're up against a calamity that you're sweating blood over, consider Jesus.

Instead of looking only at your circumstances, fix your eyes on Jesus. Take your mind off what you are facing and put it on Jesus. Consider His obedience even to death on a cross, His commitment to do God's will, and His desire to give you the power to do the same thing. When you do that, you can smile even in the midst of your tears.

The Bible says Jesus endured the cross because of the joy set before Him. Jesus looked past the cross to the exaltation that awaited Him on the other side of the cross.

Jesus was crucified on Friday and rose again on Sunday. When you're going through a tough time, that's your Friday, your cross day. But remember, there are no Fridays without Sundays!

Friday is a dark day, but Sunday is a bright new day, a resurrection day, a new life day. When you consider Jesus in the struggles of your life, when you have the same attitude in you that Jesus had, when you face your trial instead of running from it, when you are obedient to God, when Jesus is your life and your all in all, your Sunday will come. You will experience God's victory in what seemed like your greatest defeat.

Jesus is unique in His humiliation and His exaltation, but He is willing to share these with us.

CHAPTER FOUR

THE UNIQUENESS OF CHRIST IN HIS DEATH

My guess is that if you asked a large cross section of people what symbol or image comes to mind when they think of Jesus Christ, a high percentage would say the cross. That would not be a bad answer at all.

The cross became a symbol for Christianity centuries ago. It's one of the things that sets Jesus Christ apart, that makes Him unique among all religious figures in the world. The Cross marked a defining moment in Christ's life, because as we read earlier in Mark 10:45, Jesus said He came to die.

There is no way around the Cross for anyone who claims to follow Christ. Without it, Christianity loses one of its cardinal doctrines, God's offer of salvation to a lost race.

Jesus Christ was certainly not the only person to die by crucifixion. But His death was unique, because He is the one-and-only Son of God.

When it comes to trying to cover the death of Christ in one chapter, I have the same problem as in previous chapters. The death of Christ is so central to our Christian faith that it is worthy of a long treatment, and there is no lack of biblical or theological material to draw from.

But I have to limit the discussion somehow. I have put this study under four main headings, four things I want to share with you about the uniqueness of Christ's death.

THE NECESSITY OF CHRIST'S DEATH

First of all, let's talk about why Jesus had to die as our substitute to pay for our sins.

We have already talked about the problem of sin. But the Bible treats the subject from a number of different perspectives, and that's what I want to do here because we must understand why Jesus had to die.

The Contamination of Sin

The Bible says, "Through one man sin entered into the world, and death through sin, and so death spread to all men, because all sinned" (Romans 5:12).

Sin entered the world when Adam sinned. His human nature, and Eve's too, was contaminated through sin, and they passed the contamination on through the procreation of the race. So every time a baby is born, a sin nature is passed on to that baby, just as surely as its hair and eye color and other traits are transmitted by the parents.

That's why parents don't have to teach their children to lie or be selfish. No child has to take a course on how to throw temper tantrums. Why? Because sin has "spread to all men" and there's no way we can avoid it.

The doctrine Paul is teaching here is that of imputation, or crediting something to a person's account. Our plastic-crazy society can understand that. Adam's sin was charged to the account of his offspring, the human race.

It's something like a football player jumping offsides. His penalty is imputed or charged to the whole team, because that player represents a larger unit. He is not acting just for himself.

As we mentioned in our discussion of Adam as a type of Christ, Adam sinned as the head of the human race. Through him, sin entered the world. He became the sin carrier to his offspring.

This teaching has been the subject of a lot of theological debate. But Paul said all of us have sinned, so don't worry about whether you are going to have to pay for Adam's sin. We have our own sin to deal with.

Sin's contamination is universal. David wrote, "I was brought forth in iniquity, and in sin my mother conceived me"

(Psalm 51:5). Paul said of himself, "I know that nothing good dwells in me, that is, in my flesh; for the wishing is present in me, but the doing of the good is not" (Romans 7:18).

The final result of sin's contamination is death. We usually think of physical death, but actually the Bible teaches three kinds of death.

There is physical death, the separation of the body from the spirit; spiritual death, in which a person is separated from fellowship with God; and eternal death, in which a person is separated from God forever. Notice that the key element is always separation.

Jesus Christ had to die because sin is so pervasive and so corrupting that nothing short of His death could eradicate it. It took a number of concepts or words for the Bible to describe sin.

One word for sin describes it as an arrow that misses its mark. We can understand that picture. A lot of us try to aim the arrows of our lives so they will hit the target, but our aim is off and so we miss the bull's-eye.

Another word for sin means to be unrighteous, to be unlike God. Still another word describes sin as degenerate, or evil. Then there is the word that means to step over the line, to go beyond God's established boundaries. This is the term from which we get the idea of trespassing, in which someone steps over the line and goes where he is not supposed to go.

A fifth description of sin is lawlessness, the violation of God's revealed rules. The Law says this and we do that; it says don't do the other and we do that very thing. Sin contaminates, and we are all infected.

The Essence of Sin

Sin also separates, and that brings us to the attitude that is the very essence of sin. At the heart of sin is the desire to be independent of God, to do things our own way. Sin is our attempt to be autonomous from God.

A child who throws a temper tantrum is trying to break free of his parents' control. A teenager who comes in at midnight when the parents said 11:00 P.M. is exerting his will in independence and defiance of his parents.

Our human desire for independence from God is a reaction of rebellion. We don't want to be answerable to Him. The Bible describes this attitude in Romans 1:

> Even though they [unbelievers] knew God, they did not honor Him as God, or give thanks; but they became futile in their speculations, and their foolish heart was darkened. . . . Just as they did not see fit to acknowledge God any longer, God gave them over to a depraved mind, to do those things which are not proper. (vv. 21, 28)

Independence says, "I don't want to honor God. I want to do *my* thing. I want to be my own boss." Maybe you recognize this attitude, because it originated in the heart and mind of the angel Lucifer, who said, "I will make myself like the Most High" (Isaiah 14:14). Any attempt on our part to be independent of God is an expression of sin.

The Standard That Defines Sin

Romans 3:23 says the standard against which sin is measured is "the glory of God." In other words, when God measures this problem called sin, He measures it against Himself, not your neighbor or the person at work. God doesn't say, "You are a pretty good person"; He says, "You are not as good as Me."

Most non-Christians either don't understand or don't believe that, so they don't think sin is all that big a deal. They don't see why someone has to die to answer for sin. They think God judges using scales to weigh our good deeds against our bad deeds. Or else they figure God judges on the curve.

But the Bible says everyone falls short or fails to measure up to the standard, because the standard is God's perfection. God's glory is the manifestation of His person and purity, so Paul used it to describe the target we had to reach to please God. And no one has ever made it.

Think of it as two travelers missing their flight at the airport. One traveler misses the flight by just five seconds, while the other person is forty-five minutes late. Is the first person any better off? No, it's irrelevant how far short of the standard the two people fell. They are both stuck at the airport.

People need to stop measuring themselves by other people to determine their standing before God. It does not matter that you are more upright than anyone you know in your neighborhood, at your school, or on your job. God has already determined that you have fallen short of heaven, and it doesn't matter whether you miss heaven by an inch or a thousand miles.

God must respond to sin because His controlling attribute is holiness. The prophet Habakkuk said, "Thine eyes are too pure to approve evil, and Thou canst not look on wickedness with favor" (1:13). That's why the Cross was necessary.

When people in the Bible, even righteous people like Isaiah and Job, came face-to-face with God's holiness, they weren't casual about it.

Isaiah cried out, "Woe is me, for I am ruined!" (Isaiah 6:5), a word that means he was coming apart at the seams. Job met God after his testing and said, "Now my eye sees Thee; therefore I retract, and I repent in dust and ashes" (Job 42:5b–6).

Stand in Job's or Isaiah's sandals for a minute, and you'll understand why Jesus had to die for sin and why no one else but Jesus could make that payment.

THE NATURE OF CHRIST'S DEATH

Since God is the offended party when we sin, it is His prerogative to determine on what basis sin shall be atoned for and forgiven. That basis is clearly spelled out in Hebrews 9:22. "According to the Law, one may almost say, all things are cleansed with blood, and without shedding of blood there is no forgiveness."

A Blood Sacrifice

There it is. The means by which God forgives sin is the shedding of blood. Anything less than that doesn't get the job done. All of the moaning and groaning and promising and turning over new leaves that people do will not remove sin. It is a capital offense. It carries the death penalty.

A lot of people are calling on Jesus Christ's name for a lot of things these days: peace, happiness, healing, power, better relationships, freedom from debt or addictions. But none of these is what the Bible focuses on when we are told we need Christ.

We need Christ because we have sin that needs to be paid for. These other things are side benefits if God chooses to grant them. People have to have a sense of sin before they will seek a Savior. You don't look for a doctor until you realize you are sick and can't cure yourself.

Why did God decree that blood was the required payment for sin? Because the shedding of blood requires death, since the life of the flesh is in the blood (Leviticus 17:11). God had told Adam that the day he sinned, he would die (Genesis 2:17).

Obviously, God is not saying there is some magical chemical in blood that washes away sin. But the requirement of blood to deal with sin goes all the way back to Eden, when God killed an animal to cover Adam and Eve after they sinned (Genesis 3:21). The animal's death satisfied God's requirement and substituted for their deaths.

Christ's death was, therefore, a blood atonement. He offered Himself as a sacrificial substitution for the death our sins deserved.

Death on a Cross

The apostle Peter, who was present at Jesus' crucifixion, made this great statement: "He Himself bore our sins in His body on the cross" (1 Peter 2:24).

Why did Jesus have to die on the cross? Why not a heart attack or some other form of death? The Bible explains why, and when you see it you'll be grateful for the Cross.

The Bible says, "Christ redeemed us from the curse of the Law, having become a curse for us—for it is written, 'Cursed is everyone who hangs on a tree'" (Galatians 3:13). Let's take this very important verse apart phrase by phrase.

The first thing we need to notice is that the Law of Moses had a curse attached to it. Just three verses earlier Paul had written, quoting Deuteronomy 27:26, "Cursed is everyone who does not abide by all things written in the book of the law, to perform them" (Galatians 3:10).

So if you failed in one point of the Law, you blew the whole thing and came under the Law's curse (James 2:10). All of us qualify for the curse.

That's very bad, but here's something that's very good. Jesus took our curse for us. How? By hanging on a tree, another term for the cross. To demonstrate his point Paul quoted Deuteronomy 21:23, which pronounced a curse on anyone who hung on a tree. This was not crucifixion, so let me explain it.

In Old Testament days, a person who committed a capital crime would be executed, usually by stoning. If the crime was particularly hideous, the dead criminal would then be hung from a tree as the ultimate form of disgrace and shame. This also served as a warning to others, as you can imagine.

But the central idea was to bring shame to the criminal, because for the Jews to be hung up like that was disgraceful. It was obvious to all that a person hung on a tree was cursed.

Now hold that thought and fast-forward to New Testament times. The Romans had a favorite method of execution for criminals they really wanted to punish. It was crucifixion, nailing the criminal to a cross made of wood from a tree.

A good example of the kind of criminal the Romans crucified was Barabbas the thief and revolutionary who was released by Pilate at Jesus' crucifixion. Barabbas had led a rebellion against Rome, and that was considered the worst kind of offense.

So the Romans didn't just want to execute Barabbas. They wanted to shame him and make him suffer untold agony. Both were accomplished on a cross. First, it was a symbol of shame. You had to be very bad to be crucified. Second, it sometimes took crucifixion victims several days to die. The Romans wanted to make these people suffer so much they would wish for death, but it wouldn't come for many hours. So the cross was a curse too, and Jesus came under the curse of the cross. In so doing, He satisfied the curse of the Law and made it possible that you and I would never have to suffer that curse.

So why death on a cross for Jesus? Because God wanted to demonstrate to the world that Jesus was bearing the curse of the Law for us. Jesus hung on a tree as an object of open shame so it would be clear beyond any doubt that God was allowing the death blow of His curse to fall on His Son. All so that you and I could go free. I told you the Cross was good news for us!

A Full Payment

Here's the rest of the good news: God accepted Christ's death as payment in full for our sins (see John 19:30). We talked about it in the previous chapter. Let's look at the payment from the standpoint of the doctrine of imputation, which we discussed earlier. God was not "counting" or imputing or charging our sins against our account (2 Corinthians 5:19).

How could God not do that? Because "He [God the Father] made Him who knew no sin to be sin on our behalf, that we might become the righteousness of God in Him" (v. 21). God charged our sins to Jesus' account instead and credited Jesus' perfect righteousness to our account.

The Bible contains a great illustration of imputation in the tiny book of Philemon. This is the story of the runaway slave Onesimus, who stole from his Christian master Philemon and ran away—straight into Paul, who led him to Christ.

Paul sent Onesimus back to Philemon and asked Philemon to receive Onesimus, not as a rebellious slave who had ripped him off, but as a forgiven brother in Christ.

However, Paul knew there was still the matter of the money Onesimus had stolen. Obviously, it was gone, because Paul told Philemon, "If he has wronged you in any way, or owes you anything, charge that to my account" (v. 18).

In other words, Paul was ready to pick up the tab for Onesimus's wrong to Philemon, so Philemon would be free to receive his slave back without anything standing between them. That's imputation.

It's good news when the bill collector calls and says, "Someone has credited enough money to your account to satisfy the debt we have against you." That's what God did for us in Christ.

THE MOTIVATION FOR CHRIST'S DEATH

Anytime we are discussing salvation, it is good to step back and remind ourselves why God was willing to send His Son to the cross and why Jesus was willing to die. If anything sets Jesus Christ apart from all others and makes Him unique, it is His love for sinners like us, despite our lack of anything that would cause Him to love us.

This love is so hard for us to appreciate because it is so opposite to human nature. Think about it. Would you offer to sacrifice your child for a roach? That may sound hard, but that's the equivalent of what God did for us in Christ.

We were not a pretty sight to God, but He loved us even when we were at our worst. "We were yet sinners" (Romans 5:8) when Christ went to the cross. That's why if you don't understand the Cross, you will never fully understand love. If two people say they love each other, yet they don't understand Calvary, they have a limited definition of love.

God's love for us was not a feeling of butterflies in the stomach. His love is His joyful self-determination to reflect the goodness of His will and His glory by meeting the needs of mankind. That's a big definition, so let me put it in some everyday terms.

First of all, God's love is always visible. The Cross is the ultimate demonstration of love. God so loved that He *gave* His Son (John 3:16). God didn't just talk about His love; He acted on it.

God's kind of love is sacrificial. If you haven't loved someone to the point of paying a price for that person, you haven't fully loved yet.

It was a sacrifice just for Jesus to leave the purity of heaven and come to this polluted earth. You and I have enough trouble living here, and we are unholy beings. Imagine the perfect Son of God living thirty-three years in a putrid environment and then dying a horrible death.

That is the definition of sacrificial love. The one who loves you the most is the one who sacrifices the most for you.

The love of Calvary is also unconditional. According to Romans 5:8, Christ died for us before we had it all together and got our act cleaned up. In fact, God doesn't want you cleaning up your own act, because you are going to miss some spots. He didn't put any conditions on His love. Jesus died for us when we were sinners, period.

Another feature of God's love is its benefits. One of those benefits is in Romans 5:9, where Paul said, "We shall be saved from the wrath of God through [Christ]." We are delivered from judgment in the future because of Christ's death on our behalf in the present.

Finally, God's love is judicial. The Cross is also a judicial statement of God's holy determination to punish sin.

Some people have the mistaken idea that love means never having to discipline or confront anyone. That's not biblical, though. Parents who say they don't discipline their children because they love them aren't showing real love. Love always makes a distinction between what's right and what's wrong. The Bible says in effect, "Whom the Lord loveth, He spanketh" (see Hebrews 12:6). Love is judicial. It makes judgments.

THE ACCOMPLISHMENTS OF CHRIST'S DEATH

This is the final point I want to cover, and I want to do it by looking at some key theological terms that tell us what Christ's death accomplished. We have already discussed some of these, but let's review them again.

Christ's Death Brought Justification

Romans 5:1 makes a great declaration of our standing in Jesus Christ. "Having been justified by faith, we have peace with God through our Lord Jesus Christ."

Justification is a legal term that means to acquit, to find the defendant not guilty. More than that, in the New Testament it means to declare the former defendant righteous. The picture here is a courtroom in which you and I stand condemned by our sin. God has found us guilty beyond a shadow of a doubt.

But Jesus, as our "Advocate" (1 John 2:1), our defense attorney, steps in and applies His blood to our sins. He assumes our guilt, and we go free.

The reason we have peace with God once we are justified is that neither Satan nor anyone else can ever go back and bring up those sins against us again. Paul asked, "Who will bring a charge against God's elect?" (Romans 8:33a). In other words, who can make a charge against you stick in God's courtroom?

That's a legal question, the answer to which is no one, because "God is the one who justifies" (v. 33b). So when someone tries to accuse you and me before God, He says, "Not in My court. I have declared that person righteous."

Justification is a pardon from a death penalty. It's like sitting in the electric chair and having the phone ring five seconds before the switch was to be thrown. The message comes over the phone that you have been pardoned; you are free to walk out of the prison.

That would be something to celebrate! If that happened to you, you wouldn't just yawn and say, "That's nice." Not when you were in the electric chair! We ought to be celebrating the fact that we have been justified because of Christ's death.

Lest we think we must be something special for God to pardon us, Paul tells us we are "justified as a gift by His grace" (Romans 3:24).

Paul said of Abraham, "If Abraham was justified by works, he has something to boast about; but not before God" (Romans 4:2). But since Abraham was justified by faith, he has nothing to brag about. Neither do we. We are only saved because the telephone rang in the execution chamber just in the nick of time. God doesn't want any peacock Christians.

Christ's Death Brought Redemption

We have already learned that redemption means to deliver through the payment of a price (Mark 10:45; 1 Peter 1:18–19). Christ's death was the price God demanded to redeem us from slavery to sin (Galatians 1:4; Titus 2:14).

When I was growing up in Baltimore, our family saved the green stamps we got at various stores. We put them into books, and when the books were full we could purchase things from the company's redemption catalog, or even go to a redemption store to buy things with the stamps.

That's a picture of the redemption Jesus Christ accomplished for us. He paid the price that God demanded for sin. God never skips sin. Someone has to pay the price—either you or a substitute. "Jesus paid it all," the song says.

That's why 1 Corinthians 6:20 says, "You have been bought with a price."

Christ's Death Brought Propitiation

Let me go back to 1 John 2:2, which I quoted above in relation to Christ's work as our Defense Attorney in heaven. This verse goes on to say, "He Himself is the propitiation for our sins; and not for ours only, but also for those of the whole world."

I want to highlight again Christ's work of propitiation, a word that means to make satisfaction. God was righteously angry with us because of our sin, but Christ through His death has appeased or satisfied God's wrath against us. God was so satisfied with Christ's sacrifice on the cross that He averted the wrath that was due us.

Christ's Death Brought Reconciliation

Jesus also accomplished our reconciliation with God when He died on the cross. Reconciliation has to do with resolving conflict between people and bringing them back into harmony with one another.

Our sin put us "on the outs" with God. We were the ones who caused the rupture in relationship with God, so we are the ones who needed to be reconciled with Him.

But we were helpless to heal the breach in our relationship with God, so "[He] reconciled us to Himself through Christ" (2 Corinthians 5:18). God did not count our sins against us (v. 19).

God said, "You have sinned against Me and offended Me. But because of what My Son did on the cross, I do not count your sins against you. When I look at you, I will see Him. Our relationship is restored" (see Romans 5:10).

Let me point out one important thing here before we go on. The Bible says that God reconciled "the world" to Himself (2 Corinthians 5:19). What did Paul mean by this? It's obvious that it doesn't mean everyone is saved.

The simplest way to explain this is to say that Christ's death made the world "savable." In other words, Christ's death is sufficient for the sins of the entire world.

Everybody is born in sin and alienated from God. But when Christ died, God looked at that and said, "I am so satisfied with My Son's payment that I am now free to save anyone who accepts Him as the payment for their sins."

Since we are born in sin, all of us chose sin when we were old enough to understand sin and the difference between right and wrong. We repeated what Adam did when he chose to sin, so therefore we now have Adam's problem. But Christ's death reversed the effects of Adam's problem.

Because of the Cross, we can reverse our sin decision and choose Christ.

But what about babies and children who are too young to make the choice to sin and to receive Christ? What did His death accomplish for them?

Let me say first that even babies cannot get to heaven without Jesus Christ, because nobody gets to heaven without Christ (Acts 4:12). Adam's death sentence was passed on to everyone, even to those who have not sinned willfully the way Adam sinned (Romans 5:14).

But since a baby has not made the decision to sin, Christ's work of reconciling the world to God covers the inherited sin of that baby. The death of Christ cancels the penalty for original sin. It still takes the blood of Christ to get a baby to heaven, but God has made provision for these little ones. Christ's death paid the price for their sin too.

Christ's Death Brought Sanctification

Besides taking care of our sin problem, the death of Jesus Christ also has the power to help us grow and become mature in Christ—the process the Bible calls sanctification.

The Bible says, "By [God's] will we have been sanctified through the offering of the body of Jesus Christ once for all" (Hebrews 10:10). Then in verse 14 we read, "For by one offering He has perfected for all time those who are sanctified."

To be sanctified means you are now set apart. You are special, because your life is reserved for God and His glory. The key to your sanctification or Christian growth is to identify with the Cross of Christ, because it was the Cross that broke the power of Satan (Colossians 2:15).

That's why Paul said, "I have been crucified with Christ" (Galatians 2:20). Jesus told us to deny ourselves, take up our cross, and follow Him (Luke 9:23). Jesus' cross must become your cross as you die to your own interests and desires.

Christ's Death Brought Adoption

Nobody in the body of Christ is fatherless or motherless, because we were adopted as God's children when we came to Christ (Ephesians 1:5).

In the ancient world, adoption took place when a person

was an adult, not an infant. Adoption conferred on the adoptee the full rights and privileges that came with being the child of the adoptive parent.

Your adoption as a child of God was also purchased at the Cross. Jesus said He was going to His Father's house to prepare a place for you (John 14:1–3). The reason you are going to heaven is because that's where your daddy lives. It's home.

Adoption also put the adopted child in line to be a full heir of the father. Most of us leave our stuff to our children after we are gone because they are family. God has bequeathed all of the riches of heaven to you now because you are family. That's God's idea of adoption.

A SAFE PLACE

Let me try to summarize the uniqueness of Christ's death with an illustration.

Back in frontier times, a father and son were caught in a fast-moving prairie fire. The fire was rushing at them so fast, with wind blowing it their way, that they realized they couldn't outrun it.

So the father stopped, took a stick he found, and dug a circle in the grass. Then he set fire to the circle to burn off the grass. Once the spot was burned off, he and his son stood in the center of the circle.

The man's son was still afraid and said, "Dad, the fire is going to come through here and burn us. Let's get in the wagon and run."

"No," his father replied, "we're going to stand right here. The spot we're standing on has already been burned. It can't be burned twice."

That's what Christ did for us on the cross. He was burned for our sins. As long as we stand on Christ, the fire of God's judgment cannot touch us. Jesus has already died, and you cannot be burned by God's judgment.

CHAPTER FIVE

THE UNIQUENESS OF CHRIST IN HIS RESURRECTION

A lot of teachers and religious leaders have taught in history—some great, some near-great, and some not so great. These leaders taught various worldviews and philosophies, and many of them acquired great followings. Some even died for their cause, which sometimes made them seem larger than life.

But there is a dramatic difference between all of these leaders and Jesus Christ. Despite the claims of some to represent God, or even to *be* God Himself, these leaders are dead, buried, and gone. Their graves are still occupied. But Jesus Christ is alive! He stepped out of His grave on the third day.

Without the Resurrection, Christianity would have been stillborn. You can't have a living faith if all you have is a dead savior. Without the Resurrection, the Christian faith might be a commendable way of life, but Jesus would be just another great teacher who lived His life and returned to dust. Christianity would not be *the* truth from God if Jesus did not rise from the dead.

The Resurrection places Jesus Christ in a class by Himself. It makes Him unique. Other religions can compete with Christianity on some things. They can say, for example, "Your founder gave you a holy book? Our founder gave us a holy book. Your founder has a large following? So does ours. You have buildings where people come to worship your God? We have buildings where people come to worship our god."

But Christians can say, "All of that may be true, but our Founder rose from the dead!" End of conversation.

That's the uniqueness of the Resurrection. In this chapter, I want to talk about the validity, the value, and the victory of Christ's resurrection.

THE VALIDITY OF THE RESURRECTION

The Resurrection is not some pipe dream or fairy tale. You need to understand that, as Luke said in Acts 1:3, "To [the apostles] He also presented Himself alive, after His suffering, by many convincing proofs, appearing to them over a period of forty days."

Jesus' resurrection was not some hidden, private deal. He proved He was alive, and He proved it convincingly. We are not talking about a myth or a mystery here. The Resurrection is not guesswork. To reject it, you must close your mind to "many convincing proofs." You must reject intelligence itself.

Let me give you a number of proofs that validate the Resurrection. First, let me say with confidence that the evidence for the resurrection of Jesus Christ can stand beside the evidence for any historical event or person.

We confidently believe and teach that George Washington and Abraham Lincoln existed because we have reliable, written documentation of their lives. We have their own words recorded for us to read, and we have the testimony of others who saw and heard them and lived alongside them.

No one alive today has seen George Washington in the flesh. None of us was present when America won its independence from Britain. But we accept these people and events as true because of the reliability of the documentation. The same argument holds true for Jesus Christ. The documentation validates His resurrection.

The Empty Tomb

The first proof of Jesus' resurrection is His empty tomb. This is a huge problem for those who doubt and reject the Resurrection.

The issue is simple. If Jesus died and stayed dead, then why did His tomb turn up empty? Christianity could have been stopped before it got started if Jesus' enemies had simply produced His dead body. After all, they were the ones who had control over the tomb.

"Oh," some people say, "that's easy to explain. Any number of things could have happened to the body." There are several theories put forth to explain the empty tomb of Jesus.

One of these is the so-called swoon theory. This argues that Jesus did not die on the cross, but simply lapsed into deep unconsciousness. Since the people of that day were medically unsophisticated, they assumed Jesus was dead and buried Him, but the coolness of the tomb revived Jesus. He got up, shook off the effects of all His horrible injuries, unwrapped His grave clothes, pushed aside the stone without disturbing the Roman guards, and snuck away, then reappeared to claim He had been raised from the dead.

There are so many holes in this theory I don't know where to start. Physically, it would have been impossible for Jesus to do what this theory requires. If He were near death, where would He have found the strength to move the stone that covered the tomb? It weighed more than a ton. Also, imagine Him walking miles to meet the disciples on feet that had been driven through with a nail.

Even if He had done that, imagine what Jesus would have looked like with all of His wounds. He would hardly have looked to His disciples like an all-conquering King.

But the best argument against this theory is the action of Jesus' enemies themselves. They made *sure* He was dead. When the Roman soldiers came to finish off the men on the crosses, they saw that Jesus was already dead. But just to make sure, "one of the soldiers pierced His side with a spear" (John 19:33–34). When Pilate heard Jesus was dead, he checked with the centurion to make sure (Mark 15:44–45). There is no question that Jesus died on the cross.

Another theory is that the disciples went to the wrong tomb when they reported that Jesus was alive. You know, the argument goes, it was dark and they were confused and upset. But even if that happened, all the Jews and Pilate had to do was take the disciples to the right tomb and show them Jesus' body.

Another theory that was popular for a while was the idea that the disciples stole Jesus' body and then claimed His resurrection. But this theory ignores all the precautions that Pilate took to make sure that did not happen.

The Jews feared that very thing, so they went to Pilate and said, "Sir, we remember that when He was still alive that deceiver said, 'After three days I am to rise again.' Therefore, give orders for the grave to be made secure until the third day, lest the disciples come and steal Him away and say to the people, 'He has risen from the dead'" (Matthew 27:63–64).

So Pilate gave them a Roman detail to guard the tomb and permission to seal the tomb with a Roman seal (vv. 65–66). To steal Jesus' body, eleven civilian disciples would have had to overpower a well-armed detail of up to sixteen Roman soldiers and remove a stone that weighed more than a ton to get to Jesus.

But more than that, the disciples would have had to break that official Roman seal, which was a death penalty offense. It would have been suicidal for the disciples to try to steal Jesus' body. Besides, where could they have hidden a dead body so no one would detect it? And if they did pull a deception like that, why would the disciples then go out and give their lives for what they knew was a lie?

Here's another one: the ghost theory. This says that when the disciples claimed to see the risen Christ, they were just seeing some sort of vision or ghost.

But in Luke 24:36–43, the Bible says that Jesus came and stood among a group of disciples. They were afraid, because they "thought that they were seeing a spirit" (v. 37). Jesus invited them to touch Him and said, "A spirit does not have flesh and bones as you see that I have" (v. 39). Not only that, but Jesus asked for food and ate the piece of fish they gave Him (vv. 41–43). This was a hungry ghost! Maybe one person can see something that looks like a ghost, or two people might be mistaken. But more than five hundred people saw Jesus after His resurrection, including Paul (1 Corinthians 15:6–8). That's too many witnesses to fool.

The Disciples' Transformation

A second "convincing proof" that validates the Resurrection is the transformation that took place in the lives of the disciples.

You remember old "I don't know the Man" Peter. He denied Jesus three times at the Crucifixion. But just a few weeks later, Peter "[took] his stand with the eleven, raised his voice and declared" the gospel fearlessly on the Day of Pentecost (Acts 2:14).

It took a lot of courage for Peter to declare, "This Man . . . you nailed to a cross by the hands of godless men and put Him to death. But God raised Him up again" (v. 23–24). Don't think he would put himself in jeopardy like that for a lie. A couple of chapters later in Acts, Peter and the apostles were getting beaten for their message. James lost his life, and Peter wound up in jail under a death sentence (Acts 12).

What about Paul, formerly known as Saul, the persecutor of the church? Saul was present at the stoning of Stephen, giving his approval (Acts 7:58; 8:1). Saul was determined to eradicate this new sect called Christians. And he was good at it too (Philippians 3:6).

What happened to Paul? He saw the risen Jesus, first of all (1 Corinthians 15:8). After the risen Christ met Paul on the Damascus road (Acts 9:5), he was never the same. Paul became so convinced of the truth of the Resurrection that he put his life on the line for it, because his former Jewish pals tried to kill him after he became a Christian.

Not only this, but the Resurrection became a cornerstone of Paul's theology. "If Christ has not been raised, then our preaching is vain, your faith also is vain" (1 Corinthians 15:14).

Paul was transformed, as were Peter and the other apostles. And we can assume that the other five hundred plus eyewitnesses of the Resurrection (1 Corinthians 15:6) had their lives transformed as well, because they became part of the dynamic first-century church that turned the world on its ear. There is no other explanation for this mass transformation apart from the Resurrection.

By the way, before we go on let me mention that Christ's resurrection also transforms us. One of my favorite verses says, "We all . . . beholding as in a mirror the glory of the Lord, are being transformed into the same image from glory to glory, just as from the Lord, the Spirit" (2 Corinthians 3:18).

When you look into the Lord's face, His glory becomes a mirror that reflects back on you, transforming you. Look at Jesus, keep your eyes on Him, and you will be transformed by the look.

If Satan can keep you away from the mirror of the Lord's

glory and presence, there is nothing to reflect back on you and transform you. The Holy Spirit uses the mirror of Christ, as you look at Him, live in light of who He is, and think in terms of Him, to reflect Christ back on you and transform you.

The Witness of the Grave Clothes

Here is a great proof of the Resurrection that is easy to miss if you read the gospel of John too fast.

I'm talking about John's report of what Peter saw, and what John himself confirmed, when they first entered Jesus' tomb. John said they saw "the linen wrappings lying there, and the face-cloth, which had been on His head, not lying with the linen wrappings, but rolled up in a place by itself" (John 20:6–7).

John said when he saw the grave clothes, he believed in Jesus' resurrection (v. 8). Now what was it about these pieces of linen cloth that stopped John in his tracks and made him say, "The resurrection has to be real"?

Well, it was the way the grave clothes were arranged. In biblical days corpses were wrapped with one cloth around the body and a different piece of cloth around the head. The cloths were wound around the body and the head, so that the headpiece was like a turban. Then the body was laid faceup on a shelf in the tomb.

What John described was a scene in which the grave clothes were lying undisturbed. The headpiece was not unwound, but still wrapped and lying in a separate place from the other wrappings.

The only way these grave clothes could still be in position with no body in them is if Jesus came right through them. If He had not died, but revived and escaped as some say, He would have had to unwrap to get out. The clothes would have been piled in a heap on the floor of the tomb.

Or, if someone had stolen the body, the clothes would either be missing altogether, or unwrapped and discarded. Thieves are not going to stop and try to rewrap the clothes to make the grave look undisturbed.

And even if they did, they wouldn't be able to wrap the strips of cloth the way they had been wrapped around Jesus' body. That would be like trying to put toothpaste back in the tube.

There is only one explanation for the condition of Jesus' grave clothes. He simply came through them in His resurrected, glorified body. And let me tell you something sweet. The Bible says that when we see Him, we will be like Him (1 John 3:2)! We can't take these bodies to heaven, because they are limited by space and time. When Jesus came out of the grave, He had a new body.

The Change in Worship

This proof might seem like a small one, but think about what it took to change centuries of law and tradition concerning the day of worship.

The Jews had worshiped on the Sabbath, the last day of the week, since the time of Moses. But after Christ arose from the dead and His church was born, worship for these Jewish believers changed from Saturday to Sunday. For people to give up a belief they had held and practiced all their lives, something tremendous must have happened.

That something was the Resurrection. The early church believed this event was so important they met on Sunday to commemorate it. We do the same thing every Sunday when we go to church.

So the resurrection of Jesus Christ is validated. You can put the data next to the data for any other historical event, and the proofs for Christ's resurrection more than hold their own.

THE VALUE OF CHRIST'S RESURRECTION

The resurrection of Jesus Christ is not only validated, but it is incredibly valuable. I want to mention just a handful of the benefits of the fact that Jesus' tomb is empty.

It Verifies Prophecy

Since the Old Testament prophesied Jesus' resurrection (Psalm 16:10), the Bible is validated as the absolute and inerrant revelation of God.

Remember also that Jesus personally prophesied His resurrection on several occasions. "From that time Jesus Christ began to show His disciples that He must go to Jerusalem, and suffer many things from the elders and chief priests and scribes, and be killed, and be raised up on the third day" (Matthew 16:21).

Later, Jesus told the disciples they were going to Jerusalem, where He would suffer many things and be delivered to the Gentiles, who would "mock and scourge and crucify Him, and on the third day He will be raised up" (Matthew 20:18–19).

Then on Resurrection Day, Mary Magdalene came to the tomb and met an angel, who told her, "He is not here, for He has risen, just as He said" (Matthew 28:6).

If Jesus were wrong about His resurrection, then we should not believe anything else He said. If He did rise from the dead, then we believe everything else He said. So when Jesus said, "I go and prepare a place for you" (John 14:3), we can take that to the bank. Without the Resurrection, we could not believe in heaven. But I know heaven is real, not because I have been there, but because I know who told me about it—the One who rose from the dead (Romans 1:4).

It Confirms Our Salvation

Jesus' resurrection also confirms our salvation. It is the divine guarantee, God's "receipt," that Jesus' death satisfied the payment demanded for sin.

Paul said in Romans 4:25 that Jesus was delivered to the cross for our sins and "was raised because of our justification." Therefore, if you have received Jesus Christ as your Savior by faith, His resurrection is your guarantee that your salvation is secure.

You know how important it is to get a receipt when you make a major purchase. If there is a problem with the product, or if a dispute comes up about whether you actually bought the item, your receipt proves your purchase and authorizes your claim to have the problem fixed. The receipt shows that the payment for the product was made and accepted.

Jesus' resurrection serves the same purpose for us. When He cried, "It is finished!" on the cross (John 19:30), He was announcing that the price for sin had been paid in full.

So when I get to heaven, I am not going to talk about the fact that I was a preacher, or that I did the best I could. Jesus is going to show God the receipt that proves He paid for my salvation with His blood.

It Conquers Death

In his Pentecost sermon, Peter said of Jesus, "God raised Him up again, putting an end to the agony of death, since it was impossible for Him to be held in its power" (Acts 2:24).

Death was unable to hold Christ, not only because He is God, but because His death broke the power of sin. Sin is the only power that can hold a person in death. Death only exists because of sin, so when sin is done away with, death has lost its hold on us (1 Corinthians 15:55–56).

The reason sinners will never be able to escape hell in eternity is that they have never gotten rid of their sins. So sin will have an eternal hold on them.

But when Jesus rose from the dead, He broke the power of sin for all time. And since we are attached to Jesus by faith, since we hold the "receipt" that shows our sins have been paid for, we will not stay dead either. It is impossible for us to be held in death's power because it was impossible for Christ to be held in death's power. This is sweet truth!

THE VICTORY OF CHRIST'S RESURRECTION

We have seen the validity and the value of Christ's resurrection. Now let's talk about the victory we have because He walked out of the tomb.

Victory over Sin's Power

This is the other side of the truth we discussed above. In His resurrection, Jesus gave us victory over sin. That's true in the future, when the grave has to let go of us. On our resurrection day we will be free from the very presence of sin because we will be in heaven.

But Christ's resurrection also gives us victory over sin today, in the here and now:

What shall we say then? Are we to continue in sin that grace might increase? May it never be! How shall we who died to sin still live in it? Or do you not know that all of us who have been baptized into Christ Jesus have been baptized into His death? Therefore we have been buried with Him through baptism into death, in order that as Christ was raised from the dead through the glory of the Father, so we too might walk in newness of life. For if we have become united with Him in the likeness of His death, certainly we shall be also in the likeness of His resurrection. (Romans 6:1–5)

It's crucial to understand what Paul was saying. When you accepted Christ you were identified completely with Him, both in His death and in His resurrection. So when Christ was raised from the dead, you also were raised to a new way of life.

We need this new connection to Christ because of our old connection to Adam. When Adam sinned, his death sentence was passed on to all of us, as we learned earlier, because all of us have sinned.

So our connection to Adam brought death, and death is a reality for all of us. But when we believe in Jesus, we get connected to Him. And when we get connected to Jesus, we get connected to His resurrection life in the same way we were plugged in to death through Adam.

Follow me on this. No matter how hard you try, you cannot stop the ultimate impact of sin from taking its toll on your physical body. You are going to die, just as I am going to die someday, because we are connected to Adam.

But we *can* stop sin from dominating our lives because we are connected to Jesus, who gives us resurrection power *today* to be victorious over sin. This is the reason Paul could command us, "Do not let sin reign in your mortal body" (Romans 6:12).

Therefore, if you and I have sin in our lives that is overcoming us and beating us down, it is because we have adopted faulty thinking. We are living as if Christ's resurrection life within us is theoretical and not real.

The analogy is this. If death is real and not just theoretical—and we know it *is* real—then your new life in Christ and your new power over sin are real and not theoretical. If you will learn to identify with your new life in Christ (Ephesians 2:5), rather than with your old life in Adam, you will have new victory in Christ rather than old defeat in Adam.

You and I need to learn to think in terms of, "I am not what I used to be, so I don't have to act like I used to act."

But when we say, "I can't help what I'm doing," we are

calling God a liar. Paul said, "I can do all things through Him who strengthens me" (Philippians 4:13). Your ability is not the issue. Christ's ability is all that matters.

Some of us have it backward. We say, "OK, I'm going to stop doing this." So we take a deep breath and give it our best shot. We make all the resolutions, but in a few days or weeks we're back where we started. Self-effort is not the answer. If it were, you could have stopped a long time ago.

What's needed is to say to God, "I can't do it. I can't stop. I can't help myself. But here and now, I thank You that You have already given me the victory over this in Christ. I thank You that because He rose from the dead, You have given me the strength I need to live above this sin. So by faith, I am going to walk in the victory You gave me, not in the old defeat I have when I try it on my own."

That's the only way you can tap in to resurrection power that is yours in Christ. When Jesus said, "Apart from Me you can do nothing" (John 15:5), that's just what He meant.

When you connect yourself to Christ as a daily reality, you experience His resurrection power and His victory over sin. That's the key, because the Christian life is "Christ in you, the hope of glory" (Colossians 1:27).

It's like the four mountain climbers who were working their way up a steep, icy slope. There were two guides, one at the front of the line and one at the back, and two amateur climbers in between.

Suddenly, the guide at the top lost his grip and slipped over the edge of a precipice. Because all four were connected by the same rope, when the first climber slipped, his weight pulling on the rope caused the climber below him to slip too, which also pulled the third climber down. Now three climbers were dangling over the precipice.

But because the last mountain climber in line was an experienced guide, he was well dug in and had a good grip when the other three fell. Because of his sure grip, he was able to hold on to the mountain and keep the others from falling until they could regain their position. In other words, he did what the other guide could not do.

That's the difference between Adam and Christ. The first Adam slipped in the garden and took you and me with him. We were hanging over the precipice of sin and hell with him. But Jesus Christ, the Last Adam, dug in on the cross, keeping us from falling over the precipice. And when He arose, He pulled us back up the mountain.

Victory over Sin's Penalty

We don't need to take much time on this one, because we have already established the fact that Christ's resurrection is part of the victory He gives us over the penalty of sin.

In Acts 17:31, Paul said that God is going to judge the world "through a Man whom He has appointed, having furnished proof to all men by raising Him from the dead."

We know this Man is Jesus, of course, because He is the only One who has been raised from the dead. One day all people will appear before God's judgment bar. But if you have received Christ as your Savior, you won't be judged for your sin as far as salvation is concerned because you have already been judged and declared righteous in Christ. And you have your "receipt," His resurrection, to prove it!

Victory over Limitations

Here's another victory we have through the Resurrection. We mentioned it briefly above, but I want to say again that someday we will have glorified, resurrected bodies just like Jesus' body.

"Our citizenship is in heaven, from which also we eagerly wait for a Savior, the Lord Jesus Christ; who will transform the body of our humble state into conformity with the body of His glory, by the exertion of [His] power" (Philippians 3:20–21).

When you are raised from the dead like Christ was raised from the dead, you will have a body that conforms to His— which means a body like you never had before. Jesus could come through His grave clothes and walk through closed doors because His resurrected body was not subject to human limitations. Your body will also be set free from its limitations someday through resurrection.

Victory over Death

This is the final victory I want to consider, because it's the final victory we will enjoy because of Christ's resurrection.

Paul gave this promise to a group of Christians who were worried that their dead fellow believers were gone forever: "If we believe that Jesus died and rose again, even so God will bring with Him those who have fallen asleep in Jesus" (1 Thessalonians 4:14).

First Corinthians 15 is the Bible's Magna Carta on the subject of death and resurrection. Paul said in verse 20, "But now Christ has been raised from the dead, the first fruits of those who are asleep." This means He is the first of many more to come. What happened to Him will happen to us.

Paul also wrote concerning our victory over death, "As in Adam all die, so also in Christ all shall be made alive" (v. 22). And then he capped his teaching with this declaration of victory:

When this perishable will have put on the imperishable, and this mortal will have put on immortality, then will come about the saying that is written, "Death is swallowed up in victory. O death, where is your victory? O death, where is your sting?" The sting of death is sin, and the power of sin is the law; but thanks be to God, who gives us the victory through our Lord Jesus Christ. (vv. 54–57)

If you belong to Jesus, you will not get to die. The thing you fear most is the very thing that will never happen to you. Let me explain.

When you know Jesus Christ, the Bible says to be absent from the body is to be at home with the Lord (2 Corinthians 5:8). How fast will that happen? "In a moment, in the twinkling of an eye . . . the dead will be raised imperishable, and we shall be changed" (1 Corinthians 15:52).

Faster than you can blink, you'll have your new body and be in the presence of Jesus when you die. When your spirit leaves your body, you will be in heaven so fast you won't even have time to know you are dead. That's how quick it will be.

Since your spirit never dies, in the ultimate sense you will not really die. Remember, your earthly body is not the real you. It's just the tent or shell holding the real you, which is your eternal soul and spirit. That's why your body can be in the ground while you are gone.

Here's what I believe will happen. When it comes time for

you and me to die, God will give us a special grace for dying that includes a peek into heaven.

I say this because of Acts 7:55–56, which says that just before Stephen was stoned to death, he looked up and saw heaven open, with Jesus standing at the right hand of God. When he said that, the crowd rushed upon Stephen and stoned him.

If God lets you take a look into heaven before you die, then you won't have any fear about making the trip. You say, "Well, I want to see that now." But you don't need it now. When it's time for you to go and be with the Lord, you'll get it.

As the great evangelist Dwight L. Moody lay dying, he said, "Earth recedes; heaven opens for me."

Moody's son Will thought he was dreaming and tried to wake him up. But Moody said, "No, this is no dream, Will. It is beautiful. It is like a trance. If this is death, it is sweet. There is no valley here. God is calling me, and I must go." A little later he said, "This is my triumph; this is my coronation day!" Not long after that, Moody closed his eyes in death.

Moody saw something that we will see when it's time. The resurrection of Jesus gives us victory over our last and worst enemy, death.

THE CALL HOME

Just as God called D. L. Moody home on December 22, 1899, He is going to call us home someday.

Some years ago, I was invited by the president of the United States to the White House. When I got to the gate, the guards asked my name. I told them, and they asked for identification. I showed them my identification, and they said, "Your name is on the list. Come on in."

One day, you and I are going not to the White House, but to God's house. When we arrive at the gate the question will be, What kind of identification do we have to gain admittance?

We will take out our receipt, the resurrection of Jesus Christ, to show that our sins are paid for because we have put our faith in Him. If you have that receipt, your name will be on the list, and God will say, "Come on in."

CHAPTER SIX

THE UNIQUENESS OF CHRIST IN HIS ASCENSION AND PRESENT MINISTRY

Every four years, the United States government stages the closest thing our country has to the coronation of a king or queen—the inauguration of a president.

Government officials gather in Washington, D.C., for the ceremony, while the nation watches this enthronement on television. The inauguration is the moment when the new or returning president is publicly recognized as the leader of the nation.

A presidential inauguration is impressive. The old newsreel showing the coronation of Britain's Queen Elizabeth in 1953 is even more impressive. But none of these events can begin to compare with the enthronement of Jesus Christ at the right hand of God, the coronation with which He was honored when He ascended back to heaven after His resurrection.

We are talking about the uniqueness of Jesus Christ, studying His person and work from eternity past to His earthly life, death, and resurrection.

In this chapter we want to consider His ascension into heaven, His enthronement at God's right hand, and then His present ministry in heaven as He awaits the Father's appointed time for His glorious return. Let's begin with Christ's ascension, another evidence of His uniqueness.

THE IMPORTANCE OF CHRIST'S ASCENSION

The first thing to understand about the Ascension is its importance. Jesus' return in the clouds to heaven is an important confirmation of the truth of Scripture, and it has staggering implications for us today.

Its Prophetic Importance

In the course of his great sermon to the Jews on the Day of Pentecost (Acts 2), Peter indicted the nation for rejecting Jesus and putting Him to death. But he said that "God raised Him up again" (v. 24). Then Peter said:

> This Jesus God raised up again, to which we are all witnesses. Therefore having been exalted to the right hand of God, and having received from the Father the promise of the Holy Spirit, He has poured forth this which you both see and hear. For it was not David who ascended into heaven, but he himself says: "The Lord said to my Lord, 'Sit at My right hand, until I make Thine enemies a footstool for Thy feet.'" (Acts 2:32–35)

Peter's quotation is from Psalm 110:1, a prophecy made almost one thousand years before Jesus was born. David looked ahead and prophesied that Christ would ascend to God and be seated at His right hand. So the Ascension is an important validation of God's prophetic Word in the Old Testament.

Jesus' ascension also validated His own prophetic utterances. Just as He prophesied His death and resurrection, Jesus also foretold His ascension.

In John 6, some of Jesus' followers were grumbling because He had been teaching some hard things. So He asked, "Does this cause you to stumble? What then if you should behold the Son of Man ascending where He was before?" (vv. 61–62).

During the Last Supper with His disciples, Jesus said, "Now I am going to Him who sent Me" (John 16:5). Then He said the coming Holy Spirit would convict the world "concerning righteousness, because I go to the Father, and you no longer behold Me" (v. 10). And again, "I am leaving the world . . . and going to the Father" (v. 28).

Then after His resurrection, Jesus fulfilled prophecy by leaving this earth and returning to God the Father. The

Ascension is described most graphically in the book of Acts:

> After [Jesus] had said these things, He was lifted up while they were looking on, and a cloud received Him out of their sight. And as they were gazing intently into the sky while He was departing, behold, two men in white clothing stood beside them; and they also said, "Men of Galilee, why do you stand looking into the sky? This Jesus, who has been taken up from you into heaven, will come in just the same way as you have watched Him go into heaven." (Acts 1:9–11)

Notice the verbs Luke used to describe this event. Jesus "was lifted up." A cloud "received Him." He was "departing" in the cloud. The angels said He was "taken up."

In other words, Jesus' ascension was gradual, visible, and physical. This was not a mirage, not a trick or the result of any hocus-pocus. In the same way that Jesus arose bodily, He ascended bodily. The Bible prophesied His ascension, and in the presence of His disciples, Jesus ascended back to heaven.

Its Importance for Us Today

The Ascension and present ministry of Jesus are all-important for you and me and every believer as we seek to live the dynamic, victorious, Spirit-filled Christian life that is God's will for us.

During the Last Supper, after predicting His ascension, Jesus told the disciples, "I tell you the truth, it is to your advantage that I go away; for if I do not go away, the Helper shall not come to you; but if I go, I will send Him to you" (John 16:7).

This, of course, is Jesus' promise to send the Holy Spirit, of whom Jesus had said, "He abides with you, and will be in you" (John 14:17). Jesus said His ascension would initiate the ministry of the Holy Spirit and that this would be even better for the disciples than His physical presence.

How can this be? Because when Jesus was on earth, as we discussed earlier, the activity of His deity was localized in His humanity. That does not mean Jesus ceased to be the all-present God of the universe. His essence was not diminished.

But when Jesus was on earth, He functioned in one location at a time. So when someone needed Jesus to meet a serious need, as happened on several occasions, He had to leave where He was and go with the person who needed Him.

But because the Holy Spirit lives within each believer, He goes with us wherever we go. And He is always present in full power with each believer in the world, all at the same time. The Holy Spirit is not subject to the limitations of human flesh to which Jesus voluntarily submitted so He could be our Savior. That's part of the good news of Jesus' ascension.

Here's another reason the Ascension is so important for us today. Our ascended and enthroned Lord has opened the way for humanity to enter heaven. Let me explain this one.

God gave Adam the job of ruling over His creation. But Adam failed, and no human being since has qualified to fill that position, because all of us have three strikes against us. We are born with the stain of original sin, we inherit the curse of imputed sin, and then we continually commit personal sin.

And yet, God had told Satan that the woman's Seed would crush him (Genesis 3:15). Enter Jesus Christ, who became a Man that He might be our sinless Savior.

Jesus is unlike any man because He is God, and He is unlike the other members of the Godhead because He is man. Humanity now resides in heaven because Jesus Christ, in His glorified human body, is seated in the place of absolute honor, recognition, and authority at the right hand of God the Father.

In other words, because Jesus the God-man ascended into heaven, you and I as redeemed human beings will be able to go to heaven too!

Why is this so important to understand? Because when the Bible tells us that Jesus is sitting in the place of authority in heaven, the Word is telling us that finally, we have a Man who did what the first man Adam failed to do, which is rule righteously.

Heaven is getting used to the presence of humanity because Jesus is the Man in heaven. And as we will see when we deal with Jesus' present ministry, what a Man He is and what a ministry He has!

Its Importance for Us Tomorrow

Jesus' ascension is also at the heart of one of the most precious promises in the Bible. The night before His death, Jesus assured His followers, "In My Father's house are many dwelling places; if it were not so, I would have told you; for I go to prepare a place for you. And if I go and prepare a place for you, I will come again, and receive you to Myself; that where I am, there you may be also" (John 14:2–3).

The Ascension is vitally important to our hope for tomorrow and for eternity. Jesus not only ascended to return to His Father and send us the promised Holy Spirit, but to prepare heaven for our occupancy someday.

Because Jesus went somewhere, we have somewhere to go. And just as Christ ascended to heaven, you and I will leave this earth someday and ascend to heaven because Jesus is coming back for us. We could talk for a while about what heaven will be like, but that's another book. If the Ascension is true, then heaven is true.

THE ACCOMPLISHMENTS OF CHRIST'S ASCENSION

The second aspect of the Ascension we need to see is its accomplishments. What is true today because Jesus ascended to the Father?

It Enthroned Jesus in the Place of Power

When Jesus ascended and was enthroned at God's right hand, every power in the universe was made subject to Him—particularly the spirit realm, both the holy angels and the demonic world.

Peter wrote that Christ is "at the right hand of God, having gone into heaven, after angels and authorities and powers had been subjected to Him" (1 Peter 3:22).

The writer of Hebrews also established the authority of the risen and ascended Christ:

In these last days [God] has spoken to us in His Son, whom He appointed heir of all things. . . . He is the radiance of His glory and the exact representation of His nature, and upholds all things by the word of His power. When He had made purification of sins, He sat down at the right hand of the Majesty on high; having become as much better than the angels, as He has inherited a more excellent name than they. For to which of the angels did He ever say, "Thou art My Son, today I have begotten Thee?" (Hebrews 1:2–5)

Christ was exalted over the angelic realm in His ascension, and that has huge implications for you and me. Paul said that because of our identification with Christ, we are raised up with Him and "seated . . . with Him in the heavenly places" (Ephesians 2:6). We are rulers in the heavenly realm with Christ! In His ascension, redeemed mankind was elevated to a position of authority over the angelic world.

Here's why this is so hugely important for us to understand and believe. Hebrews 2:7 says we humans were created as a lower order than the angels. That's obvious. The angelic realm has far more power and authority than any mere human being possesses.

It was Satan, the original fallen angel, who ruined Paradise and plunged mankind into sin. And all your problems today as a believer are rooted in Satan and the angels who fell with him.

We know this because of Ephesians 6:12. "Our struggle is not against flesh and blood, but against the rulers, against the powers, against the world forces of this darkness, against the spiritual forces of wickedness in the heavenly places."

You see, your problem is not other people. They are merely the vehicles through which the Enemy often attacks you. Your battle is against spiritual forces, which means you need Someone with greater authority than the angels to address the problem. You need Jesus, and as a Christian you share in His exaltation over your spiritual Enemy. You have all the power of heaven at your disposal to win at spiritual warfare.

And what about the holy angels of God? They are your servants, "ministering spirits, sent out to render service for the sake of those who will inherit salvation" (Hebrews 1:14). Satan and the demons are your enemies, and the angels are fighting on your behalf in this struggle called spiritual warfare.

You are in the best position possible, because you are enthroned with Christ above the spirit realm and you have the angels of God acting on your behalf.

You have to exercise your spiritual authority in everyday practice, but it belongs to you by virtue of your position right now. That is why Paul told us, "Stand firm" in the armor of God (Ephesians 6:14).

One of the hardest things for us to do, and yet one of the surest ways to have victory, is to live in light of our position in Christ. This is the one thing Satan cannot address, because our position has lifted us higher than Satan, higher than the demons, and higher than our circumstances. We are seated with the ascended Christ in heaven (Ephesians 2:6).

It Gives Us Authority

The ascension of Jesus, and our identification with Him, also gives us tremendous authority for service to Him.

Just before His ascension, Jesus told His disciples, "All authority has been given to Me in heaven and on earth" (Matthew 28:18). Then He commissioned them, and us, to make disciples of all nations.

The authority of Jesus Christ abides today in His church. "He [God] put all things in subjection under His [Jesus'] feet, and gave Him as head over all things to the church, which is His body, the fulness of Him who fills all in all" (Ephesians 1:22–23).

When we understand the limitless spiritual authority we have in Christ, we will realize that none of the weapons of Satan formed against us can defeat us. If they do, it is because we let Satan win, not because he has more power than Christ.

Paul said *all* things are subject to Christ. That's every angel, every person, and every circumstance. They all must bow to Christ.

And since in this age Christ does not exercise His authority apart from His body, the church, to the degree that we use and display His great authority, to that degree the world will see Jesus Christ operating in its midst.

OUR RESPONSE TO CHRIST'S ASCENSION

Now that we see something of the importance and the accomplishments of Jesus' ascension, let's consider what our response should be to this facet of His uniqueness. What should we do in light of the fact that Jesus has ascended and has been inaugurated as King of the universe?

Exalt His Name

Our first response should be to exalt Jesus' name, because that's what His Father has done. "God highly exalted Him, and bestowed on Him the name which is above every name" (Philippians 2:9). In other words, God has conferred celebrity status on Jesus.

Everyone loves to be around a celebrity. Well, God has designated Jesus Christ as the Celebrity of the universe. In the Bible, a person's name has to do with his authority and recognition. And Jesus, the ascended God-man sitting at the right hand of God the Father, has the highest name of all. He is "King of kings, and Lord of lords" (Revelation 19:16).

This is why Peter said at Pentecost, "Let all the house of Israel know for certain that God has made Him both Lord and Christ—this Jesus whom you crucified" (Acts 2:36).

What does Jesus' exalted name and celebrity status mean? It means that from the moment of Jesus' ascension on, God is judging and evaluating every creature in the universe by the standard of whether that creature honors or dishonors His Son.

Jesus had said earlier, in anticipation of this moment, "The Father . . . has given all judgment to the Son, in order that all may honor the Son, even as they honor the Father. He who does not honor the Son does not honor the Father who sent Him" (John 5:22–23).

So people who say they believe in God, but who reject Jesus Christ, have dishonored God. That is why Jesus told the religious leaders of His day that they did not really know God the Father, because if they knew the Father they would have recognized Jesus as His Son (John 8:18–19).

Give Him Our Lives

We should also respond to Christ's ascension and exaltation by giving Him the place of full authority in our lives.

The more of yourself you withhold from Jesus, the more you take away from His celebrity status and try to share that status with Him. John the Baptist said of Jesus, "He must increase, but I must decrease" (John 3:30). Jesus should have more of you and me today than He had yesterday or last week or last year.

What does Jesus want from us? Everything! He wants us to do everything for His glory (Colossians 3:23).

Bow Before Him

Someday, every knee will bow in submission and honor to Jesus Christ (Philippians 2:10). Our privilege is to bow before Him now in voluntary worship and submission and honor, rather than later in forced submission at the judgment.

The book of Revelation gives us a glimpse into heaven, where we see glorious beings called "the four living creatures" worshiping God incessantly, and "the twenty-four elders" falling down before "Him who sits on the throne" (Revelation 4:8–10). They give "glory and honor" to the enthroned Christ.

For all eternity, Jesus will receive full homage as God, because He is the God-man. Jesus is the Celebrity of the universe because He is unlike anyone else. He is unique in His ascension.

In light of this glorious fact, our prayer today ought to be, "Lord Jesus, I thank You that I am now seated with You at the right hand of the Father. I thank You that in this position there is all power, and all authority, and all strength. Help me to live this day in terms of who I am because of who You are. And because of who You are, I thank You for the victory I can experience today. I thank You that I can do anything through You, the One who gives me strength."

THE UNIQUENESS OF CHRIST IN HIS PRESENT MINISTRY

The fact that Jesus Christ is ascended and enthroned in heaven leads naturally to the question, What is He doing in heaven today as He awaits His return?

In the remainder of this chapter, I want to give you seven biblical portraits, seven pictures, that convey the present ministry of Christ, the work He assumed when He ascended back to heaven and is carrying on even now as He rules from on high.

The Leader of a New Creation

Portrait number one of Christ's present ministry is His role as leader or head of a new, redeemed creation.

The key here is the contrast Paul presents in 1 Corinthians 15, a theme we have discussed pretty thoroughly in previous chapters: "As in Adam all die, so also in Christ all shall be made alive" (v. 22). "'The first man, Adam, became a living soul.' The last Adam became a life-giving spirit" (v. 45). "The first man is from the earth, earthy; the second man is from heaven" (v. 47).

Adam's sin not only plunged the human race into sin and death, but it also put the whole creation under a curse of sin because Adam was placed in rulership over creation. Now, all of creation groans under the curse of sin (Romans 8:20–22).

But as the Last Adam or new Adam, Jesus Christ is in the process of undoing the destruction wrought by the first Adam.

Just as Adam's sin brought death and deterioration to mankind and his environment, Christ's complete obedience brings life and hope and restoration to the environment that had been cursed.

Jesus Christ reversed the sin curse of Adam. Adam once ruled as earthly head of the race. But now Jesus sits on the heavenly throne as Head of a redeemed and transformed people, those who have put their faith in Him and have passed from spiritual death to spiritual life (1 John 3:14).

That's why Jesus told Nicodemus, "You must be born again" (John 3:7). We must be born again, or born from above, because we were born the first time in Adam. We were born under the curse and the penalty of sin, which is physical death and eventually, spiritual or eternal death.

But Jesus' act of righteousness, His death on the cross, brought "justification of life" (Romans 5:18). And the goal of this new life is our complete transformation as "new creature[s]" (2 Corinthians 5:17).

This new creation over which Jesus Christ rules today involves more than just our salvation. That's the entry point, to be sure. But the Christian life is a complete package, a life-long process of becoming more and more like Jesus Christ. It's the process by which a butterfly frees itself from the cocoon and emerges to soar in its freedom and beauty.

Jesus' friend from Bethany, Lazarus, is a good picture of what I'm talking about. When Jesus raised Lazarus from the dead, he came out of the grave still wrapped tight in his grave clothes. Lazarus was already alive; he just needed to be set free. So Jesus said, "Unbind him, and let him go" (John 11:44).

Many Christians have life, but they haven't gotten around to living yet. They are still wrapped up in some form of bondage to the old life. That's why the greatest thing you can do to be transformed is what we talked about previously, which is to understand your new standing or position in Christ.

Ephesians 2 explains it so well. We were dead in our sins (vv. 1–3), but we were given new life in Christ, raised and seated with Him in the place of authority in the heavenly realm (vv. 4–6). Your identity with Christ is crucial.

We are saved by grace (vv. 8–9), but we are also created for good works (v. 10). God wants to re-create us inside so that we might live differently on the outside. Jesus is the Head of this new creation today.

The Head of His Body the Church

Colossians 1:18 says that Jesus is the "head of the body, the church." He is the Head "from whom the entire body, being supplied and held together by the joints and ligaments, grows with a growth which is from God" (Colossians 2:19).

Headship over the church is a second aspect of Christ's present work. The metaphor of the head and the body is Paul's favorite analogy of the present relationship between Christ and His church.

What is the job of your body? Your body has only one job description—to obey and carry out the instructions of your head, your brain. When your head says, "Right hand, move," your right hand is supposed to move. If your right hand, or any other part of your body, refuses to move in response to a command from the head, better call a doctor. Something is wrong.

You can see the analogy between Jesus Christ, who is Head of His body, the church, and we Christians who make up the parts of that body. When we are not following the dictates of our Head, there is sickness in the body. There is rebellion against the Head, which is absolutely contrary to Christ's intent that "the entire body" grow together to spiritual health and maturity.

You are not the whole body of Christ, and neither am I. But we are important parts of the body, because Christ's body is constructed like the human body. If just one part of your body is hurting, your whole body is miserable.

Jesus is the authoritative Head of the church. And just as a human body looks to its head for direction, so the members of Christ's body, the church, look to Him for direction.

Let's extend the body analogy a little further. Without intending any suggestion that the Spirit is less than God, we could say the Holy Spirit is like the neck, which connects the head to the body and supports the central nervous system that carries the commands from the head to the various parts of the body.

That's why the Bible commands us to "Walk by the Spirit" (Galatians 5:16). The Holy Spirit's job is to keep the connection between us and Christ healthy, open, and flowing.

In Colossians 1:18 we find the goal of Christ's headship over the body: "So that He Himself might come to have first place in everything." That's what Jesus is after in His ministry as Head of the church, in the church collectively and in us individually.

Therefore, the degree to which Jesus Christ is prioritized in your life is the degree to which you will grow into the spiritual maturity that is His will for you.

Too many Christians are trying to "find" themselves. But if you don't know who you are in Christ and yet you are trying to find yourself, you won't know what you have when you *do* find yourself. Don't look for yourself. Look to your Head as your divine reference point.

The Shepherd of the Sheep

This is the third of our word portraits that describe Jesus' present ministry, and it is one of the most reassuring.

Jesus said, "Truly, truly, I say to you, I am the door of the sheep. . . . If anyone enters through Me, he shall be saved, and shall go in and out, and find pasture. . . . I am the good shepherd; the good shepherd lays down His life for the sheep" (John 10:7, 9, 11).

Jesus Christ is our Good Shepherd today. He is also our "Chief Shepherd" (1 Peter 5:4) and our "great Shepherd" (Hebrews 13:20).

What all is involved in Jesus' present ministry as our Shepherd? The operative word is *provision*. A shepherd in Jesus' day provided everything his sheep needed. And this is what we must have today, because left to themselves sheep are about the most helpless and directionless of all God's creatures.

So a shepherd makes provision for his sheep. Jesus said, "I am the door of the sheep." This wasn't as odd an image as it sounds, because in those days the sheepfold had an opening through which the sheep went in and out to pasture. The shepherd would literally lie across that opening at night to keep the sheep in and the predators out.

When we enter the sheepfold through Jesus, we are saved (John 10:9). Our Shepherd provides us with *salvation*. We know that Jesus is the only way to heaven (John 10:1; 14:6).

Our Shepherd also provides us with *security* or protection. We are free to "go in and out" (John 10:9).

If I were to say to you, "It's dangerous to be out at night," you would know exactly what I meant. You'd be better off to stay in at night because it isn't safe to go in and out.

But with Jesus as your Shepherd, you have security. That doesn't mean bad things will never happen to you, but it does mean that nothing can happen to you outside of His will. And nothing can touch the secure relationship you have with Him.

Jesus is not only providing us with salvation and security today, but we also have *satisfaction* in Him. We shall "find pasture" (v. 9).

Sheep need pasture both for nourishment and as a place where they can lie down for refreshment and rest. Jesus supplies us with all the pasture, all the satisfaction, we could ever want as His sheep. Jesus put it this way, "I came that they might have life, and might have it abundantly" (John 10:10).

God not only wants us to live, He wants us to live life to the full, to enjoy spiritual fullness. Sheep who are seeking satisfaction are much better off following their shepherd than they are leaving him and striking off on their own in search of the abundant life.

But sheep are prone to go astray. Have you ever wandered off on your own, trying your own way rather than the Shepherd's way, only to get lost and wind up in a ditch?

That doesn't have to happen. Jesus says to us, "I am your Provider, the Good Shepherd. I will lead you in the way you ought to go. I will provide you with abundant life, abundant satisfaction." Psalm 23:1 says, "The Lord is my shepherd, I shall not want."

As our Shepherd, Jesus also provides us with *direction*. "He makes me lie down in green pastures; He leads me beside quiet waters" (Psalm 23:2). When I need to know which way to go, the Shepherd leads me down the right path.

Along with direction, Jesus provides us with *peace*, even when we walk "through the valley of the shadow of death" (v. 4). What a wonderful thing to be in a fearful situation and yet not be afraid. Only Jesus can provide that.

Another provision of our Shepherd is *comfort*. "Thy rod and Thy staff, they comfort me" (v. 4). This comfort has to do with providing "a table" even in the presence of enemies— which for a shepherd meant feeding his sheep even though he knew that wolves and foxes and other predators were nearby.

The sheep were able to eat in safety and comfort even in the presence of their enemies, because the shepherd was there with his rod and staff to drive away any predator.

Take the first line of Psalm 23, "The Lord is my Shepherd," put it with the last lines, "all the days of my life" and "I will dwell in the house of the Lord forever," and that covers this life and eternity and everything in between!

Now you may say, "Tony, that's wonderful. But sometimes I don't sense the Lord's presence as my Shepherd. I don't seem to experience His provision and protection."

If you ever have that problem, here's the key to the solution. In John 10 Jesus said that His sheep will hear and recognize His voice (vv. 3, 5, 16).

What does it mean to hear Christ's voice? It does not mean listening for an audible sound, because God is spirit.

As a saved person, you are indwelt by the Holy Spirit. God's method of conversing with you is Spirit-to-spirit, when His Holy Spirit speaks to your human spirit primarily through God's revealed Word.

Paul made this important point in 1 Corinthians 2 when he said that God has revealed His things to us "through the [Holy] Spirit." Then he continued:

> For the Spirit searches all things, even the depths of God. For who among men knows the thoughts of a man except the spirit of the man, which is in him? Even so the thoughts of God no one knows except the Spirit of God. Now we have received, not the spirit of the world, but the Spirit who is from God, that we might know the things freely given to us by God, which things we also speak, not in words taught by human wisdom, but in those taught by the Spirit, combining spiritual thoughts with spiritual words. (vv. 10–13)

Paul was saying that the only way we can know the things of God is when the Spirit of God communicates them to us. And as believers, we can know the voice of God because "we have the mind of Christ" (v. 16). Therefore, when God's Spirit communicates with your human spirit, it will register in your mind. That is, God will begin to shift and adjust your thinking so that His thoughts become your thoughts, and you begin to think like Jesus Christ.

And in the process of this mind renewal (Romans 12:2), you will begin to detect and enjoy the provision, comfort, guidance, and satisfaction of your Shepherd.

The Vine Supporting the Branches

A fourth word picture or analogy that describes Jesus Christ's present ministry is that of the vine and the branches.

At the Last Supper, Jesus said, "I am the true vine, and My Father is the vinedresser. Every branch in Me that does not bear fruit, He takes away; and every branch that bears fruit, He prunes it, that it may bear more fruit" (John 15:1–2).

Then He told the disciples, "I am the vine, you are the branches; he who abides in Me, and I in him, he bears much fruit. . . . I chose you, and appointed you, that you should go and bear fruit, and that your fruit should remain" (vv. 5, 16).

The fruit Jesus was talking about here is spiritual—the good works God has ordained for us (Ephesians 2:10) and our personal growth to spiritual maturity and Christlikeness. Notice the progression from "fruit" to "more fruit" to "remaining fruit." That's what God wants from us.

Let me give you three characteristics of fruit. First, fruit reflects the nature of the vine or tree of which it is a part. Grapes don't grow on apple trees. You don't get pears from peach trees.

Second, fruit is always visible. There is no such thing as invisible apples or oranges or pears.

Third, fruit always grows for the benefit of someone else. You never see a grapevine eating the grapes or the grapes eating themselves.

So when God says He wants you to be a fruitful Christian, He wants you to produce the character of Christ in a very visible way, so that others will see it and want to take a bite out of your life, and in so doing will be drawn to Christ.

If a cluster of grapes wants to grow to be nice and big and juicy, that cluster has one overriding concern. It must stay intimately connected to the vine. If the grapes break off and start doing their own thing, they will shrivel up and die. The life flow the grape needs is not in the grape, but in the vine.

Why must we stay connected to Jesus our true vine? He tells us why. "Apart from Me you can do nothing" (John 15:5). Do you believe that? Do you *live* like you believe that?

If you believe you cannot produce anything in your life of lasting value without an intimate attachment to Jesus Christ, then you won't want to do anything detached from Him. That takes us back to Paul's statement in Colossians 1:18 that Christ needs to have first place in everything.

How do you stay connected to Jesus every moment? One way is through prayer. Remember the command, "Pray without ceasing" (1 Thessalonians 5:17)? You don't have to be on your knees moving your lips to pray. Prayer can be the atmosphere in which you exist. You can bring the Lord to bear on every aspect of your day by staying in touch with Him, communing with Him in your spirit.

Prayer is an expression of your dependence on Christ.

And because He is also your Great High Priest as well as the vine, He can do something about your situation.

The Lord who is sitting at the right hand of God in the place of authority wants to work in your life to bear spiritual fruit. The key to fruit bearing is abiding in Him, and the key to abiding is obedience.

Jesus said, "If you keep My commandments, you will abide in My love; just as I have kept My Father's commandments, and abide in His love" (John 15:10). Then He made the statement, "These things I have spoken to you, that My joy may be in you, and that your joy may be made full" (v. 11).

Jesus obeyed His Father all the way to the cross, which He endured for the joy that was beyond it (Hebrews 12:2). Now He wants to share His joy, the joy of obedience, with us.

It's important to see that the joy is from Jesus, not something we have to try to drum up ourselves. Someone says, "I can't find joy." Jesus says, "My joy is available to you, and it will make your joy full." So don't go looking for joy; look for Jesus. Joy is found in obeying Him and bearing much fruit.

The Foundation and the Cornerstone

Jesus Christ is also the foundation and cornerstone of the church today—anchoring His church, tying the parts of the building together, and giving it stability.

Paul wrote in 1 Corinthians 3, "As a wise master builder I laid a foundation, and another is building upon it. But let each man be careful how he builds upon it. For no man can lay a foundation other than the one which is laid, which is Jesus Christ" (vv. 10–11).

You know how important the foundation is to the superstructure of a building. It determines whether the building will stand or not. It determines the building's size and shape. If the foundation is weak, it doesn't matter how pretty a building looks, because when the storm hits the building will topple.

A lot of pretty-looking Christians have weak foundations, so when trouble comes they collapse. You can go to church every Sunday, but if you aren't building your life on the foundation of Jesus Christ, you are not a wise builder.

Jesus is the only foundation that will stand. No one can supplant Jesus as your foundation. Whenever you abandon the kind of dependence on Christ talked about above, your life is in trouble. Paul told the Corinthians, "Be imitators of me, just as I also am of Christ" (1 Corinthians 11:1).

"Be careful how you build on the foundation," Paul cautions us. In other words, don't build a cheap building on the strong foundation of Jesus Christ. Use "gold, silver, precious stones" (1 Corinthians 3:12).

Jesus Christ is also the cornerstone of the church. Peter wrote:

> Coming to Him as to a living stone, rejected by men, but choice and precious in the sight of God, you also, as living stones, are being built up as a spiritual house for a holy priesthood, to offer up spiritual sacrifices acceptable to God through Jesus Christ. For this is contained in Scripture: "Behold I lay in Zion a choice stone, a precious corner stone, and he who believes in Him shall not be disappointed." (1 Peter 2:4–6)

The cornerstone of a building is the alignment stone, the stone the builder uses to properly align the other stones in the building. By saying that Jesus Christ is the church's cornerstone, Peter was talking about the unity of the church.

We are the living stones God is using to build His church. The only way the church can be built properly and fit together the way God intended is if we are aligned with Christ.

Verse 9 of this chapter speaks to the church's unity. Notice all the singular words Peter used. The church is "a chosen race, a royal priesthood, a holy nation, a people for God's own possession." Even though believers are of different colors, different classes, different cultures, and different backgrounds, the thing that should characterize us is that we are lined up together under Christ.

But what often happens is that we Christians start aligning ourselves by a stone other than Christ. We start lining up behind our race, our social standing, our background, or some other criteria. There's nothing wrong with these things, but they become a problem when they get us out of alignment with our cornerstone, Jesus Christ.

If you and I are out of alignment, then anyone who aligns with us is going to be off too. That's the problem with the church today. That's why there is so much division. We have chosen to align ourselves with other stones. But there is only one cornerstone. Jesus Christ must be our standard.

The Bridegroom of the Church

The relationship between the ascended and reigning Jesus Christ and His people is a love relationship, and nothing captures that more than the biblical portrait of Christ as the church's bridegroom.

Human marriage is an illustration of Christ's husbandly love for the church. "Husbands, love your wives, just as Christ also loved the church and gave Himself up for her" (Ephesians 5:25).

Marriage includes a time of engagement or betrothal, the wedding ceremony, and then the wedding banquet or reception. The same thing is true of Christ and the church. He betrothed us to Himself in salvation, He is coming to take us for Himself as His bride at the Rapture, and then will come "the marriage supper of the Lamb" (Revelation 19:7–9).

The wedding ceremony and marriage supper of Christ and His church are still future. We are in the period of betrothal or engagement. And in preparation for the wedding, Christ is preparing for Himself a pure and attractive bride.

The church isn't very pretty sometimes. We have a lot of stains and wrinkles and ugly spots on us. How is Christ making us pure and attractive? He is sanctifying us, cleaning us up "by the washing of water with the word, that He might present to Himself the church in all her glory, having no spot or wrinkle or any such thing; but that she should be holy and blameless" (Ephesians 5:26–27).

We need to be cleaned and purified to get us ready for the environment of heaven. That means if you have any ugly spots or wrinkles in your life, Jesus Christ will not let you go until He has scrubbed you clean, because He wants a pretty bride.

The Great High Priest

Our seventh and final word picture is a glorious one. Jesus Christ in heaven today is serving as our Great High Priest, our Intercessor before God.

The high priest in Israel was the mediator, the intercessor, the go-between who stood before God and offered sacrifice for the people's sins, to make them acceptable to God (Hebrews 5:1).

That's what Jesus did for us when He offered Himself on the cross, and He is presently standing in the temple in heaven, interceding with God for us and applying the benefits of His blood sacrifice to our sins.

Hebrews 7:26 describes the kind of high priest we have. Jesus is "holy, innocent, undefiled, separated from sinners and exalted above the heavens." Human high priests had to offer sacrifices for their own sins first, and human priests died off and had to be replaced. Plus, their animal sacrifices could not permanently deal with sin.

But Jesus has none of these defects. His sacrifice was perfect and once-for-all, and He serves in heaven as our perfect High Priest forever.

And best of all, even though Jesus Christ is perfect and separated from sinners in that He had no sin, He is able to identify with us because He became a man like us (Hebrews 2:17). Therefore, we have a High Priest who can "sympathize with our weaknesses" (Hebrews 4:15).

That's good news. Jesus "has been tempted in all things as we are, yet without sin" (v. 15). We can come to Him with our needs, "For since He Himself was tempted in that which He has suffered, He is able to come to the aid of those who are tempted" (Hebrews 2:18).

So no matter what you are facing right now, or what Satan is trying to do to you, you are not alone. Your High Priest in heaven is praying for you, asking the Father to give you all the strength you need.

Jesus has been there. He has been attacked by Satan. He has been tempted by sin. He has been rejected by others. He has been in intense physical pain. Any category of trial you could face, Jesus can say, "I have been there. I will help you."

This is Jesus Christ . . . stepping on a cloud and ascending to heaven, receiving a crown as the King and being seated at the Father's right hand in the place of highest power and authority, yet getting up from His throne to serve as our Great High Priest.

CHAPTER SEVEN

THE UNIQUENESS OF CHRIST IN HIS RETURN

I hope you are getting the idea by now that the uniqueness of the Lord Jesus Christ is woven through almost every page of Scripture, particularly the New Testament.

In the last two chapters of this section I want to extend our study of His uniqueness into two more areas, both of which are related. These are His return in the clouds to take His people to be with Him—called the Rapture—and His return in power and glory to crush sin and Satan and rule—what we call His millennial reign.

When Jesus got ready to leave this earth, He promised His disciples that He would return for them (John 14:3). That promise was restated and reinforced at Jesus' ascension, when the angels said, "This Jesus, who has been taken up from you into heaven, will come in just the same way as you have watched Him go into heaven" (Acts 1:11). No one else has ever left this earth by ascension the way Jesus left it, and no one is coming back the way Jesus is coming back. That makes Him unique in His return, which is the next item on God's program as far as we are concerned today.

The Bible says that Jesus will first return for us. That's the Rapture. Then He will return *with* us. That's the event most often referred to as the Second Coming. We'll talk about that in the next chapter. But the first aspect of Christ's return is the Rapture.

THE RAPTURE OF THE CHURCH

We have referred briefly to 1 Thessalonians 4:13–18, the passage in which Paul said believers will be "caught up" someday to be with the Lord forever. The term *rapture* comes from the Latin translation of this phrase.

The background to this teaching is found right in the text. The church had been around long enough that some believers in Thessalonica had died. This was very upsetting to the surviving believers there, since the church did not know what would happen to these people, and since the church in that day was expecting Christ to return at any time. So Paul had to address the question of whether dead believers would miss out on the return of Christ.

His answer begins in verse 13. "We do not want you to be uninformed, brethren, about those who are asleep, that you may not grieve, as do the rest who have no hope."

Hope in Spite of Grief

We have grief when we lose a loved one. But there is a big difference between grief and hopelessness. Since those who are outside of Christ have no hope for the future, it's not surprising that their grief at death takes on a sense of hopelessness and despair.

But because Christ is returning for His own, we can grieve in hope instead of *without* hope. The Thessalonians were ignorant of this truth, so they were grieving over their dead as if they would never see them again. Ignorance of biblical truth can lead to emotional instability.

I'm amazed at how many Christians today are uninformed concerning what the Bible teaches about Christ's return and heaven. Anyone who thinks we are going to be floating around on clouds in heaven for billions of years is uninformed about the glory that awaits us.

Paul addressed the ignorance of the Thessalonians by referring to dead believers as "those who are asleep." This is a term we need to understand, because it describes the death of all Christians. The word is never used of non-Christians in the Bible, only of God's people.

The "Sleep" of Death

We use the term *death* to describe the cessation of life because from the human perspective, death is the end. But in the Bible, physical death never means the end of a person's existence.

Some groups of people who may come to your door will use 1 Thessalonians 4 to teach "soul sleep," the idea that the believing dead exist in an unconscious, sleep-like state until Christ returns. But that is uninformed teaching, because that is not what the Bible says.

When a person dies the body goes to sleep, but not the spirit. The person whose body has ceased to function is still alive and functioning in another realm. For unbelievers, that realm is the torment of hell. But for Christians, physical death or sleep means that we go immediately to be in God's presence.

We can demonstrate that in 1 Thessalonians 4: "God will bring with Him those who have fallen asleep in Jesus" (v. 14).

Follow me on this one. Paul had just said that dead believers were asleep. If they were simply buried in the ground awaiting the resurrection, how could Christ bring them *back* from heaven with Him at the Rapture? You can't come back with someone unless you are already with him. But Paul clearly said that sleeping saints will come back with Jesus when He returns.

Here is proof that at the instant of death, while the body falls asleep the soul and spirit of a Christian go to be with Jesus. In other words, you will be very much alive after your body dies—and a lot better off, even though we still await our resurrection bodies (2 Corinthians 5:4).

This is why Paul could use the term *sleep* to describe the physical death of a Christian. The reality is that death will never occur for you if you know Jesus Christ. In fact, you will not even be at your own funeral!

Paul had the hope of being with Christ. For him, "absent from the body" meant "to be at home with the Lord" (2 Corinthians 5:8). Another time he said, "I am hard-pressed from both directions, having the desire to depart and be with Christ, for that is very much better" (Philippians 1:23).

Earlier we noted that before Stephen was stoned to

death, he looked into heaven and saw Jesus Christ waiting to welcome him (Acts 7:55–56).

So don't think you are stuck in a casket and sealed in a grave when you die. If you die in a hospital, you will enter paradise before they can take you off the hospital bed, because to be absent from the body is to be present with the Lord.

Because of the hope of Christ's return, we don't have to attend the funerals of our loved ones as people who have no hope. We attend as hopeful grievers.

We can still grieve; even Jesus cried at the grave of Lazarus (John 11:35). Grief is a part of the temporary human condition, even for Christians. But hopelessness is not.

Our Guarantee of Jesus' Return

Someone may say, "How do we know all of this is true?" The answer takes us back to the uniqueness of Jesus Christ.

We can trust the word of the One who died and rose again when He said He will return for us. "If we believe that Jesus died and rose again, even so God will bring with Him those who have fallen asleep in Jesus" (1 Thessalonians 4:14).

Jesus' promise to return from heaven and catch away His people is as sure as the truth of His death and resurrection. These events stand or fall together. We can't say we believe in the death and resurrection of Jesus Christ but we don't know what's going to happen to us when we die. We must give the Rapture the same weight we give to these other doctrines.

This ought to give you hope! It ought to change how you think about this fearful thing called death. Death is fearful for us, because it is the unknown.

But Jesus has been to death and back, so death is not unknown to Him. And if He said He is coming back to raise the dead, you can stake your eternal destiny on it.

Otherwise, we have no real hope, because Paul said, "If we have hoped in Christ in this life only, we are of all men most to be pitied" (1 Corinthians 15:19). Believing in Christ is not only good for time, but for eternity.

Our New Bodies

Before we get to the actual events of the Rapture, I want to remind you that this is the moment when believers in Christ—all of us, dead and alive—will receive our new, resurrection bodies.

Dead believers will receive their new bodies first, in fact, because "the dead in Christ shall rise first" (1 Thessalonians 4:16). The bodies of those who are asleep in Jesus will be awakened and changed, all in an instant.

This issue of what happens to the human body after death, and in some cases at death, is a problem for some people. That's because we know that when we die, our bodies become worm food. We return to the dust from which we came. And even the worms that eat our bodies will someday die and return to the dirt themselves.

Some people also wonder about those whose bodies were destroyed at death, such as in an accident or explosion. Others have wondered how cremating a body might affect the promise of resurrection.

The answer is that reassembling the molecules and atoms of a human body is not a problem for the God who could bring the universe into existence using nothing but words. Let's recall another aspect of Christ's uniqueness here. The Lord who died and rose again, and who is returning for us, is the Lord of creation. Creation was the work of Jesus, so re-creation is not hard for Him. He has done this before!

So the dead, and then the living, will receive new bodies as we are caught away in the clouds to be with Christ. Our bodies will rise to be joined again to our souls and spirits, which left the body the moment we died to be with the Lord.

Our resurrection bodies will be perfect, eternal, no longer subject to the limitations of time or space or illness or injury. The Bible says we will have bodies like Jesus' glorious body (Philippians 3:21). This was the body in which He could walk through a locked door or suddenly disappear from sight.

When God gives you a new body, He is not going to negate what He made you to be. He is just going to glorify your body. So at Christ's return we will be black people without flaws, white people without flaws, Hispanic people without flaws, Asian people without flaws. Whatever race God made you will remain the same in eternity. This is why John was able to recognize people from different nationalities in heaven (Revelation 7:9).

Now here's another question to consider. If your spirit and soul, the real you, goes immediately to heaven when you die, why do you need another body—even a perfect one? The reason is that you are coming back to a new earth to live, a subject we will take up in the next chapter.

The problem with the bodies we have now is that they are not suited to the new environment of eternity. God says these bodies won't work where He is taking us. They are not fitted for the glory of heaven.

In 1 Corinthians 15:52, Paul said we will be changed "in a moment, in the twinkling of an eye." Do you know how fast that is? Too fast to worry about. No sightseeing on this trip! In the time it takes you to move your eye in any direction, the transformation will be made. New bodies for all of us!

The Events of the Rapture

According to 1 Thessalonians 4:15–16, three things will occur when Jesus Christ returns for us. These are probably simultaneous announcements of the Lord's coming:

> For this we say to you by the word of the Lord, that we who are alive, and remain until the coming of the Lord, shall not precede those who have fallen asleep. For the Lord Himself will descend from heaven with a shout, with the voice of the archangel, and with the trumpet of God; and the dead in Christ shall rise first.

The first thing Paul mentioned is the shout. This is the same shout Jesus gave at the tomb of His friend Lazarus, when Jesus had the stone removed from the opening and said with a loud voice, "Lazarus, come forth" (John 11:41– 43).

This shout was a command. Jesus didn't whisper; He shouted like an army officer giving a command. The command was, "Death, let Lazarus go!" Someone said if Jesus had not called Lazarus by name, every corpse in that cemetery would have been raised!

The only thing holding a Christian's body in the ground is death, and death only has power because of sin. So when

Christ descends from heaven with a shout, He will be speaking against the only thing holding our bodies back, because sin and death will no longer have any claim on us.

Christ will command death concerning us, "Let them go!" Then no casket in the world will be able to hold you! All of the believing dead will respond to the command of Christ.

Second, there will be the voice of the archangel. The Bible says Michael is the archangel (Jude 9). The term means the number one angel, the head guy, the one in charge. Michael is the perfect being to announce the coming of Jesus Christ.

But Michael's presence at the return of Christ also means the angels are coming to escort you and me to heaven. Angels are ministering servants to the people of God (Hebrews 1:14), so when it comes time for us to go and meet the Lord, we will have an angelic escort service to take us there.

That's what happened to a different Lazarus, the poor man who begged food from the rich man's table and then died. Jesus said in Luke 16:22 that Lazarus "was carried away by the angels to Abraham's bosom," another term for heaven or paradise.

Why do we need an angelic escort service? Because we are leaving a familiar realm and traveling to an unfamiliar realm. Whenever you go on a tour in a place you've never visited before, it's helpful to have a guide.

So the archangel will dispatch the angels to every believer to whom they have been assigned, to escort them into the presence of God (Luke 16:22). God views you as so special He's not just going to call you to Himself, He's going to send an escort for you, because you are His prized possession.

The third manifestation of the Rapture is "the trumpet of God" (1 Thessalonians 4:16). When God showed up at Mt. Sinai to give Moses the Law, a loud trumpet sounded (Exodus 19:16). That trumpet blast meant God was on the scene, in the house, and people had better get ready for His marching orders.

When I was growing up in Baltimore, my father would whistle for our dog with a special sound he could make. Dad would go to the back door and make this whistle, and our

dog's ears would shoot up. He knew this wasn't just any whistle. It was his master calling.

The trumpet of God is a call for the ears of believers who
know Him, to let them know it's time to march home. It's a
signal you will know when you hear it, because you've been
redeemed by the blood of the Lamb.

Our Preparation for the Rapture

The return of Jesus Christ is sure, it's wonderful, and it
could happen anytime. It's like a telephone answering
machine that tells you, "I'm not home now, but when I return
I will call you."

If the person we have called is reliable, we can expect a
return call even though we don't know whether it will be five
minutes or five hours before it comes. Jesus is coming back.
What should we be doing now to prepare ourselves for His
coming and live in the light of it?

Every year I go to a clinic in Dallas for my annual
checkup. It's a time when I find out how well I have taken
care of my body during the year. When I remember that this
time of evaluation is coming, I get serious about watching
what I eat and exercising. When I forget about this time of
evaluation, I get slothful.

Paul tells us: "For the grace of God has appeared, bringing salvation to all men, instructing us to deny ungodliness
and worldly desires and to live sensibly, righteously and
godly in the present age, looking for the blessed hope and the
appearing of the glory of our great God and Savior, Christ
Jesus" (Titus 2:11–13).

We should be looking for and anticipating Christ's return
every day. We are looking for the "upper taker," not the
undertaker! But during the waiting period, at least two
things should characterize us.

First, Paul said that while we are looking for Jesus to
return, the best way to prepare for Christ's coming is to live a
life that pleases Him, one characterized by godliness and
righteousness.

John said the hope of Christ's return should have a purifying effect on us (1 John 3:2–3). Looking for Jesus to return
does not mean just sitting and staring into the sky or living in
some dreamy world. It means you are so aware of His pres-

ence and so focused on seeing Him someday that you want to
live like Him now, so you won't disappoint Him at His coming.

Looking for Jesus Christ to return should also deepen our
love for Him. God does not want us to be focused on an
event, but on a person. We are looking forward to the return
of Someone we love, not just the occurrence of an event.

Peter puts it in perspective when he said, "Though you
have not seen [Christ], you love Him, and though you do not
see Him now, but believe in Him, you greatly rejoice with joy
inexpressible and full of glory" (1 Peter 1:8). You don't have
to see Jesus Christ to love Him. And your love for Him will
only intensify your desire to see Him.

When a loved one who has been away and is coming back
home is scheduled to arrive on a certain flight, you don't just
sit home and say, "Well, I guess the plane will arrive OK and
my loved one will get a ride home."

No, you go to the airport to meet that plane. You find out
if the flight is on time. You sit at the gate and wait for the
arrival announcement.

You don't go to the airport because of an event, the
arrival of an airplane. You go because of a person. Someone
you love very much is on that flight. The relationship dictates
that you watch and wait with eagerness.

You may not know the exact moment the plane is going
to touch down, but someone does. The tower can tell you
because the tower is in constant communication with the
plane that is coming in.

God the Father knows exactly when His Son is due to
return. He tells us to keep watching and waiting for the person we love.

The world may think we are talking religious science fic-
tion when we talk about the return of Christ. But the Bible
urges us to live in the realm of the unseen, not the realm of
the visible. "We look not at the things which are seen, but at
the things which are not seen; for the things which are seen
are temporal, but the things which are not seen are eternal"
(2 Corinthians 4:18).

THE JUDGMENT SEAT OF CHRIST

The second event I want to talk about in this chapter is
what the Bible calls "the judgment seat of Christ" (2

Corinthians 5:10). I am connecting this event with the Rapture because this is the first order of business on Christ's agenda for the church after we are caught away to be with Him.

Evaluation for Rewards

Even though this event is called a judgment, it is not a judgment for salvation. Anyone who is not saved did not make this trip. The judgment seat of Christ is an evaluation of us as believers to determine the rewards, or lack of rewards, we will receive based on the quality of our Christian lives and service.

Don't think that because your eternal destiny is not at stake here, this review is not important. Let me tell you, it was of great concern to the apostle Paul. Just before he declared that we must all appear at this judgment, Paul wrote, "We have as our ambition, whether at home or absent, to be pleasing to Him" (2 Corinthians 5:9).

The Greek term for "judgment seat" is *bema*, which was a platform erected for the judges during the Isthmian Games, a first-century version of the Olympics that were held near Corinth. The judges sat on the *bema* to determine who won and who lost, or who was disqualified (see 1 Corinthians 9:24–27). The prizes given to the winners were also handed out at the *bema*.

You can see why this was such an ideal analogy for Paul to use in describing the time following the Rapture when we Christians will account to Jesus Christ for what we did as His children.

A Serious Occasion

Let me give you the full statement in 2 Corinthians 5:10. Paul wrote, "For we must all appear before the judgment seat of Christ, that each one may be recompensed for his deeds in the body, according to what he has done, whether good or bad."

Does this sound serious to you? It does to me. Anyone who says, "Well, I don't really care whether I get any rewards or not as long as I make it to heaven," doesn't understand what's going on here.

There is a lot at stake here. Our degree of authority and privilege in heaven will be determined at Christ's judgment seat. The kind of Christian life we have lived will be revealed there. We will have to stand before Jesus Christ and give account for how we have managed the gifts and resources He entrusted to us.

This is serious stuff. Paul wrote, "But you, why do you judge your brother? Or you again, why do you regard your brother with contempt? For we shall all stand before the judgment seat of God. . . . So then each one of us will give account of himself to God" (Romans 14:10, 12).

The problem with these believers is that they were judging each other in areas such as food and drink and condemning each other for things that were nonessential matters of personal conscience.

Paul told them they had better stop judging each other and start worrying about themselves. Why? Because each one of them was going to stand before the judgment seat where the questions were going to be about them, not someone else. Jesus Christ is going to ask you about you, not about your brother or sister.

So let me say it again. The judgment seat is important. The Bible uses at least three analogies to help us see what we will be judged for at the *bema* of Christ.

The Analogy of a Steward

In Luke 16:1–13 Jesus told the parable of a steward who was dishonest in the way he handled his master's business and was fired from his position. We are more familiar with the word *manager*, but the concept is the same. A steward is responsible for the resources his master entrusts to his care.

In Jesus' story, when the master realized his steward was cheating him, he said, "Give an account of your stewardship" (Luke 16:2). Stewardship always involves accountability.

Peter said, "As each one has received a special gift, employ it in serving one another, as good stewards of the manifold grace of God" (1 Peter 4:10). Spiritual gifts are part of the stewardship for which we will give account at the *bema* of Christ. Our material resources, our families, and the opportunities for ministry God gives us are also included in our stewardship. Even our bodies are given to us by God and are included in the responsibility of stewardship (1 Corinthians 9:27).

Our goal as God's stewards or managers is to do the best possible job we can with what He has given us. That's all you need to worry about, what God has given you. You won't have to answer for anyone else. And the standard by which we will be measured is clear: "It is required of stewards that one be found trustworthy" (1 Corinthians 4:2).

The Analogy of a Builder

The second image I want to show you is that of a builder. To do that, I need to cite an extended passage:

> According to the grace of God which was given to me, as a wise master builder I laid a foundation, and another is building upon it. But let each man be careful how he builds upon it. For no man can lay a foundation other than the one which is laid, which is Jesus Christ. Now if any man builds upon the foundation with gold, silver, precious stones, wood, hay, straw, each man's work will become evident; for the day will show it, because it is to be revealed with fire; and the fire itself will test the quality of each man's work. If any man's work which he has built upon it remains, he shall receive a reward. If any man's work is burned up, he shall suffer loss; but he himself shall be saved, yet so as through fire. (1 Corinthians 3:10–15)

We are builders in God's kingdom, and we have been given the most magnificent foundation ever laid for a building, Jesus Christ Himself.

With a foundation like that, you don't want to build junk. The quality of our work for Christ will be revealed at "the day," which is a reference to Christ's judgment seat.

The test will be the quality of our work—not just the quantity, or the flashiness, or the busyness of what we tried to do for Christ. The question will be, Did you give God the leftovers of your life or the best you had? Did you invest the precious things of life in His service, or were you content with any old building material you could find?

Building with gold, silver, and precious stones is another way of saying you gave Christ the place of supreme value in your life. That commitment will be rewarded at the *bema*.

But you can even go to a junkyard and find wood, hay, and straw lying around. These things burn, whereas precious metals and stones do not. So Jesus Christ will use fire to test the quality of our Christian walk and our service for Him. And the fire will reveal the quality of our building materials.

The Analogy of an Athlete

A third analogy of the judgment seat is that of an athlete. We have already referred to 1 Corinthians 9:24–27, so let's look at these verses in more detail.

Paul compared the Christian life to an athletic contest. "Do you not know that those who run in a race all run, but only one receives the prize? Run in such a way that you may win" (v. 24). Then he said that when it comes to serving Christ, he is running to win (v. 26).

How do you win the prize Jesus Christ has for you? By running the race of life in such a way that you fulfill God's will and hear Jesus' commendation, "Well done." In other words, "Congratulations, you won the race. Here's your prize."

Now look at verses 25 and 27 of this passage, because they reveal the key to being a winner and receiving the prize at Christ's judgment seat. The key is self-discipline.

I know you don't want to hear about this. Neither do I. But it's inescapable. If you want to win the race, you have to get in shape. And that means saying no to a lot of things that are not wrong in themselves, and saying yes to a lot of exercise and sweating when you don't feel like exercising and sweating.

Paul told Timothy, "Discipline yourself for the purpose of godliness" (1 Timothy 4:7). It won't happen automatically. The Spirit of God is not going to levitate you out of bed tomorrow morning and float you into a chair with your Bible. You have to discipline yourself to get up.

You may say, "But I'm not a disciplined person." Really? Do you make it to work every day? Even though you may not feel like getting up, I'm guessing that you get up and get to work on time because you know the payoff is worth the effort.

Paul said if athletes in the Isthmian Games exercised strict self-discipline to win a wreath of leaves that would fade

away, we should be much more willing to discipline ourselves to win the "imperishable" prize Jesus will give us at
His *bema* (1 Corinthians 9:25).

That's why Paul said, "I buffet my body and make it my
slave, lest . . . I myself should be disqualified" (v. 27). He didn't
want the Judge at the *bema* to review the tape of his race and
say, "Disqualified. No prize."

PREPARING FOR THE PARTY

Let me mention one more thing before we get to the next
chapter and study the thousand-year reign of Christ known
as the millennial kingdom.

In Jesus' day the engagement period before a wedding
was much more official and serious than it is today. The
bride and groom were betrothed to one another, then the
bridegroom would go off and prepare for the wedding day.

When everything was ready, the bridegroom would
return for his bride and take her to the marriage feast, where
they would celebrate with their friends. We would call this
party a reception, but it was much grander than our wedding
receptions and lasted for several days.

This is how Christ is dealing with His bride, the church.
We'll go into this in detail in the next chapter, but I want to
set the stage a little bit here.

In His first coming, Jesus betrothed us to Himself. He
paid the dowry price for us on the cross. Then He went away
to prepare the bridal home, heaven, and someday He is coming back for His bride.

At the Rapture, Jesus is going to take His bride to Himself. The church is going to complete and consummate its
relationship with the Savior, and then He is going to take us
to "the marriage supper of the Lamb" (Revelation 19:9), the
biggest party that has ever been held because it is going to
last for a thousand years! The marriage supper is another
term for the millennial kingdom.

John said the bride of Christ "has made herself ready" for
the wedding (Revelation 19:7). We will be dressed in "fine
linen, bright and clean . . . the righteous acts of the saints"
(v. 8).

How did the bride get herself ready to wear this linen of
pure righteousness? At the judgment seat of Christ, anything

unholy and impure that we brought with us will be purged and cleansed away in the fire that Jesus Christ will use to judge our works.

In other words, at the judgment seat all the useless stuff will be edited out of our lives.

The messages that are broadcast nationwide over our radio program, *The Alternative,* are edited versions of the sermons I preach at our church. A lot of things in the original messages don't get broadcast over the airwaves.

My wife, Lois, goes through the manuscripts and pulls out things that would be inappropriate for a national radio audience. These include things such as specific references to our church in Dallas and things there that wouldn't make sense to anyone else. Or comments about local people and events that have no application to the radio listener.

By the time the editing process is done, a one-hour sermon may be down to forty-five minutes. Fifteen minutes of things that are of no benefit to a larger audience have been removed.

Some people may have been saved for twenty or thirty years, but by the time Jesus Christ finishes editing their lives at His judgment seat, those twenty or thirty years may be down to one or two years of worthwhile stuff. That's why you and I need to make sure we are ready for His evaluation.

I first met Lois in 1968. Her father invited me over to dinner, Lois and I began to talk, and we had a few days to get to know each other. When I left, I told Lois, "I will come back." Our homes were three thousand miles apart, but I told her I would come back.

How did Lois know she could trust me to keep my word? I told her, "The way you know I will be back is that I will write you every day, even if it's just a line or two." So Lois had my word that I would return, even though she couldn't see me.

I wrote her every day, just like I promised. One time the letters got delayed in the mail and Lois didn't get one for a week. So she called me, wanting to know what in the world was going on that she wasn't getting her daily letter. But I wrote her faithfully, and then I returned to take her to be with me where I was.

Jesus Christ has met you and won you as part of His bride. He wants to take you to be with Him in heaven, and He said, "I am coming back."

How do you know He is coming back? Because He said, "I am going to write you and remind you of My promise to return." We have Christ's love letter, the Bible. So the question is, Do you believe the Author of the letter? If Jesus died and rose again, and He did, then He's coming back. Let's be ready.

CHAPTER EIGHT

THE UNIQUENESS OF CHRIST IN HIS MILLENNIAL RULE

As I write this book, the world is waiting apprehensively for the arrival of the new millennium and whatever computer catastrophes or end-time events it may bring.

Even without the Y2K problem, this is an unusual and exciting time as we anticipate the beginning of a new thousand-year period (the word *millennium* means one thousand years).

Some people wonder if the new millennium will bring in what the Bible recognizes as the golden age of human history, the thousand-year millennial reign of Jesus Christ.

This glorious kingdom will be ushered in when Jesus Christ returns in what the theologians call His second advent, the event most people have in mind when they talk about the second coming or return of Christ. This is when sin and Satan are judged and righteousness is established.

Christ's thousand-year reign is preceded by the Battle of Armageddon (Revelation 19:17–21). The Lamb is Jesus, coming to consummate His marriage to His waiting bride, the church. The church is seen preparing herself for her bridegroom by putting on her wedding garments, "fine linen, bright and clean" (v. 8).

I get to perform my fair share of weddings. I go into the bridal room just before the wedding to pray with the bride and her bridesmaids for the ceremony we are about to enter into.

You know what a bride is doing in that room. She is making herself ready, in great detail. And she usually has other women there to help her make herself ready for the wedding ceremony.

When the marriage of the Lamb comes, Christ's bride is going to be ready. He will see to that. We, the church, will be wearing wedding garments that are called "the righteous acts of the saints" (19:8).

The reason only our righteous acts will make it into the Millennium is that the stubble in our lives was burned off at the judgment seat of Christ, which occurred after the Rapture (1 Corinthians 3:10–15). So Christ's bride will be glorious and perfect in every detail.

This marriage supper is something like a reception. It is basically a party, a celebration when people gather together to congratulate the newlyweds and celebrate their union.

Well, the marriage supper of Jesus Christ is a *real* party! I say that because this bash is going to last one thousand years. The millennial reception will bring time to an end and usher in eternity. Let's find out more about this unique period called the millennial kingdom (Revelation 20), ruled over by the unique person of all time and eternity, Jesus Christ.

THE PURPOSE OF
CHRIST'S MILLENNIAL REIGN

Why did God ordain and decree in His eternal plan that there would be a thousand-year period on earth that His Son would rule with absolute, sovereign control and perfect righteousness?

To Vindicate Jesus

One reason is to vindicate Christ. Jesus was rejected by the nation Israel when He came the first time to be their King. But it is impossible that the second person of the Trinity could ultimately be prevented from taking His rightful throne.

That's why Jesus will rule His kingdom with Jerusalem as His capital. Remember the Magi asked in Jerusalem, "Where is He who has been born King of the Jews?" (Matthew 2:2). That title was written over Jesus' cross, and it still belongs to

Him. In the Millennium, He will finally claim His throne and receive all the glory that is His due.

To Vindicate God's Plan

The millennial kingdom will also prove the wisdom of God's original plan for mankind. God created man to rule the earth in His behalf (see Psalm 8:5–6; Hebrews 2:7) in response to the conflict in heaven when Satan and one-third of the angels rebelled and were booted out of heaven.

God wanted to demonstrate His glory to the angels by fashioning human beings, creatures inferior to the angels, whom He would use to rule the earth and overcome the sin and ruin caused by the angel Lucifer, or Satan. This will happen in the Millennium, the "world to come" (Hebrews 2:5) that the writer of Hebrews said will be ruled by Christ and His redeemed people.

This goes all the way back to Genesis 1–2, when God took the chaos of the original creation, re-created it, and put man in the Garden of Eden with the command to subdue and rule the earth. God told Adam, "I have created this world for you to rule."

But Satan snuck in and ruined the renovation (Genesis 3). Adam and Eve sinned, and in so doing handed the rulership over to Satan. The devil took the earth, and creation has been on a steady decline ever since.

But God made a promise in Genesis 3:15 that the Seed of the woman, Jesus Christ, was going to come and destroy the serpent. Jesus would overthrow Satan's overthrow of Adam in the garden.

So the spiritual battle lines were drawn, and the rest of the Bible is the unfolding story of the coming of the Seed, God become Man, who defeated Satan in fulfillment of God's promise.

God made the statement that He has "put all things in subjection under his feet" (Hebrews 2:8a), that is, the feet of mankind. "But now we do not yet see all things subjected to him" (v. 8b).

In other words, the creation has not yet been restored to man's rule, although we can see traces of man's former dominance in the fear that some animals have of humans. If you run into a lion, you'd better run because that lion will have no respect for you. Lions are not subjected to man today, although God originally made it that way.

But in earth's coming golden age called the Millennium, mankind will realize his original destiny and purpose to rule because of the person and work of *the* Man, Jesus Christ.

We will rule and reign with Christ for a thousand years (Revelation 20:6) as God demonstrates to the angels what He can do with mankind, a lesser creation, when mankind operates according to His Will and His Word.

THE PROCESS OF CHRIST'S MILLENNIAL REIGN

The second aspect of the Millennium is what I call the process, the succession of events by which Christ's kingdom is established.

With the bride of Christ adorned and ready for her marriage, the apostle John said:

I saw heaven opened; and behold, a white horse, and He who sat upon it is called Faithful and True; and in righteousness He judges and wages war. And His eyes are a flame of fire, and upon His head are many diadems; and He has a name written upon Him which no one knows except Himself. And He is clothed with a robe dipped in blood; and His name is called The Word of God. And the armies which are in heaven, clothed in fine linen, white and clean, were following Him on white horses. (Revelation 19:11–14)

This will be quite a sight. Jesus Christ will ride out of heaven to inaugurate His kingdom and begin the wedding reception. We are with Him, because no bridegroom goes to his reception without his bride.

Judgment of Christ's Enemies

But in order to inaugurate His thousand-year rule, Jesus Christ must deal with His enemies. So His first task will be judgment. That's the purpose of the army following Him.

According to verses 15 and 16, "From His mouth comes a sharp sword, so that with it He may smite the nations; and

He will rule them with a rod of iron; and He treads the wine press of the fierce wrath of God, the Almighty. And on His robe and on His thigh He has a name written, 'King of Kings, and Lord of Lords.'"

Here is Jesus Christ coming back from His throne in heaven to rid Himself of all opposition as He sets up His throne on earth. The earth has just gone through the seven-year period known as the Tribulation, and God is ready to conclude this portion of His judgment in preparation for the millennial reign of Christ.

Jesus described His return in Matthew 24:27, where He said, "Just as the lightning comes from the east, and flashes even to the west, so shall the coming of the Son of Man be." Then He continued, "Immediately after the tribulation of those days the sun will be darkened, and the moon will not give its light, and the stars will fall from the sky, and the powers of the heavens will be shaken, and then the sign of the Son of Man will appear in the sky, and then all the tribes of the earth will mourn" (vv. 29–30a).

This is the return we just read about in Revelation 19. We are not told what this sign is or how the whole world will see it, but it will definitely capture the attention of everyone living on earth. The whole world will see Jesus Christ returning in glory. It will be like a lightning strike that gains worldwide attention. Christ's return to establish His reign is going to be a climactic event.

The great battle in which Jesus Christ eliminates His enemies prior to His kingdom is called the Battle of Armageddon, which will take place in the huge valley of Jezreel in Israel at the end of the Tribulation.

The enemies of Christ will join behind the Antichrist and the false prophet to go to battle against Christ as He rides out of heaven (Revelation 19:17–21). The Antichrist and the false prophet are judged at this point and thrown into the lake of fire. Then their armies will perish in a great slaughter. The armies of the earth will be wiped out.

If the church is coming back with Christ, and a good portion of the earth's population is wiped out at Armageddon, who will be left on earth to populate the millennial kingdom?

It will be populated by people who became believers in Christ amid great suffering and persecution in the Tribulation, but who survived and are brought into the Millennium.

Revelation of Christ to Israel

In Revelation 1:7, Jesus said that when He returns, "Every eye will see Him, even those who pierced Him."

This is a reference to the nation of Israel. At Jesus' coming to establish His kingdom, the remnant of Israel that survives the Tribulation will see Him and realize He is their Messiah whom the nation rejected and who was crucified (see Zechariah 12:10). Then Zechariah says the nation will weep and mourn over the rejection of its Messiah.

Many people in Israel are still looking for Messiah to come. On one of our trips to Israel, no matter where we went or who we talked to, it seemed that everybody was looking for Messiah.

One of our Jewish tour guides told me at dinner, "When Messiah comes, he is going to solve our problems here in the Middle East."

Another man told me, "I don't know who Messiah is or when he is going to come, but I sure wish he would hurry up and get here." A woman who lost her son in the 1967 Six-Day War said she prayed that Messiah would come and bring peace.

Israel rejected Jesus as its Christ, its Messiah. But when He comes again, the truth of who He is will be revealed to Israel.

The Imprisonment of Satan

When we were talking about Christ eliminating His enemies, you may have noticed that we did not mention the greatest Enemy of all—Satan.

Satan will be dealt with separately, because God has a special judgment awaiting Satan for the duration of the Millennium. John said:

> I saw an angel coming down from heaven, having the key of the abyss and a great chain in his hand. And he laid hold of the dragon, the serpent of old, who is the devil and Satan, and bound him for a thousand years, and threw him in the abyss, and shut it and sealed it over him, so that he should not deceive the nations any longer, until the thousand years were completed; after these

things he must be released for a short time. (Revelation 20:1–3)

The reason the Millennium will be a golden age is that the devil will be put out of commission for the entire time. Our Enemy who has been tempting and corrupting the human race since Genesis 3 will not have access to the nations for one thousand years. There will be no deception from the devil in Christ's kingdom.

This is the process of Christ's millennial reign. He will come with His saints, win the Battle of Armageddon and judge the Antichrist and false prophet, resurrect the Tribulation martyrs, and usher in His kingdom.

THE PATTERN OF CHRIST'S MILLENNIAL REIGN

What will Jesus Christ's millennial kingdom look like? How will it function? Since He is the unique person in all of eternity and in all of history, we would expect His kingdom to be unlike any other—and it will be. Let's describe some of the elements so we can better understand this golden age of which you and I will be a part.

A Theocratic Rule

The first thing we need to understand is that Christ's kingdom will be a theocracy, literally the "rule of God." No democracy here, no voting for your favorite candidate, no majority to carry the day. Jesus will rule "with a rod of iron" (Revelation 2:27; 19:15). His authority will be absolute.

If you want a biblical picture of Jesus' reign, look at Daniel 7:13–14, which describes the One who will have total dominion. And the prophet Zechariah says, "The Lord will be king over all the earth; in that day the Lord will be the only one" (14:9). Everyone will conform to Christ's will during this age.

Let me clarify something here. The millennial kingdom will not be a perfect age because there are still non-resurrected human beings living on earth—people still possessing the sinful nature, in other words.

You and I will be perfect because we will have been raptured and judged for rewards and given our new bodies. And only righteous people will be brought into the kingdom. But these people will have children and grandchildren and great-grandchildren, because human life will continue. And these descendants will not all follow in the spiritual footsteps of their ancestors.

In other words, sinners will be born and grow up during the Millennium. This is why the Bible says Jesus will rule with an iron rod. This rod is a picture of judgment. What it means is that no rebellion will be tolerated during Christ's reign. The only possible rebellion will be internal, in a person's heart. There will be no allowance for external rebellion.

So there will be no crime or anything like that when Jesus Christ sits on His throne. To put it in today's terms, He will not take any stuff from anybody. Any attempted rebellion will be dealt with instantly. The earth will finally function the way it is supposed to function.

A Righteous Rule

Jesus' rule will also be totally righteous. No one will have to fear any injustice or wrongdoing from the government.

Isaiah 11:1–9 is a prophecy of the coming millennial kingdom, not a prophecy of heaven as a lot of people assume. The "shoot" and "branch" from the line of David is Messiah, Jesus Christ (vv. 1–2). Notice what Isaiah says about His rule:

He will not judge by what His eyes see, nor make a decision by what His ears hear; but with righteousness He will judge the poor, and decide with fairness for the afflicted of the earth; and He will strike the earth with the rod of His mouth, and with the breath of His lips He will slay the wicked. Also righteousness will be the belt about His loins, and faithfulness the belt about His waist. (Isaiah 11:3–5)

The Millennium will be an era of total righteousness. Jesus Christ can carry out this kind of rule because He is God, and He will decide every case in absolute righteousness.

A Harmonious Planet

The Millennium will also be an era of total peace. We're talking about the kind of peace the world has been longing for and striving for, and failing to achieve, since sin entered the Garden of Eden.

Isaiah 11:6–9 gives us this picture of peace, when even the animal kingdom will be restored to the peace and harmony it enjoyed before sin entered. Wolves and lions and bears and leopards can't live in peace with lambs and goats and calves today because of sin. But that's not the way God created the world.

When sin entered, nature went crazy, and now the wolf is going to eat the lamb. But in the golden age of the Millennium, nature will be restored, and the effects of Adam's mess will be reversed.

Mankind will no longer have to fear things like lions and poisonous snakes, because nature will be brought back under man's control. But not just any man. We are talking about Jesus Christ, the God-man.

Isaiah also says, "They will not hurt or destroy in all My holy mountain" (11:9). There won't be any harm coming to anyone from the animal world or from humans. We have already seen that there won't be any crime or other human ugliness because Jesus Christ will take care of it instantly. He will keep the peace like it has never been kept before.

A Spiritual Atmosphere

The atmosphere in Christ's millennial kingdom will also be permeated by the knowledge and presence of God. "The earth will be full of the knowledge of the Lord as the waters cover the sea" (Isaiah 11:9).

God and His Word, and the knowledge of Him, will be everywhere. Everybody will function in harmony with the knowledge of God because everybody will have it. The knowledge of God will completely saturate the atmosphere of earth.

In the Millennium, nobody will be able to do anything that does not bring him or her into contact with God.

A Prosperous Era

The millennial kingdom of Christ is also going to usher in an era of prosperity like the earth has never known before.

Isaiah wrote, "He will give you rain for the seed which you will sow in the ground, and bread from the yield of the ground, and it will be rich and plenteous; on that day your livestock will graze in a roomy pasture" (Isaiah 30:23). "And the scorched land will become a pool, and the thirsty ground springs of water" (35:7).

I could cite a number of passages that describe the bounty and fertility of the earth in the Millennium.

Christ's kingdom will also be a time of health and long life for the people who live and are born during this golden age. Isaiah 29:18 indicates that deaf ears will be able to hear and blind eyes able to see in that day. And "the lame will leap like a deer, and the tongue of the dumb will shout for joy" (Isaiah 35:6). Isaiah 33:24 says, "No resident will say, 'I am sick.'" There will be no illness whatsoever.

This does not refer to you and me, because we will already have our perfect resurrection bodies. This is talking about the people who will inhabit the earth during the Millennium.

Now here's a passage for you. According to Isaiah 65:20, "No longer will there be in [the kingdom] an infant who lives but a few days, or an old man who does not live out his days; for the youth will die at the age of one hundred and the one who does not reach the age of one hundred shall be thought accursed."

Can you imagine it? No crib deaths in the kingdom! Now remember, this is not us, but the people we will help Christ rule in the kingdom. It will be such a golden age that if someone dies at the age of ninety-eight, people are going to say, "What happened to him? What did he do wrong? How did he mess up to die so young?"

This is the restoration of the way the earth was intended to operate before sin messed up everything.

Isaiah 65:21–22 says, "They shall build houses and inhabit them; they shall also plant vineyards and eat their fruit. They shall not build, and another inhabit, they shall not plant, and another eat." In Christ's millennial kingdom, prosperity will abound.

THE PROGRAM OF CHRIST'S MILLENNIAL KINGDOM

Before we conclude this study of the kingdom and this section on the uniqueness of Jesus Christ, I want to talk about what you and I will be doing during His millennial reign.

Jesus Christ's Administrators

We know that the resurrected saints will return with Christ, and we will be very busy during the kingdom. Our involvement in the Millennium answers the question of how Jesus is going to administer the program of His kingdom.

Jesus will be ruling from His throne in Jerusalem, and He will need administrators to carry out His program. Enter the saints who make up His church. We will serve as administrators in Jesus' government. We will be "fellow heirs" with Him (Romans 8:17).

The extent of our individual privilege and responsibilities will already have been determined at the judgment seat of Christ. Remember Jesus said He would make some of His faithful servants rulers over ten cities and others rulers over five cities (Luke 19:11–27). The kingdom is where these rewards are handed out.

Some Christians will be administering entire regions, while others will be sweeping streets in the kingdom, depending on their faithfulness to Christ.

After the rich young man had turned away from Jesus one day, Peter went up to Him and asked, "Jesus, what's in this deal for us? After all, we're committing our lives to You. Is there a payback here?"

Jesus said to all the disciples, "You who have followed Me, in the regeneration when the Son of Man will sit on His glorious throne [the millennial kingdom], you also shall sit upon twelve thrones, judging the twelve tribes of Israel" (Matthew 19:28).

And then Jesus broadened the promise. "And everyone who has left houses or brothers or sisters or father or mother or children or farms for My name's sake, shall receive many times as much, and shall inherit eternal life. But many who are first will be last; and the last, first" (vv. 29–30).

The Importance of Faithfulness

That last statement Jesus made is crucial as it applies to the kingdom age. He is telling us not to get too hung up on our roles down here because a lot of things will be turned around in the kingdom. Some up-front people will be background people there, and vice versa.

We just need to worry about serving Christ faithfully with what Christ has given us. That's why it is incumbent on us to do everything we do to the glory of God (Colossians 3:23).

So we are going to rule with Christ in His kingdom, and the extent of our responsibility will be determined by our faithfulness to Him.

THE CONCLUSION OF
CHRIST'S MILLENNIAL REIGN

I need to show you how the thousand-year reign of Christ will conclude. That takes us back to Revelation 20:

When the thousand years are completed, Satan will be released from his prison, and will come out to deceive the nations which are in the four corners of the earth, Gog and Magog, to gather them together for the war; the number of them is like the sand of the seashore. And they came up on the broad plain of the earth and surrounded the camp of the saints and the beloved city, and fire came down from heaven and devoured them. (vv. 7–9)

The Final Rebellion

It's amazing that after one thousand years of unbelievable prosperity, peace, and righteousness on earth, Satan will still find a large following in his final attempt to overthrow God.

By the end of the Millennium, with people being born and living longer lives, there will be quite a massive population on earth. Apparently, among the earth's population will be a huge group of people who have wanted to rebel against Jesus Christ but never had the chance. Satan will bring out the rebellion that's already inside of these people.

This final world battle is called Gog and Magog, which are probably symbolic terms for God's enemies. Satan gathers around him everyone on earth who has any gripe at all against God, and fire comes from heaven to devour the last remnants of a rebellion against God that began way back in Eden.

Judgment of Satan and the World

Then the devil will receive his awful eternal sentence, joining the Antichrist and the false prophet in the lake of fire (Revelation 20:10). Notice that even though these other two were thrown into the lake more than a thousand years earlier, they are still alive and being tormented.

The doom of Satan is followed by the great judgment called the Great White Throne judgment (v. 11), in which all dead unbelievers are resurrected and hear their own doom. When God finishes this judgment and all unbelievers are cast into hell, then the kingdom and time as we know it is finished, and we enter into eternity in heaven (Revelation 21–22).

The Eternal State

Remember we said that Christ's kingdom is the reception party for the marriage supper of the Lamb. When a newly married couple finishes with all the celebration and the festivities, they eventually come home to begin their life together.

That's what happens with Christ and His people when we leave time behind and enter the eternal state of heaven. This is when we enter the New Jerusalem and when God wipes away all tears from our eyes (Revelation 21:1–4).

You know what Jesus Christ is doing right now. He is preparing the place He promised for us in His Father's house, and He is awaiting the day when He will return for us and take us to be with Himself (John 14:1–3).

When the millennial reign of Christ draws to a close, when righteousness has been vindicated, and when sin and Satan have been judged, then Christ will deliver up His kingdom to the Father. Paul tells us how it will happen:

Then comes the end, when He [Jesus] delivers up the kingdom to the God and Father, when He has abolished all rule and all authority and power. For He must reign until He has put all His enemies under His feet. . . . And when all things are subjected to Him, then the Son Himself also will be subjected to the One who subjected all things to Him, that God may be all in all. (1 Corinthians 15:24–25, 28)

This is the conclusion to the millennial reign of Jesus Christ, the unique Son of God who will hand His kingdom over to His Father and reign as God the Son for all eternity.

GETTING READY FOR CHRIST'S COMING KINGDOM

As we close this section of the book, I want to suggest four things we can do today in response to the coming thousand-year kingdom of the unique Son of God.

First, we can model the kingdom right where we are. That's what God wants us to do, set up replicas of Christ's kingdom on earth so people can see what it looks like when Christ controls a person's life.

Second, we also need to prepare for the kingdom. If you want a high post of authority and honor in the Millennium, live a life of faithfulness to Christ now.

Third, we can honor the King of the kingdom. We can live in such a way that we bring honor and glory to Jesus Christ by our lives.

Fourth, we need to prioritize the kingdom. Jesus said, "Seek first His kingdom and His righteousness; and all these things shall be added to you" (Matthew 6:33). Are you getting ready for Christ's return?

PART TWO

THE AUTHORITY OF CHRIST

CHAPTER NINE
THE AUTHORITY OF CHRIST OVER NATURE

I want to turn now from a consideration of Jesus Christ's uniqueness to a study of His authority. What we are going to see in this and the following chapters of this section is that just as Christ's uniqueness as the Son of God extends to every area of life and to every corner of earth and heaven, so His authority over every other force and power on earth or under the earth is complete, absolute, and never ending.

We're going to begin by talking about Christ's authority over nature, using one of my favorite stories in the gospel of Mark. This is a confrontation between Jesus and the forces of nature that served notice on the disciples, and serves notice on all of us, that Jesus Christ is in a class all by Himself.

You see, whenever people say the answer to anything is Jesus plus anything, or Jesus plus anybody, they've said too much. Jesus is incomparable. He is God in the flesh, and when He comes on the scene you have to make a decision. You can acknowledge or reject His authority, but you cannot ignore it or add to it.

As I said, Jesus' authority affects every realm of life. There is no area in which Jesus does not have total authority. He *is* Lord of all, and the best thing we can do is confess His lordship and live under it.

Jesus demonstrated His authority over nature a number of times in the Gospels. One of these is the occasion described in Mark 4:35–41, at the end of a long day.

THE PLAN

Jesus had been teaching from a boat at the edge of the Sea of Galilee (see 4:1), and that evening He turned to the disciples and said, "Let us go over to the other side" (v. 35). He was referring to the western shore of the Sea of Galilee opposite the Galilee side, about a seven-and-a-half mile trip. That was the plan.

When that boat set out on its trip, Jesus was very tired. He had been teaching the multitudes and answering the disciples' questions all day long. You need to read Mark 4:1–34 to get the picture of the kind of exhausting day Jesus had experienced. Jesus lay down in the boat and was asleep as soon as His head hit the cushion (v. 38).

We have talked enough about the two natures of Christ that it should not be hard to understand how the eternal Son of God, the second person of the Trinity who created everything, could be exhausted. Jesus' humanity was real.

In fact, Christ was so tired He didn't even want to go back to shore or try to deal with the crowds anymore. Mark tells us, "Leaving the multitude, they took Him along with them, just as He was, in the boat; and other boats were with Him" (v. 36).

Jesus didn't want to hang around. But even though they left as soon as He finished teaching, some people in other boats tried to follow Jesus. That was the kind of day it was for Him.

THE PROBLEM

Even though Jesus had made a simple statement of His intention to go with His disciples to the other side of the lake, they obviously weren't listening.

The Threat of the Storm

We know that they weren't listening because as soon as they got out on the water, a storm came up and they panicked, thinking for sure they were going to drown right there.

The Sea of Galilee is situated in such a way that the winds can come sweeping down from the surrounding mountains and create ferocious storms. This is the kind of storm that engulfed the boat carrying Jesus and the disciples. "There arose a fierce gale of wind, and the waves were breaking over the boat so much that the boat was already filling up" (Mark 4:37).

These men had heard Jesus say they were going to the other side, but all of a sudden their experience was not matching Jesus' word. They began to see that they were in danger of not making it to the other side. They had a major problem.

So the disciples did what you and I probably would have done in the same situation. They looked at Jesus asleep in the back of the boat, "awoke Him and said to Him, 'Teacher, do You not care that we are perishing?'" (v. 38).

Do you see how tired Jesus must have been? He was sleeping in spite of this fierce storm that was filling the boat with water and rocking it from side to side. This was a serious situation, not some minor inconvenience. Jesus must have been getting wet, but He was still asleep.

The Fear at Jesus' Seeming Unconcern

Have you ever been in a circumstance like this? You believe you are acting in God's will, but then hell attacks. When you call on Jesus, it seems like He is asleep. No one picks up on the other end of the line.

The disciples felt like that, and they asked themselves, "How could Jesus sleep at a time like this?" So they woke Him up to inform Him of the terrible problem they had. As far as they could see, they were about to die, and Jesus didn't even care.

The disciples were saying, "Jesus, even if You don't care that much about us, You ought to at least care about Yourself, because if this boat goes down You are going down with us."

It wasn't the storm or the danger that woke Jesus. It was the disciples who woke Him up, because they were beginning to allow their circumstances to control their theology. They were measuring the love of Christ by the amount of water in the bottom of the boat.

Have you ever asked the question, "God, don't You care? It doesn't seem like it, because if You cared it wouldn't be raining this hard. If You cared, my boat wouldn't be filling with water and rocking back and forth like this."

The disciples forgot what Jesus had said when it was calm and began to doubt His care based on their problem. Let me tell you, many times in life the problems will appear to negate the promises of God or make it seem like He doesn't care.

The disciples suddenly developed a "circumstantial theology" in the middle of that storm. They determined what they believed by what they were going through.

But the middle of a storm is not the place to work out your theology. You need to determine what you believe in the good times, so you'll know what to believe when the bad times hit. You need to decide who Jesus Christ is when everything's going right, so you'll know who He is when everything's going wrong.

The disciples forgot what they had learned about Jesus when the sea was calm, so they raised a very serious question: "Jesus, don't You care?"

THE PROVISION

The dangerous storm and the disciples' question led to a miraculous provision by Jesus Christ, who exercised His authority over the natural world He had created.

Jesus Calms the Sea

"And being aroused, He rebuked the wind and said to the sea, 'Hush, be still.' And the wind died down and it became perfectly calm" (Mark 4:39).

The disciples had allowed fear of their circumstances to start dictating their theology, but at least they knew where to go for help. Jesus was asleep and they were desperate, so they came to Him and shook Him awake with their need. And they definitely came to the right person, because Jesus quickly and effortlessly calmed the wind and the sea. No problem there.

But notice that nothing happened until the disciples asked Jesus for help. So often when we get in a mess, instead of going to God for help we go off and try to fix the mess ourselves.

We figure if we just keep rowing our boat "gently down the stream" we will reach calm waters. The disciples tried that, but they got to the place where all their efforts at rowing were meaningless, and someone finally said, "Let's ask Jesus."

So they aroused Jesus. They didn't just gently whisper until He woke up or lightly tap Him, either. They made sure He was awake, because they were in a desperate situation.

One reason God allows us to face trials is to remind us of something that Jesus wants His people to learn: "Apart from Me you can do nothing" (John 15:5). In other words, independent Christian living is failed Christian living.

The storms show us that unless God shows up, we are in trouble. As long as we insist on doing it all ourselves, He will allow the storm to get worse and worse.

Jesus wasn't going to do anything until the disciples asked Him. The apostle James wrote, "You do not have because you do not ask" (James 4:2). If you don't have a determination to get hold of God, don't be surprised if He seems to be sleeping through your storm.

People often ask me how long they should pray about something. My response is, "Until you get an answer." You talk to God until He says yes or no.

The disciples had an external problem, the storm, that led to an internal problem, their fear and belief that Jesus didn't care about them. When they woke Jesus up, He dealt with the external problem. The elements immediately obeyed Him.

When Jesus fixes stuff, it's fixed. One way you know Jesus has done something is that it's done perfectly. Jesus doesn't do anything halfway. When we try to work things out, we do a piecemeal job. But when Jesus addresses an issue, He addresses it comprehensively.

A Lesson for the Disciples

The stilling of the storm was a miracle, but that's the kind of authority Jesus has. I'm surprised there are so many Christians who do not believe the authority of Christ still works miracles today. Sometimes we just do not understand the nature of the Christ whom we serve.

We serve a Christ who can tell the wind to stop blowing, because He made the wind. He can tell the sea to be calm, because He made the sea. So what is there in your life that Jesus cannot handle?

We would fare a lot better if we allowed Jesus to be Lord in our lives. He *is* Lord, make no mistake. But He will not rule as Lord in your life until you come to Him and say, "Jesus, I need You. I can't make it by myself."

Jesus wants to take control of our lives, but so many of us are like a wild mustang that needs to be broken. The first time the rider puts a saddle on the mustang and attempts to ride, the horse goes wild. The uncertainty and confusion of this new weight on its back sends the animal into hysteria, and so it begins to buck and resist the new pressure.

This goes on until the mustang learns to submit to the rider's will and discovers that the rider is not a threat but an ally. When God puts the saddle of trials on us, they are designed to bring us into submission to Him. But as long as we buck and resist, we are expending energy trying to throw off the very One who wants to help us realize the purpose for which we were created.

Having Jesus in your boat may not keep you out of the storm, but He is the provision you need to get you through the storm. Jesus is unique. He could be tired and sleep because He was human, and yet He could stand up and calm the wind and waves because He is God.

In other words, Jesus knows what you feel because He's Man, and He can do something about it because He's God!

When you are tired, Jesus knows how that feels because He got tired. When you're hungry, Jesus can identify because He was hungry. When you cry over painful circumstances, Jesus understands because He cried over the death of His friend Lazarus (John 11:35).

If you have ever been betrayed, Jesus knows how you feel because His best friend Peter denied Him three times. Jesus also knows what it feels like to be lonely, because when He was arrested all the disciples forsook Him and ran away. And Jesus even knows what it feels like when you are burdened down with sin, because He carried the weight of the whole world's sin on the cross.

So no matter what your problem, when you come to Jesus you will find a Lord who understands and can provide for your need. Jesus knew the disciples were scared out of their wits. He knew the storm was terrorizing them.

The disciples could empathize with each other, but they couldn't do anything about the problem. Oh, but Jesus could!

I've had people come to me with a problem and leave mad because I couldn't fix it. But I never said I was Jesus. The issue is, Where are you taking your problem?

There's nothing wrong with human counselors. But if you are talking to a human counselor more than you are talking to the heavenly Counselor, you've got the wrong focus. The disciples held a group counseling session and decided to try to get out of their mess by themselves.

But that didn't work, so they had another very brief session and decided they had better take this mess to Jesus, because they needed Someone with authority over nature.

A NEW PERSPECTIVE

You can be sure the disciples got a new perspective on themselves and on Jesus after He quieted the storm.

A New Perspective on Themselves

Jesus performed the miracle, then He said to His disciples, "Why are you so timid? How is it that you have no faith?" (Mark 4:40). Now Jesus was dealing with the *real* problem, which was not the wind or the waves or the water in the bottom of the boat.

The problem was the disciples' wimpy lack of faith. That's the idea behind the word *timid.* The disciples wimped out on Jesus. Their faith collapsed in the face of the storm.

Men don't like to hear that they are wimps, that they are weak. So I can imagine the disciples thinking to themselves, *Wait a minute, Jesus. You obviously don't understand. This is the real world, and in the real world when your boat gets full of water you get scared. It's just natural. We know how bad these storms can be.*

Why did Jesus rebuke the disciples for their lack of faith? Not just for becoming afraid in a bad situation. The problem was they had missed the whole point. Before they ever left, Jesus had said, "Let us go over to the other side."

Jesus was rebuking His men for allowing their bad situation to take over so that they reacted to the storm instead of believing what He said. They allowed their circumstances to dictate their theology, as we said above, and that's a very bad perspective. The disciples forgot what Jesus had told them.

He didn't say, "*I'm* going to the other side while you drown." And He certainly didn't say, "Let's all go out to the middle of the sea and drown." He intended to complete the trip with them. But Jesus also did not say the trip would be trouble free.

Do you see where I'm going? The disciples had the assurance of God's word that they would be fine, because they had Jesus and He is the Word of God incarnate. But they forgot what God had said—and when circumstances come between you and God's Word, your fear of the storm will overwhelm your confidence in the Word.

What we need today is confidence in a Savior who has all authority. When you have that, your boat of circumstances may start taking on water, and it may look like you're going to drown. But you can go back to the Word with the confidence, "God says we are going to the other side."

The choice is pretty clear. Either you cling to the truth, or you give in to the circumstances. Jesus could sleep through the storm because He knew where He was going. So when the storm started someone should have said, "Well, Jesus is sleeping, so we must be all right. All the oars are taken already, so hand me a pillow."

Are you facing a problem that no human being can solve? Are you holding on to Jesus, clinging to what His Word says? Since Jesus is the only One who can calm the sea with a word, we had better be spending our time getting to know Him. Until we get to Jesus, the storm will still rage.

The disciples had no faith. They didn't believe Jesus' word. They needed to see for themselves their lack of faith.

A New Perspective on Jesus

After Jesus gave the disciples a new look at themselves, they got a new perspective on Him. Seeing the miracle, "They became very much afraid and said to one another, 'Who then is this, that even the wind and the sea obey Him?'" (Mark 4:41).

At first the Twelve were afraid of the storm. But now they were afraid of the storm stopper. The Greek text says literally, **"They feared with a great fear."**

We are too often afraid of the wrong thing. We are awed by the circumstance when we need to be in deep, reverential awe of God. If we are going to get our emotions stirred, they need to be stirred up over who Jesus Christ is.

Now the disciples were afraid of Jesus because they did not yet fully understand or appreciate who it was in the boat with them.

They did not know that "very God of very God," to use the theologians' term for Jesus, was in the boat with them. They didn't realize what kind of person they were dealing with.

Our Need for Perspective

We lose sight of this too. That's why we need to keep our focus on Christ, especially when everything else breaks loose. Any carpenter will tell you that if you want to avoid hitting your thumb with the hammer, keep your eye on the nail you're driving, not on your thumb. If you take your eyes off Jesus, don't be surprised if you smash your spiritual thumb.

One day a farmer was teaching his son how to plow. He said, "Son, in order to plow a straight furrow, don't look down at the ground, look ahead. Find something on the other side of the field, fix your eye on it, and head toward it. That way, you'll plow straight furrows."

The farmer left his son to plow, but when he came back he saw crooked furrows going all over the field. The farmer asked his son, "What in the world happened?"

"Dad, I picked out something to keep my eye on just like you said. I kept my eye on the cow." The problem was, of course, that the cow kept moving. Keep your eyes on Jesus, because He's not going anywhere.

You don't have to deny your hard circumstances. A storm is a storm. Call it what it is, but don't yield to it. Remember that all the authority belongs to Christ.

That way, you can make your trials work for you. They can become stepping-stones to a new level of spiritual maturity and blessing, rather than stumbling blocks to take you to the bottom of the sea. The disciples were getting a new perspective on Jesus that they wouldn't have gotten if it had not been for the storm.

It takes wind for a kite to fly. The opposition of the wind against the kite lifts it higher and higher until it is soaring.

That's exactly what God wants for us. He wants us to soar, but that means some wind is going to have to blow against our lives. If you haven't felt the wind yet, just keep living. I suspect, though, that you've felt the wind against you plenty of times, just as I have.

When the wind starts blowing, go to Jesus. Remind Him of the promises in His Word. Remind Him that He said that you're going to the other side, not that you will drown in the middle of the lake.

One day a young boy was on an airplane flight when the plane got caught in a storm and hit some very bad turbulence. The plane was rocking back and forth, and trays were sliding around. People were getting scared, and some began to scream as the plane pitched back and forth and dipped up and down.

But in the middle of all this chaos, the boy just kept on playing. When the plane dipped, he said, "Wheee!" while everyone else was screaming.

A little old lady sitting next to the boy asked him, "Son, how can you play and be happy at a time like this?"

The boy looked at her and said, "Oh, it's easy, my daddy's the pilot."

Once you know who's in charge, it doesn't matter whether your plane or your boat is rocking in the storm. Jesus is in charge of nature. He's the One with all authority. He can calm any storm. Does He have authority over your life?

CHAPTER TEN

THE AUTHORITY OF CHRIST OVER SATAN

History may be defined as the outworking of the cosmic conflict between God and Satan in the realm of mankind. We see moves and countermoves between God and the devil.

God made the first move by creating the world, which included all the angelic host. Satan countered that move by rebelling and taking a third of the angels with him in his rebellion.

God countered that move by creating Adam, who would be His man to rule over planet Earth. Satan countered that move by tempting Adam and Eve to rebel against God's authority. God promised a coming Seed through the woman who would redeem mankind so we could be brought back into fellowship with Him.

Satan tried to counter that move by getting Cain to kill Abel, in order to cut off the godly line. But God blocked that move by creating Seth to reintroduce the godly line. So Satan induced the whole world to rebel against God.

But God found a righteous man named Noah and told him to build a boat on dry land, providing salvation for Noah and his family while wiping out the rest of the world.

Satan wasn't finished yet, though. He found a man named Nimrod and got him to lead a world movement that tried to declare its independence from God by building the Tower of Babel.

That's when God pulled off one of His great counter-moves. He went to Ur of the Chaldees to a man named Abraham and told him, "Through you I am going to build a nation that will obey Me."

Satan countered that move by sending Israel into bondage in Egypt. God, however, sent Moses to Egypt to tell Pharaoh, "Let My people go."

Satan tried to block that move by sending the Egyptian army to wipe out Israel. But God countered by opening the Red Sea for the Israelites and closing it over the Egyptians.

Throughout the Old Testament, this is the way it went. Israel rebelled against God, who raised up a prophet or a judge to bring the nation back to Him. But Satan would be there to tempt the nation to go back into idolatry and sin.

I'm not suggesting that God and Satan were equal foes, each struggling for supremacy. There was never any question that God is absolutely sovereign in His power. But on the chessboard of biblical history, the outcome of the battle was still unclear to human observers by the time the Old Testament closed.

This was followed by four hundred silent years, a period in which there was no word from God. But that silence was broken with the birth of Jesus Christ. Up to this point, God had used men to counter the devil. But now He was saying, "It is time to demonstrate My authority over Satan once for all. I am coming down to take care of this Myself."

PREPARATION FOR THE GREAT BATTLE

So God became a Man in the person of Jesus Christ, who took on Satan in head-to-head battle and emerged totally victorious. This battle is recorded in Matthew 4:1–11, the temptation of Jesus Christ in the wilderness.

This is the great contest between the authority of Christ and the authority of Satan, and there emerges a clear winner. Let's look at Jesus' preparation for this battle and then study the battle itself in detail.

Just prior to our text is the story found in Matthew 3:13–17, the baptism of Jesus. Jesus came to John the Baptist to be baptized, and as He was coming up out of the water, the Bible says, "the heavens were opened, and he saw the Spirit of God descending as a dove, and coming upon Him, and behold, a voice out of the heavens, saying,

'This is My beloved Son, in whom I am well-pleased'" (vv. 16–17).

This was Jesus' preparation for ministry, His public coming out, if you will. God the Father clearly identified Jesus as His Son, and Jesus was commissioned for His ministry. And the first step in that ministry was His temptation, a time of testing and proving in which Jesus established His authority over Satan in no uncertain terms.

Jesus on the Offensive

Matthew 4:1 says, "Then Jesus was led up by the Spirit into the wilderness to be tempted by the devil." Please notice that this confrontation did not come about by Satan's will, but by God's will. It's already clear who is calling the shots here. Jesus went into the wilderness on the offensive, not on the defensive. He was going to demonstrate His superior authority.

By the way, God also allows you and me to be tempted so that we might demonstrate the supreme authority of Christ through our lives. God does not permit Satan to tempt us to make us fall, but that we might prove the superiority of Christ.

Temptation becomes your opportunity to validate the truth, "Greater is He who is in you than he who is in the world" (1 John 4:4). God allows us to be tried and tested in order to validate and verify that Jesus Christ is who He said He is.

The Battleground Decided

Why did God decide that His Son would be tempted in a hot, dry, barren wilderness instead of somewhere else? Because the purpose of Jesus' earthly ministry, which culminated in the Cross, was to reverse the effects of Adam's sin and failure.

The first Adam was tempted in a garden. Satan came onto God's territory and got Adam to sin. As a result, Adam was kicked out of the garden into a world that was now a hot, dry, barren wilderness. It was now Satan's territory.

But Jesus Christ, the Last Adam, paid Satan a return visit. He went onto Satan's territory and defeated him. Why?

To bring us back into the garden, that which God intended mankind to have. Jesus gave us back what was taken from us by the sin of our forefather Adam.

Jesus' Spiritual Preparation

Jesus did not just rush into battle against Satan. What a lesson for us. The Bible says, "After He had fasted forty days and forty nights, He then became hungry" (Matthew 4:2). Until you have fasted over a problem or a need or a circumstance in your life, you have not fully addressed it as far as God is concerned.

Far too many of us give up in the face of trouble before we have used all of our spiritual resources. Jesus knew that He was facing a test from His Father and a temptation from the devil. He needed all the spiritual resources He could get.

So He fasted, going without food for forty days. Jesus gave up a natural and normal need of the body in order to address a greater need of the spirit. That's what fasting is all about. Instead of eating that meal or that day's meals, you commit to spend that time in prayer.

Fasting is a reversal in priorities. We usually eat when we are hungry, but when we fast we ignore our hunger to feed our spirits. Fasting says to God, "The spiritual is more important to me than the physical." God is pleased when we value the spiritual over the physical.

Jesus knew He was heading into a titanic spiritual battle. So He fasted. If Jesus needed to do this, what do you think we need to do when we are facing a spiritual trauma, a trial, or a temptation?

The Tempter's Identity

As we see the stage being set for the confrontation between Christ and Satan, it's important to understand who is doing the tempting here. God the Holy Spirit led Jesus into the wilderness, but God did not tempt His Son to sin.

The Bible says, "God cannot be tempted by evil, and He Himself does not tempt anyone" (James 1:13). Jesus was in the wilderness "to be tempted by the devil." The temptation began when "the tempter," Satan, came to Jesus (Matthew 4:3).

God tests us, but does not tempt us. The difference is that a test is designed to validate your victory in Christ and help you grow stronger spiritually. But a temptation from the devil is designed to defeat you spiritually.

The same event can be both a test and a temptation. In other words, what God uses as a test in your life, Satan may try to use as a temptation. While God seeks to show you that He is powerful in your life, Satan is trying to prove he's powerful.

So don't be surprised if the same circumstance includes both testing and temptation. God is testing you to see whether your "amen" on Sunday is workable on Monday. Satan is tempting you to see whether he can make what you said on Sunday to be only words from your lips rather than the commitment of your heart.

A lot of us are like the three-year-old girl whose mother caught her standing on a chair in the kitchen, eating cookies she wasn't supposed to have. The mother said, "What are you doing up there?"

"Well, Mommy," the girl said, "I just climbed up here to smell the cookies, and my teeth got caught." We make excuses because sin trips us up, but Jesus prepared Himself thoroughly for His battle with the devil. Jesus had just been publicly validated by God, and now it was time for Him to demonstrate His authority over Satan.

THE FIRST ATTACK IN THE BATTLE

After Jesus had fasted for forty days and nights, it was time for battle. So the tempter came at Jesus with three powerful attacks.

The first is recorded in Matthew 4:3, where we read, "The tempter came and said to Him, 'If You are the Son of God, command that these stones become bread.'"

Why did Satan suggest that Jesus launch "Operation Breadbasket"? Because he knew Jesus was hungry! The devil knew what was going on in the wilderness.

The Tempter's Suggestion

This first temptation hit Jesus where He was vulnerable physically. Remember, because Jesus became fully human

He experienced things the way we experience them. Jesus was just as hungry and weak as you and I would be if we fasted that long.

Since God had not stepped in and fed His Son for all that time, the devil's first temptation was for Jesus to act independently of His Father and feed Himself.

The devil was saying, "Jesus, You have been fasting for forty days and Your Father hasn't fed You yet. You have the power to turn these stones into bread. Why should You go hungry when You can do something about it? It's obvious to me that God doesn't intend to supply Your legitimate need for food."

Do you feel that way? It has been forty days and God hasn't supplied your need yet. You've been hunting for a job this long and He hasn't given it to you yet. You've been expecting a raise that you've been praying for. He hasn't supplied it yet. You've been waiting and longing for a mate. He hasn't given those things to you yet. Satan said to Jesus, "God is really not that good because if He was that good, You would have eaten by now."

The Answer of the Word

Jesus answered Satan, "It is written, 'Man shall not live on bread alone, but on every word that proceeds out of the mouth of God'" (Matthew 4:4). Jesus used the Word of God against the devil.

You say, "I know that, Tony." We know it, but we need to let the lesson sink in. If Jesus, the very Word of God in the flesh, needed to use the written Word to deal with the Enemy, how much more do you and I need to use this same Word to deal with the devil when he's trying to tempt and defeat us?

God did not give us the Bible to decorate our coffee tables or just be carried under our arms to church. He gave us the Bible so we could learn it and wield it like a sword.

"The word of God is . . . sharper than any two-edged sword" says the author of Hebrews (4:12). When Satan shows up, you are to take the Word and say, "On guard!"

But you can't use what you don't know. I'm afraid most Christians would have been saying, "It is written . . . somewhere. It's in the Bible somewhere. I know it is. What is that verse again?"

When was the last time you used the Bible on the devil? See, Satan has tricked us into neglecting our primary weapon, because he can beat anything else we have. He can always deal with what we say or think, but he can't handle the Book.

Jesus' answer to the first temptation was a quotation from Deuteronomy 8:3, where Moses was explaining to Israel how God brought the nation through the wilderness. "[God] humbled you and let you be hungry, and fed you with manna . . . that He might make you understand that man does not live by bread alone, but man lives by everything that proceeds out of the mouth of the Lord."

Manna was the little breadlike wafers God miraculously sent from heaven to feed the Israelites. The Hebrew word *manna* means "What is it?"

Why would anyone call a food by a name that's actually a question? Because it was a question God wanted Israel to answer. When the people saw these cornflakes coming down from above and asked, "What is it?" the correct answer was, "This is the supernatural provision of God."

In other words, Israel didn't make it through the wilderness just because the people had something to eat. They made it because they had a God who fed them. And remember, the manna supply only lasted for one day. God wanted His people to look up every day, see the manna falling down, and say, "Thank You, Lord, for giving this to us. We are going to depend on You to give us tomorrow's supply tomorrow."

If God doesn't give something, you shouldn't have it. And if you go and get it anyway, it's going to wind up eating you rather than you eating it. Jesus was hungry and needed bread, but He was not going to get it from the devil.

Too many times we will say, "Well, I'm hungry, and I know God doesn't want me to starve."

That's true. God doesn't want you to starve, but He wants you to trust Him to feed you. He doesn't want you getting your menu from the devil. He doesn't want you compromising with Satan to satisfy what may be a legitimate need.

Satan wanted Jesus to act independently of God by questioning His Father's provision. When you start doing that, you start listening to Satan's suggestions. "Go ahead and get it. You deserve it. You're hungry, aren't you? God doesn't want you to starve, does He?"

Jesus Christ could dismiss the devil's temptation because He has authority over the devil. And through His Word and His name, He delegates His authority to us.

THE SECOND ATTACK IN THE BATTLE

Satan wasn't through with Jesus yet. He fired the second volley in the battle when he took Jesus into Jerusalem and had Him stand at the highest point of the temple.

From this high pinnacle Satan said to Jesus, "If You are the Son of God throw Yourself down" (Matthew 4:6).

Satan's Pattern of Testing

The devil said to Jesus, "Come with me so I can tempt you," and Jesus went. His authority was such that He did not put Himself in any danger at all by allowing Satan to take Him to a place of temptation.

We can't say that about ourselves, but the fact is that God still permits the devil to take us on occasion to see whether we will be faithful to Him. The classic biblical example is Job. God allowed the devil to take Job almost to the grave. The devil took everything Job had and his ten children too, then he took Job's health. But Job's reaction was, "Though [God] slay me, I will hope in Him" (Job 13:15).

God's authority was never in doubt throughout Job's trial. God drew the line each time, and Satan had to stop (see Job 1:6–12; 2:1–6). God's authority is firmly in control in your trial, but sometimes the only way you can see that is by going through the trial and proving God faithful. That's what happened to Job, who ended up with more than he had before Satan's attacks.

Job understood something we need to understand. After all his calamities had hit, Job said to his wife, "Shall we indeed accept good from God and not accept adversity?" (Job 2:10).

Job understood that God was not what we might call today a "Santa Claus" God whose only reason to exist is to shower us with the things we want and never allow discomfort to touch us. God permits Satan to take us sometimes.

The Tempter's Suggestion

Satan took Jesus to the pinnacle of the temple, about 450 feet above the ground, and tempted Him to jump. Then look at what Satan said: "For it is written, 'He will give His angels charge concerning You'; and 'On their hands they will bear You up, lest You strike Your foot against a stone'" (Matthew 4:6).

Satan had been doing some reading in Psalm 91. He knew these verses and used them against Jesus to try to get Him to bypass God's plan, which included the agony of the cross. This was the second temptation, to get Jesus to take the easy way out.

Satan's idea was that if Jesus jumped off the temple in full view of Israel, the angels would ease Him to the ground, He would land safely, and the people would see the miracle and fall down before Jesus in awe and worship and say, "You are the Messiah."

Was Jesus Israel's Messiah? Of course. Did the nation need to fall at His feet and confess Him as Messiah? Certainly. Will they do that someday? Yes, someday *every* knee will bow and confess, "Jesus Christ is Lord" (Philippians 2:11). But it won't happen Satan's way.

Before we look at Jesus' second answer, let's talk about this thing of the devil quoting Scripture. Satan knows the Bible. If he knows the Bible and you don't, you are in big-time trouble, right?

Satan tried "It is written" on Jesus because his first temptation failed. So he said to Jesus, "If I can't get You to act independently of God, let me try some religion on You." Don't get all ruffled when people use the Bible for their own twisted purposes. They're not being original. Hell uses the Bible.

Satan was trying to convince Jesus that he wanted to help Him out by giving Him a way to achieve God's purpose for Him without all the mess of dying on a cross.

If Satan tried that line on Jesus, he'll use it on you. But God doesn't need Satan's help to get you where He wants you to go and be what He wants you to be. You don't need to buy into Satan's plan to make it in the Christian life.

The Answer of the Word

I love this part. Jesus wasn't ruffled at all by Satan's quoting a few Scripture verses out of context.

Jesus countered the devil by saying, "On the other hand" (Matthew 4:7). Don't believe everything you hear until you have checked out "on the other hand." This is where we get the rest of the story.

Jesus was saying, "Satan, if you are going to quote Scripture, tell the whole story." "On the other hand, it is written, 'You shall not put the Lord your God to the test.'" In other words, you can't back God into a corner so that He is obligated to perform a miracle for you.

That's what Satan tried to make Jesus do. But God had a plan, and when it was God's time for Jesus to be revealed and worshiped as Messiah, He would be revealed.

God will not change His plan or hurry it up just because we get tired of waiting and go looking for a temple to leap from. You can't bypass God's will and get God's result. There are no shortcuts on the Christian walk.

The only way Jesus could gain the glory of the crown was by enduring the agony of the cross. Even so, the way we can experience God's blessings is by enduring under trials (James 1:2).

THE THIRD ATTACK IN THE BATTLE

In the third temptation Satan laid aside all the pretense of caring about whether Jesus was hungry or received the worship due Him. In his final attempt, we see Satan revealing himself in all his evil. Now he was standing there in his red jumpsuit, with two horns, a pitchfork, and a pointed tail.

The Tempter's Suggestion

"Again, the devil took Him to a very high mountain, and showed Him all the kingdoms of the world, and their glory; and he said to Him, 'All these things will I give You, if You fall down and worship me'" (Matthew 4:8-9).

This was Satan's bottom line. He was saying, "Jesus, let me tell You what I've been trying to get at here. Bow!" This was Satan's attempt to get Jesus to bow down and hand over to Satan His authority and the worship due Him as God.

This is what Satan has wanted since the day in eternity past when He rebelled against God and tried to take over heaven. He was tired of bowing to God and wanted God to bow to Him.

It was impossible that Jesus Christ would yield to Satan and forfeit His divine authority. But Satan is still trying to rob God of the worship due Him by coming to us as God's people, dangling things in front of us, and saying, "You can have it all. All you have to do is bow."

Satan wants us to worship him—and it's working in too many cases. Too many people are bowing at Satan's altars, whether it's materialism or power or prestige or fame or lust or whatever.

Satan can give you that stuff, because the kingdoms of this world belong to him temporarily. But the cost is astronomical. Satan wanted to be like God, and that's the line he used to seduce Adam and Eve in the garden. He got Eve to bow to him because of her desire to be like God in the wrong way.

See, Satan can offer you "all these things," but that's all he can offer you. However, Jesus said, "Seek first His kingdom and His righteousness; and all these things shall be added to you" (Matthew 6:33).

That doesn't mean God is obligated to give you all the stuff you want. But the beauty of following Him is that you don't have to break your neck or sell out to the devil to have what you need. You can enjoy rest, the way God rested on the seventh day.

You can come to a day every week when you say, "I'm finished. I'm not going to do anymore. God, I'm trusting You to give me what I need. I'm going to enjoy what I've done, which is what I was supposed to do. And if it wasn't enough, I trust You to add these things to me as You see best."

The Answer of the Word

Now that Satan had put aside his pretenses and revealed his true purpose of trying to dethrone God, the temptation was over. Jesus dismissed Satan with the Word. "Begone, Satan! For it is written, 'You shall worship the Lord your God, and serve Him only'" (Matthew 4:10).

Here's a tremendous example of Jesus' authority. Satan had nothing in Him, as Jesus Himself said (John 14:30). Jesus had no obligation to the devil, and neither do you. Jesus' quotation, also from the book of Deuteronomy, puts the issue squarely.

A lot of people observe half of that command. They worship God on Sunday, but they serve all kinds of other agendas and other gods during the week. But if Jesus is the ultimate authority in the universe, then He deserves our exclusive worship *and* our service.

THE AFTERMATH OF THE BATTLE

According to Matthew 4:11, "Then the devil left Him; and behold, angels came and began to minister to Him."

Jesus resisted Satan, and Satan had to flee. Jesus had absolute authority to command Satan to leave, but we have His delegated authority against Satan because James says, "Resist the devil and he will flee from you" (James 4:7).

After Jesus' temptation, God sent angels to minister to Him. Where were those angels all that time? Waiting for the battle to be concluded. Sometimes God leaves us out there with nothing but the sword of the Spirit in order to demonstrate that the Word of God is enough to whip Satan. And when the battle is over, angels show up to minister to us.

Those angels brought food to Jesus because He was hungry. They also brought Him spiritual strength from heaven because that's what He needed. And they brought Him worship because that's what He deserved.

Did you know that every believer has a guardian angel? Jesus said that children have "their angels" (Matthew 18:10), and the believers in Acts thought it was Peter's angel who was knocking on the door (Acts 12:15). The book of Hebrews says the angels are "ministering spirits" sent out to serve the heirs of salvation (Hebrews 1:14).

The job of angels is to deliver the blessings of God according to the timetable of God when we are doing the will of God. When it comes to dealing with Satan, that means we are going to have to keep our eyes firmly fixed on Jesus, "the author and perfecter of faith" (Hebrews 12:2).

Jesus Christ is the One who has total authority over the devil. You can't beat the Enemy on your own. It is the authority of Christ magnified through His Word that wins the battle.

We need to react to Satan and temptation the way a well-trained dog resists a piece of meat thrown at his feet if his master doesn't give him permission to get it.

That kind of discipline doesn't just happen naturally. It comes from a process of training in which the trainer throws out a piece of meat and disciplines the dog when he goes for it. The trainer will do this again and again until the dog learns not to move without the trainer's command. In fact, when the dog is fully trained he won't even look at that tempting piece of meat. He keeps his eye on the trainer, waiting for the trainer's command.

That's one side of the equation, keeping our eyes on Jesus. Here's the other side: When Satan does come, we need to treat him like we would an intruder in our home. You don't welcome an intruder and let him take over and run your home. You pick up the telephone and call 911. Then the police show up with enough firepower to evict and arrest the intruder.

God has an emergency number that will bring the authority of Christ to your side when the devil intrudes. That number is, "It is written." When you dial that number, heaven comes down with all the firepower needed to remove the intruder from your life!

CHAPTER ELEVEN
THE AUTHORITY OF CHRIST OVER DISEASE

Probably no area of Jesus Christ's authority is more discussed, debated, and disagreed about than the issue of Christ's authority over disease and how God intends that authority to be exercised in this age.

The disagreement isn't about whether Christ does or does not have authority over the diseases and deformities that ravage the human body. As we will see in this chapter, the Bible proves unmistakably that Jesus Christ has absolute control over the problem of disease.

The controversy is over whether God intended for every disease and illness to be miraculously healed by the power of Christ, or whether God sometimes allows and uses disease for His greater purposes in the lives of His children.

Two extremes operate here—both of which are a misrepresentation of what the Bible teaches. One is the extreme that *demands* healing from God for every sickness because all disease is from the Enemy and never part of God's will for believers. It seems that God can't make any decisions for Himself because He is controlled by what we want.

In reacting to this extreme, other believers wind up putting God in a box and restricting His power in such a way that He can't do anything about physical illness. It's all up to the doctors.

As with most extremes, the truth lies somewhere in between. What I want to do is try to let the Bible speak for itself as we go to Matthew 8:1–17, a passage in which Jesus healed three people in quick succession. As we unfold this text, I want to extract five key principles that will help us understand the authority of Christ as it relates to disease.

CHRIST'S AUTHORITY IS SOVEREIGN

The first principle Matthew 8 reveals is that Christ's authority over disease is exercised by His sovereign choice. The scene for these three healings is set in verse 1. Jesus had finished the Sermon on the Mount and was coming down from the mountain. Multitudes of people met Jesus at the foot of the mountain, because He had developed quite a reputation.

Verse 2 says, "A leper came to Him, and bowed down to Him, saying, 'Lord, if You are willing, You can make me clean.'" Leprosy was such a feared disease in biblical days that a leper had to live apart from people. A leper was defiled from the standpoint of the Mosaic Law (Leviticus 13:44).

An Appeal to Sovereignty

This man was desperate for help. The leper may not have known the theological concept of *sovereignty*, but his appeal recognized that Jesus was the person with ultimate authority in his case. God's sovereignty means His freedom to act for His own purposes and glory. Jesus Christ has the right to choose what He will and will not do. None of us can presume on Him.

This flies in the face of a current theology that says, "God must heal, and if God does not heal you, the problem is you don't have enough faith." This view presumes on God. It puts man in the position of sovereignty and makes God our servant who is bound to carry out our demands.

Many times it is within the Lord's sovereign purpose to heal. The people in Matthew 8 all experienced healing. But it was by Jesus' choice and His initiative, not theirs or anyone else's.

It's very important that we understand God's sovereignty because, as you know, He does not always choose to do what we want Him to do.

Our children often ask us for things that we, for our own "sovereign" parental purposes, decline to give them. There may be things we cannot do for our children even if we wanted to. But God does not have that problem. His sovereignty involves His will, not His ability. This leper was correct to say that Jesus could heal Him if He chose to do so. It's false to say Jesus *must* heal you because He can heal you. It is correct to say He *may* heal you if your healing is part of His sovereign purpose.

The experience of Shadrach, Meshach, and Abednego in Babylon is a classic example of this distinction. These Hebrew boys were standing before King Nebuchadnezzar, and old "Nebby" warned them that if they didn't bow down to his image, he was going to throw them into the fiery furnace. Then the king asked, "What god is there who can deliver you out of my hands?" (Daniel 3:15).

They answered, "Our God whom we serve is able to deliver us from the furnace of blazing fire. . . . But even if He does not, let it be known to you, O king, that we are not going to serve your gods" (vv. 17–18). That is a proper understanding of God's sovereignty in relation to His power to deliver us from a trial by fire or a trial by disease.

The Part That Faith Plays

Luke says the man who came to Jesus was "full of leprosy" (Luke 5:12). That's worth noting because it suggests his faith in Jesus was strong. When we say that Jesus' authority over disease is exercised sovereignly rather than on the basis of our faith or lack of it, this doesn't mean that faith plays no part in the process.

God still responds to our faith, just as Jesus responded to this man's request. But we can't make the mistake of saying that faith becomes the way we maneuver God into doing what we demand of Him.

Jesus exercised His authority immediately and comprehensively in healing this leper. "He stretched out His hand and touched him, saying, 'I am willing; be cleansed.' And immediately his leprosy was cleansed" (Matthew 8:3). There were no intermediaries, no delay, and no material used.

This is one of the ways Jesus healed people. In Mark 8:22–26 Jesus used saliva to heal a blind man, and He healed him progressively. Another time Jesus used clay, which the blind man had to wash off (John 9:6–7).

The point is that God may intervene directly or progressively, through full, instantaneous healing or through doctors and medication over a period of time. But in all cases, it is the authority of Christ that pulls off the healing.

I'm amazed at the number of Christians who will call on the doctor before they call on God. There's nothing wrong with calling on the doctor. There's everything wrong with treating the doctor as though the doctor were God.

We may shy away from a "name it, claim it" healing theology, but we evangelicals suffer from a reluctance to believe that God miraculously intervenes today in our physical well-being. That's wrong, because Jesus Christ is the same today as He was when He healed the leper (see Hebrews 13:8).

God's Reasons for Illness

God allows disease for a number of reasons, but they come under the banner of His sovereign will and purpose. One of the clearest examples of this is the case of the blind man in John 9, which we mentioned above.

Jesus' disciples had a "godly people don't get sick" theology, so they asked Him, "Who sinned, this man or his parents, that he should be born blind?" (John 9:2).

Jesus set the record straight. The man's blindness was not because of sin, but "in order that the works of God might be displayed in him" (v. 3). This illness was sovereignly created so that God might be glorified in this man's healing.

In Exodus 4:11, God asked Moses, "Who has made man's mouth? Or who makes him dumb or deaf, or seeing or blind? Is it not I, the Lord?" God takes sovereign responsibility for the negative events of life because of His sovereign purposes—some of which He reveals, and some of which He does not reveal. But in the case before us in Matthew 8:1–4, Jesus responded to the leper's plea and healed him. Then Jesus told him to go to the priest and offer the sacrifice specified in the Mosaic Law when a leper was pronounced cleansed. He was to do this "for a testimony to them" (v. 4), to the Jews, of Jesus' power and authority over even the most dread of diseases.

CHRIST'S AUTHORITY IS POSITIONAL

Christ's positional authority is the second principle we can learn from the healings in Matthew 8. In Capernaum Jesus was approached by a centurion, a Roman commander:

> A centurion came to Him, entreating Him, and saying, "Lord, my servant is lying paralyzed at home, suffering great pain." And He said to him, "I will come and heal him." But the centurion answered and said, "Lord, I am not worthy for You to come under my roof, but just say the word, and my servant will be healed. For I, too, am a man under authority, with soldiers under me; and I say to this one, 'Go!' and he goes, and to another, 'Come!' and he comes, and to my slave, 'Do this!' and he does it." (vv. 5–9)

This man paid high tribute to Jesus' authority. He knew that as a soldier he had to carry out the commands of his superior officers, even if they weren't there in person to give the command. And he knew that all he had to do was speak the word to get the soldiers and servants under him moving.

Jesus' Position of Authority

In other words, this man understood authority. He knew that when a person is in a position of authority, that person's presence is not necessary for his commands to be carried out. The people under him just need to know who gave the command.

This soldier was saying to Jesus, "I know what it's like to be under authority and to have authority over others. And if I as a mere man can make things happen just by saying the word, I know You can do it by Your word. So if You will just speak from Your position of total authority, You can heal my servant."

Jesus Christ has authority over disease by means of His supreme position as Creator and sustainer of the universe. He can simply speak away an illness or disease because He created the heavens and the earth (John 1:3; Colossians 1:16) and because the whole creation is held together by His power (Colossians 1:17).

So Jesus has total authority over any environment that can cause sickness, and He has authority over our bodies because He also created us. Christ's position of authority is such that He did not need to be present to heal the centurion's servant. All He had to do was speak the word.

Knowing Someone in the "Corporate Office"

One time I was in Miami, and my business there finished a lot earlier than expected, so I wanted to leave and go home.

Another airline had a flight leaving two or three hours earlier than the flight on my airline, but I couldn't take the earlier flight because the ticket I had would not transfer between the airlines. The airline I was on said they couldn't transfer the ticket, and the airline I wanted to get on said I would have to buy a new ticket.

But then I remembered something. I knew somebody back in Dallas in the corporate office of the airline I was trying to fly home. So I picked up the phone and placed a call. I said, "I've got to get home. I don't want to wait around here three hours for the next flight. Can you help me?"

My problem was in Miami, but the person in Dallas was in a position of authority. It was all about position. This friend picked up the phone and dialed the airline ticket counter in Miami and said, "We have got somebody at the airport there who needs to be on your next flight. He doesn't have a ticket, but put him on the plane based on my word. And by the way, give him a first-class seat."

My friend did not have to be in Miami to help me. That position of authority within the airline solved my problem.

Let me tell you, when you know Christ, you know Somebody in the corporate office! You know Someone who is in heavenly places, but who has access to where you are. All Jesus has to do is speak the word, and your impossible situation becomes possible.

CHRIST'S AUTHORITY IS IMPARTIAL

We are still in the story of the centurion with the sick servant. After this Roman commander made his insightful statement about authority, the Bible says:

Now when Jesus heard this, He marveled, and said to those who were following, "Truly I say to you, I have not found such great faith with anyone in Israel. And I say to you, that many shall come from east and west, and recline at the table with Abraham, and Isaac, and Jacob, in the kingdom of heaven; but the sons of the kingdom shall be cast out into the outer darkness; in that place there shall be weeping and gnashing of teeth." (Matthew 8:10–12)

This is an interesting section of Scripture, which I won't deal with in great detail because it's not within our purpose in this chapter. The point is that Jesus' authority is available to anyone in any place who exercises faith in Him.

At this point in Jesus' ministry, He was ministering to the lost sheep of the house of Israel. The mission to the Gentiles had not yet begun in earnest, but incidents like this gave a sneak preview of what was to come.

Jesus marveled at the centurion's faith. No wonder. Remember that Jesus' own disciples had such little faith that they shook Him awake in the boat for fear they were going to die. But here was a Gentile, saying, "Just say the word, and my servant will be healed."

So Jesus took this occasion to remind His Jewish hearers that in His coming kingdom, there would be many people at the banquet table from "east and west," from all corners of the earth.

In other words, Jesus is accessible from east or west, from anywhere. You don't have to be anyone special or some spiritual giant to access His authority. You just need to know who He is. You need to understand His position of authority.

Many of us are not seeing the deliverances we could be seeing because we don't really understand who Jesus is or believe in the authority He has. And the proof of this is that we go to Jesus last, not first.

We do this in so many areas, such as money. We go to the credit cards first, and only when they are full do we go to Jesus. We don't go to Him first, so we don't see Him work.

Jesus is saying that great faith brings great blessing, which is the point of His mention of the kingdom. Those who recline at the table with the patriarchs are those who have exercised great faith in their lives.

Let me outline what I believe Jesus is saying and how it relates to His authority.

I take the view that the "sons of the kingdom" here are believers, based on Matthew 13:38. So the "weeping and gnashing of teeth" is not hell, but profound regret over the loss of blessing in the kingdom.

In other words, those believers who never accessed Christ's authority on earth by exercising great faith will lose their reward in the kingdom. The Roman centurion did not have that problem. "Jesus said to the centurion, 'Go your way; let it be done to you as you have believed.' And the servant was healed that very hour" (Matthew 8:13).

The centurion was a Gentile who was not part of the covenant community of Israel. But he understood and believed in Jesus' authority, and his servant was miraculously healed.

CHRIST'S AUTHORITY IS POWERFUL

Jesus sent the centurion on his way and then went to Peter's house, where Peter's mother-in-law was sick with a fever (Matthew 8:14).

Luke's account tells us that the people in the house asked Jesus to heal this woman (Luke 4:38–39). Matthew leaves out that detail, but leaving it out doesn't diminish the account of Jesus' authority. "He touched her hand, and the fever left her; and she arose, and waited on Him" (v. 15).

The power of Jesus' authority is seen in what happened after Peter's mother-in-law was healed. Usually, if you are down with a fever and you get better, you are left feeling weak. But after Jesus healed this woman of her fever, she immediately got up and was able to serve her special Guest. Her healing was complete.

It doesn't matter what method Jesus used, the result was the same. Here He touched the sick person without saying anything. He touched and spoke to the leper, but didn't see or speak to the sick servant He healed. The power of Christ's authority operates under any circumstances. It is not diminished by the severity of the disease or the greatness of the distance.

Jesus not only raised this woman up from her bed, but He also gave her strength so she could return to her normal duties. There is power in His touch and in His words because of the authority He has over disease.

CHRIST'S AUTHORITY IS PROPHETIC

The fifth and final principle I want to talk about is more complicated than the others, so we need to address it more fully. It is a very important principle and crucial to understand if we are going to have a fully developed view of Jesus' authority over disease.

The setting is still Capernaum, the evening of the day that Jesus healed Peter's mother-in-law:

> And when evening had come, they brought to Him many who were demon-possessed; and He cast out the spirits with a word, and healed all who were ill in order that what was spoken through Isaiah the prophet might be fulfilled, saying, "He Himself took our infirmities, and carried away our diseases." (Matthew 8:16–17)

Matthew quoted the prophecy of Isaiah 53:4 to explain what was happening that evening in Capernaum. Isaiah 53 is one of the prophet's Servant Songs, prophecies about the ministry and sacrificial death of the Messiah.

Prophecy Fulfilled in Jesus

These prophecies were fulfilled in the ministry of Jesus Christ, who is God's Messiah. In Isaiah 53:5, the prophet went on to say of the Messiah, "By His scourging we are healed."

Some people believe this verse teaches that in His substitutionary death on the cross, Jesus not only paid for and conquered sin, but took all our sicknesses on Himself so that no believer ever has to be sick anymore. These are usually the people who also say that all you have to do is command your healing, because Christ purchased your healing on the cross.

It's true that Jesus' death is the basis on which someday all sickness and disease will be banned forever. The accomplishments of Christ's death were so comprehensive that they are the foundation upon which both your spiritual and your physical well-being rest. That's why John could write, "I pray that in all respects you may prosper and be in good health, just as your soul prospers" (3 John 2). The two areas are intricately related for the believer.

But the full realization of Christ's authoritative defeat of disease will come in His glorious kingdom. So I believe a better understanding of this passage is that Jesus' earthly healing ministry was a foretaste of the kingdom, when the full glories of all that His suffering purchased for us will be realized.

But whatever your view of the way Jesus' death has dealt with physical disease, the point is the same we have been making all along. That is, the power for healing can be found only in the person and the authority of Jesus Christ.

Here's where it gets interesting and a little complicated. Jesus not only gave the people of His day a foretaste of this aspect of His kingdom, but He also has given us a foretaste too. The question with this quotation from Isaiah 53 is not whether it is true, but how we are to apply it.

Should we seek out so-called faith healers who can draw on the healing authority of Jesus' suffering as they touch us and make all our diseases go away? Should we go over to Israel and bathe in the Jordan River? What is the process today by which we can experience a foretaste of the blessing of healing that Jesus purchased in His death on the cross?

The Application of the Prophecy

For the answer to that question, we need to leave Matthew 8 and spend the rest of our time in James 5:13–16, a powerful and controversial passage on healing that directs sick believers to Christ's body, the church.

The prophecy of Isaiah 53, which says the death of Christ would bring physical as well as spiritual well-being, carries over today in the ministry of the church, the entity that Jesus Christ left here on earth to continue and fulfill His ministry (Ephesians 1:22–23; 4:13).

The Sick Person's Responsibility

James begins with several questions:

Is anyone among you suffering? Let him pray. Is anyone cheerful? Let him sing praises. Is anyone among you sick? Let him call for the elders of the church, and let them pray over him, anointing him with oil in the name of the Lord. (James 5:13–14)

The Greek word *sick* here means "weak." This word could cover any of the different kinds of weaknesses, whether physical or psychological or emotional or spiritual.

James directs the sick or weak person to the elders of the church. If you are ill, you can go to Christ in prayer, but you cannot go to Christ physically. However, you *can* go to the church physically by calling for the elders.

The sick person must take the initiative, which shows that he or she really wants God to intervene in his or her situation. It's a demonstration of faith, the way the centurion sought out Jesus.

The Meaning of the Anointing

The elders are to "pray over [the sick one], anointing him with oil in the name of the Lord" (James 5:14). This was not oil as we normally think of it, but the oil used in biblical times for grooming and soothing of the body.

For example, Jesus told us to anoint ourselves when we fast so we won't appear to be fasting (Matthew 6:17). In other words, groom yourself with oil so you look good. Oil also had a medicinal use, as when the Good Samaritan poured oil on the wounds of the man lying by the side of the road (Luke 10:34).

In general, then, oil was used for refreshment and restoration. This is what the anointing of James 5 is referring to. The elders were to anoint the sick or weak person with oil as a symbol of the refreshment and restoration that God would bring into the person's life in fulfillment of the following promise: "And the prayer offered in faith will restore the one who is sick, and the Lord will raise him up" (v. 15).

The Promise of the Anointing

This verse is usually taught as promising full physical healing to anyone who follows the procedure. That interpretation is problematic for two reasons. First, it is obvious that not everyone who is anointed and prayed for is healed, and second, the focus of the verse is wider than just healing.

Let me say right off that if an illness is the direct result of sin, and if the sin is confessed and removed, then the sick person can expect to be restored to health. That's why James says, "If he has committed sins, they will be forgiven him. Therefore, confess your sins to one another, and pray for one another, so that you may be healed" (James 5:15b–16).

But what about believers who are physically sick, or weak and weary in some other way, such as emotionally or spiritually? The promise is that if they will call for the elders and allow these representatives of Jesus to minister to them, they will be restored.

Why the anointing with oil by the elders? Because they are the formal representatives of the church, and it is the church's job to act on Christ's behalf. The anointing communicates the same kind of human presence and caring touch Jesus gave to people when He was here among us, except that now Jesus does it through His body. The presence of the elders means the local church is there to help.

Jesus is no longer present with us physically, but His servants are. And when you're sick or weary, you need somebody you can touch. You need somebody who can relate to you face-to-face, person to person.

The elders may not be the means of your healing, but they can make sure the church brings you the restoration and refreshment that Jesus has for you. He wants you to feel His encouraging, grooming touch.

James is telling believers, "Let the elders pray for you and anoint you with oil. Let them and the local church body encourage you and see to your well-being. Let them care for you."

The anointing and prayer are a way of showing the same kind of immediate, personal concern that Jesus would show for a sick believer if He were here physically. And if healing results, praise God. You've been given a foretaste of kingdom blessing, just like the people whom Jesus healed in Matthew 8.

Let me emphasize again, James 5 is not saying that everyone will be healed. But it does promise that everyone will be restored, for the church is God's community of restoration.

Restoration and being free of a disease aren't necessarily the same thing. As an illustration of this, I would point you to Isaiah 40:31, which says, "Those who wait for the Lord will gain new strength; they will mount up with wings like eagles, they will run and not get tired, they will walk and not become weary."

Some people whom the Lord has touched will be like eagles. They will get well. They will soar out of their sickbed.

Others may not soar, but they will be able to run. And still others will be able to walk—not quite like flying or running, but still a restoration.

When God restores you, regardless of whether you fly, run, or walk, He keeps you going. Some believers will be supernaturally healed, and the doctors will be amazed. Others may take medicine for years, but they will still be moving forward with God. Still others won't have enough energy to run; they will have to walk, but they still will keep on keeping on. They will not faint.

So when Matthew said that Jesus fulfilled prophecy by exercising His authority over disease, he was looking ahead to the complete application of that authority in the kingdom. But God gave the people in Jesus' day, and has given us today, a preview of Jesus' complete victory over disease.

ACCESSING JESUS' AUTHORITY

How do we access Jesus' authority? It is accessed by prayer, as seen in the pleas of the leper and the centurion (Matthew 8:2, 5–6).

This prayer is accompanied by an attitude of humility. The leper bowed before Jesus. The centurion came humbly, realizing that as a Gentile he had no claim on Jesus' time. He threw Himself completely on God's will.

Access to Jesus' authority over disease must also be accompanied by active faith. God responds to faith. But it's not the amount of our faith, it's the focus of our faith that makes the difference.

The centurion had great faith because he knew the One with whom he was dealing. The greatness of your faith is in the Christ of your faith, not just the amount of your faith.

Finally, remember that Jesus' authority is exercised according to His sovereign determination. God makes the final decisions. He may choose to intervene instantly, miraculously, and completely, or He may choose to use the skills of doctors and the benefits of medications. Or God may say to you, as He said to Paul, "My grace is sufficient for you" (2 Corinthians 12:9).

Whatever the case, Jesus' authority over disease is complete—and someday, it will be fully manifest in our bodies.

CHAPTER TWELVE
THE AUTHORITY OF CHRIST OVER DEMONS

When my father calls from Baltimore, he often asks, "How is Martin Hawkins doing? Has he learned to play checkers yet?"

Martin is my dear friend and longtime associate pastor at our church in Dallas. My dad loves to play checkers, and he's very good at it. Whenever he visits, Martin challenges him to a game of checkers—and usually loses, because my father is a consummate checkers player.

On a number of occasions, Martin brought in better players than himself to challenge my father, and they did not fare any better. Dad welcomes the challenge because my father is excellent at playing checkers.

God is excellent at running the universe. He has never lost, but Satan insisted on challenging God for the control of the universe. For reasons we will never fully understand until we get to heaven, God allowed Satan to challenge His authority, and God allows the challenge to continue today.

One reason the Bible suggests for this is that God's glory is manifested, and will be manifested throughout eternity, by His triumph over Satan. Somehow the rebellion of Satan made God's greatness appear that much more great and glorious.

God also permitted sin and rebellion to enter the universe so that it could be judged once and for all. In other words, once Satan and his demon hordes are finally and eternally defeated, no one is ever going to challenge God again.

SATAN'S EVIL EMPIRE

We talked about Christ's authority over Satan himself, and now we are going to see Christ's authority over the demons who followed Satan in his rebellion. Revelation 12:4 indicates that one-third of heaven's angels defected with Satan. This must be an enormous number of spirit beings, because the Bible pictures the angels as an innumerable host.

These fallen angels came to be known as demons or unclean spirits. They, like Satan, have already been judged and will one day be consigned to hell, which Jesus said was created not for human beings, but for "the devil and his angels" (Matthew 25:41). Human beings go to hell because they choose to join Satan's rebellion.

Satan knows his doom is sure, but in the intervening time he is doing all he can to thwart the plan of God. He has emulated heaven by creating an organizational structure and hierarchy of his own among the demons. Satan has a demonic government whose job it is to carry out hell's agenda in attempting to defeat the program of God.

Satan's Organizational Structure

According to Ephesians 6:12, Satan's demonic hierarchy includes "rulers," "powers," "world forces of this darkness," and "spiritual forces of wickedness." These words denote governmental terms lifted out of the Roman world. Paul used them to describe the organization of demonic forces that do Satan's bidding.

Rulers are the princes who guide the affairs of the satanic realm. Then there are the powers who execute Satan's program. The next group is something like the officers and sergeants who make sure the program is properly implemented. The last group includes the troops who take the marching orders to the field of battle.

Notice the reach of Satan's government. It extends to all the world. When you become a Christian, you are targeted for Satan's attacks, because he does not want your influence working against his kingdom.

As we said in the chapter on Christ's authority over Satan, if you are dealing with a spiritual realm and you don't have your spiritual weapons ready, you are in trouble. We are under spiritual attack from well-organized, well-developed, and dedicated spiritual forces under the command of Satan.

Since Satan is not God, he is neither omnipotent, omnipresent, nor omniscient. He doesn't have unlimited power, he can't be everywhere at one time, and he doesn't know everything. He's certainly more powerful than we are, but he must carry out his agenda through his organization of demons.

One of the best illustrations of Satan's organizational scheme I can think of is the Mafia. Do you know the address of the Mafia? Can you tell me where their international head-quarters is located?

No, you can't. But the Mafia's influence is everywhere. The Mafia may be more or less an invisible empire, but its influence is very real. And sometimes the Mafia's structures and programs are disguised as legitimate businesses.

The Attributes of Demons

Satan has the power to hide his true identity and agenda too. The Bible says, "Satan disguises himself as an angel of light" (2 Corinthians 11:14).

Satan has all the attributes of personality, and so do his demons. As we will see in Mark 5, they exhibit intellect, emotion, and will. In fact, demons must have an intellect superior to ours because they can deceive people. They are master masqueraders.

Demons also have limited knowledge of future things. They can overpower men, interfere with the laws of nature, and pass through physical barriers. They can cause muteness, blindness, deformity, seizures, and insanity. So we are dealing with beings who, though they are invisible, are very powerful.

Since all of this is true, it's obvious that trying to battle demons using only our five senses will result in frustration and defeat. Demons are masters at getting people to fight and attack each other rather than recognize the true source of the problem. And as long as the demons can get us to do that, they win, because we are fighting the wrong enemy.

Our Need for Christ's Authority

I can't overemphasize the importance of taking seriously the reality of the demonic world. Part of Satan's strategy is to get us to think he is imaginary and that all this talk of an unseen spiritual world is sort of a fairy tale. If Satan can cause you to ignore him, he has won half the battle in your case. That's something of the nature and program of demons. They are formidable enemies, just like their commander.

But here's the good news. Jesus Christ has absolute, eternal authority over the demonic world. In fact, the only way we human beings can address the problem of demons is through the authority of Christ.

Because we are dealing with a spiritual realm and a spiritual conflict, we must draw on spiritual power. We need to be aware of the reality and power of demons—not so we can fear them or go looking for a demon behind every bush, but so we can take up the armor of God to defeat them (Ephesians 6:13).

JESUS' CONFRONTATION WITH DEMONS

Demonic activity is evident all through the Bible, from Genesis to Revelation. But demons were particularly active during the ministry of Jesus Christ.

That shouldn't surprise us, since the devil's overarching agenda is to oppose and thwart the program of God. Jesus came to do the will of God and to do it as no one else has ever done it. So we would expect the demons to show up where Jesus showed up, and that's the case throughout the Gospels.

The Initial Contact with the Demons

Of all Jesus' confrontations with demons, the incident described in Mark 5:1–20 is probably the most graphic. It's also a wonderful illustration of Jesus' authority over demons.

Jesus and His disciples had crossed to the eastern shore of the Sea of Galilee when the action started. "When He had come out of the boat, immediately a man from the tombs with an unclean spirit met Him" (v. 2).

Here we are introduced to a man most people would call a madman. The doctors would have said, "This man is dangerously disturbed. He needs to be sedated and taken to a mental ward." If he had approached police officers in this wild condition, they would probably have tried to restrain him and take custody of him. He was a mess.

But the man's problem was not medical or psychological or environmental. He had "an unclean spirit," a demon. It turns out the man was possessed by a multitude of demons, but the bottom line is the same. He was under the control of demons.

Notice what demons produce when they take over a life. This man was living among the tombs that dotted the hillside of the area. He lived in the realm of death. Demon activity makes a person morbid. The person suffering from demonic oppression often has a fixation on death and self-destruction. This man was also "gashing himself with stones" (v. 5). Don't ever think demonic activity is harmless.

He also possessed superhuman strength; no one could restrain him (v. 3–4). Drugs, by the way, are one of the primary means through which demons work. There are plenty of cases of a person high on drugs who was able to throw off five or six police officers like rag dolls.

Luke says the man had also been naked for a long time (Luke 8:27). One of Satan's goals is to rob people of their God-given modesty, so that inhibitions are broken down and people become obsessed with sex and nudity. Sexual immorality is a major item on the agenda of the demonic realm.

The Demons' Recognition of Jesus

In the middle of all this evil, Jesus showed up. "And seeing Jesus from a distance, he ran up and bowed down before Him; and crying out with a loud voice, he said, 'What do I have to do with You, Jesus, Son of the Most High God? I implore You by God, do not torment me!'" (Mark 5:6–7).

This man recognized Jesus, bowed before Him, and acknowledged His deity. Actually, this was probably the demons speaking through him, since the man had apparently never met Jesus before.

What a powerful example of Jesus' authority. Demons have to acknowledge Jesus, and they have to bow before His authority. All they could do was beg Him not to command them to leave the man. Jesus had already told them, "Come out of the man!" (v. 8). Demons seek to inhabit a body through which they can express themselves. Otherwise, they are restless.

The Completeness of the Possession

Throughout this story it's hard to tell when the demons were speaking and when the man was speaking. When the devil takes over a life, everything gets confused and you don't know who anybody is. That's why people can say, "I don't know why I did that. That wasn't like me." The demonic world creates confusion.

Don't misunderstand. I'm not saying that every time a person has an emotional or a marital problem, or goes through a crisis, it's the work of the devil. But on the other hand, we have to bring the reality of the devil's influence to the table as we deal with serious issues.

The Bible tells us to "test the spirits" (1 John 4:1). This is specifically said in relation to false teachers, but it applies in other areas as well. Notice that Jesus had discerned and identified the evil spirit before a word was spoken.

The demons had taken such complete possession of this man that his identity had fused almost completely with theirs. Let me make a clarification: Believers in Jesus Christ cannot be demon possessed. The Holy Spirit inhabits our bodies and spirits. So a demon cannot take up residence in a believer's life. But believers can be oppressed and harassed by demons.

If you are saved, Satan can't own you, but he can put a whipping on you. He can so oppress you that you come under his influence. That's why it's possible for Christians to hit bottom like non-Christians and to fall into the same sins as unbelievers.

The Boldness of Demons

If demons won't leave us alone, they certainly aren't going to leave the unsaved alone. Demons are far more active and present than our secular world will ever admit. Many of the terrible evils we see today are the result of demon possession. The Bible makes it clear that hell can take over a life or a family.

Hell can also rule over nations. Daniel 10:13 talks about a demonic being called "the prince of the kingdom of Persia." In other words, this demon was assigned to the Persian government. Is there any doubt that Nazi Germany was demonically driven in its desire to destroy the Jews?

Hell can even dominate religion. Jesus referred to "a synagogue of Satan" in Smyrna (Revelation 2:9). In fact, "The whole world lies in the power of the evil one" (1 John 5:19). Satan is in the business of hostile takeovers. There is no human explanation for some of the things that are happening today. They come from a different realm.

The man from the tombs was a true split personality. He was demonically tormented, but a part of him was crying out for Jesus' help. The demons within him begged Jesus not to torment them, because when Jesus shows up they are exposed for who they are, and they know they have been placed under sentence.

The Demons' Need for a "Home"

These evil spirits did not want to leave the man's body, because demons seek a body through which to express themselves and carry out the devil's agenda. They are only content when they are tormenting someone, not just floating around in space.

Jesus taught that demons seek a human home. "When the unclean spirit goes out of a man, it passes through waterless places seeking rest, and not finding any, it says, 'I will return to my house from which I came'" (Luke 11:24). The house is the body which the demon left. Evil spirits don't find rest until they have a body to inhabit.

This is why the demons begged Jesus not to make them leave the man from the tombs. What had sent them into a frenzy was the word of Jesus, "Come out of the man" (Mark 5:8). All it takes to bring the powerful, supernatural demonic world to its knees is the authoritative word of Jesus Christ.

The Word of God is torment to the demons. If Jesus had not spoken to them again, they would have had no choice but to leave the man immediately. The demons are just like their commander, Satan. He can't hang around in the presence of the Word either. That's why Jesus said to him, "It is written."

Actually, we experience something similar when we hear the Word and know what we need to do. But what we need to do may be hard or may require letting go of something to which we have become attached—or even addicted. The Holy Spirit is saying yes to us, but the Enemy is saying no, and the battle is creating havoc within us. The spiritual conflict is raging. The demons within this man were creating havoc in him.

The Destructive Nature of Demonic Activity

Let's pick up the story at Mark 5:9. "And He [Jesus] was asking him, 'What is your name?' And he said to Him, 'My name is Legion; for we are many.'"

Here's the dual-personality thing at work again. Jesus was simply asking the man for his name. But the demons were so totally in control that they answered with *their* name.

A legion in the Roman army was up to six thousand soldiers, so this was a horde of demons. Yet Jesus addressed the demons in the singular, and they answered in the singular. That's because this huge legion of demons was operating as one. They were unified. There is no defection among Satan's troops (Matthew 12:22–29).

This tells you how potent the demonic hosts are. All hell was breaking loose in the poor man's life, but the demons were working in total unity. When a demonic legion is present, you're going to need more power than any person can give you. It takes the authority of Christ to handle a legion.

When the demons realized Jesus was not going to rescind His command that they leave the man, "he [the demons] began to entreat Him earnestly not to send them out of the country. Now there was a big herd of swine feeding there on the mountain. And the demons entreated Him, saying, 'Send us into the swine so that we may enter them'" (Mark 5:10–12). Remember, demons only fulfill their purpose when they are tormenting someone.

Pigs were unclean animals to the Jews, so if these unclean spirits had to leave this unclean man, they wanted to enter the closest available unclean thing. Jesus granted them permission, and this huge herd of two thousand pigs went wild, running over a cliff and drowning themselves in the sea.

Why did Jesus do that? In order to teach an object lesson about the havoc that evil spirits can wreak in a life. This man had been written off by the people in that region as wild, insane, and dangerous. Jesus wanted to point out to them, "There is more going on here than what you see. Let me show you the real situation."

So He allowed the legion of demons to inhabit the pigs, and the pigs were driven to madness and self-destruction. In the meantime, the former madman was regaining his senses and his modesty. His problem was demonic, and only Jesus could do something about it.

This tells me that no matter what help you may get for your problem, no matter what counseling you seek for your marriage or other relationship, unless you are getting your life together with Jesus Christ you are going to continue plunging downhill and be drowned in the circumstances of life. Jesus Christ has to be the authority of your life.

The Commotion After the Cleansing

This scene caused quite a commotion. Those who were watching the pigs ran away and told everyone they met what had happened (Mark 5:14). So a crowd came out to see the excitement. They saw Jesus and "the man who had been demon-possessed sitting down, clothed and in his right mind, the very man who had had the 'legion'; and they became frightened" (v. 15).

When the authority of Christ moves into a situation, people are going to talk about what God is doing. The pig herders were certainly talking about it (vv. 14, 16), and the people from the city and the countryside must have been talking about it as they saw the former demon-possessed man sitting there completely healed.

Then they made the wrong decision, because they became afraid and asked Jesus to leave (v. 17). The man who had been healed and delivered wanted to follow Jesus, but Jesus sent him back to his own people to keep on talking about what God had done for him (vv. 18–20).

You may read this story and say, "That's all well and good. Jesus could simply speak and the demons had to obey. But that was two thousand years ago. How can I appropriate Jesus' authority over the demonic world in my struggles and temptations today?" Let me close with some good news.

A STRATEGY FOR
DRAWING ON JESUS' AUTHORITY

First of all, I want to reaffirm that Jesus' authority is the same today as it was two thousand years ago (see Hebrews 13:8).

But He also told His disciples, "I have given you authority . . . over all the power of the enemy, and nothing shall injure you. Nevertheless do not rejoice in this, that the spirits are subject to you, but rejoice that your names are recorded in heaven" (Luke 10:19–20).

Jesus was saying if you are going to get excited, get excited about what your salvation has done for you. Understand who you are in Christ, in other words, because it's in Christ that you find your authority. There are at least three things you need to know about your identity in Christ as it relates to the demonic realm.

Recall What Christ Has Done

First, you need to recall that Christ has completely and eternally smashed Satan and his realm on your behalf.

Through Jesus' death on the cross, God has "disarmed the rulers and authorities, [making] a public display of them, having triumphed over them through Him," that is, through Christ (Colossians 2:15). Even though Satan may still temporarily have an army, God has taken the bullets out of their weapons. Satan's government has no ultimate authority.

Peter said that Jesus is "at the right hand of God, having gone into heaven, after angels and authorities and powers had been subjected to Him" (1 Peter 3:22). Jesus' authority over demons did not end when He left the earth. He is still in total control from His place at the right hand of God.

The demons are still subject to Jesus. So the issue is not whether you have power over demons, but whether you know Jesus. There's a dramatic example of this in Acts

19:14–16, when seven sons of a Jewish priest named Sceva tried to imitate Paul's power in casting out demons.

Those men thought they would try it the way Paul did it. But the demon looked at them and said, "I recognize Jesus, and I know about Paul, but who are you?" These men had no authority because they didn't know Christ, and authority comes only from Christ. So they got the beating of their lives from the demon-possessed man.

Resist the Devil

A second step in appropriating Christ's authority is to resist. James 4:7 is a familiar verse which says, "Submit therefore to God. Resist the devil and he will flee from you." This also applies to the devil's underlings he may send to carry out his evil agenda.

Actually, what makes our resistance effective is our surrender to God. To submit to God is to reject compromise with the world, which lies in the control of the Evil One. We can stand against the devil and his forces when we stand in the name and authority of Jesus Christ.

We do that by putting on the armor of God as outlined in Ephesians 6:13–17. Notice that it takes the "full armor" (v. 13) to get the job done. That includes the belt of truth, because the devil is "the father of lies" (John 8:44); the helmet of salvation, because the devil attacks us with doubt; and the sword of the Spirit, the Word of God.

We talked in a previous chapter about wielding the sword of the Word against the devil, and the same truth applies against his demonic forces. When Jesus speaks His authoritative Word, they have to go.

Rely on Jesus Christ

This is the third part of the formula for drawing on Jesus' authority. We must depend on Christ to do in and through us what we could never do for ourselves.

If God thought you could live the Christian life in your own power, He would not have sent the Holy Spirit to indwell you. You are indwelt by the Holy Spirit because you need a power bigger than anything you can muster yourself. You need Somebody who is experienced in spiritual warfare.

The Holy Spirit is an experienced general in God's army. He has been fighting demons for eons. He knows how they move, when they move, and where they move.

So what you and I need is to be filled with the Spirit (Ephesians 5:18). We must give the Lord control of our lives and say, "Not my will, but Your will be done." That's what Jesus did, and it gave Him authority. When the Holy Spirit fills you, there is no place for demons to dwell.

By the time Jesus got finished, the former madman of Mark 5 had found a garment and put it on, and his mind had returned to him. He started thinking right again—all without medication or psychiatric help or hospitalization or any of that. The demons had left because Jesus had the authority to make them leave.

Let me give you one final word about Jesus' authority over Satan and the demon world. He not only commands and controls this sphere; He can even use it for His own purposes.

A good example is the man who was committing incest in the church at Corinth. Paul said he was delivering the man over to Satan for severe discipline (1 Corinthians 5:5). Satan was to be the instrument of God in this man's correction.

Paul himself said his thorn in the flesh was "a messenger of Satan to buffet me—to keep me from exalting myself!" (2 Corinthians 12:7). We're not sure how this worked, but Paul literally said this problem was "an angel of Satan."

This did not happen because Paul was out of God's will or because he had opened himself up to demonic attack. It was sent to keep him living in humility and dependence on God so that God would get all the glory from Paul's life.

In all of these cases, whether it was a demon-possessed madman or an apostle of Jesus Christ, there was no question about who was in charge. Jesus' authority is absolute.

CHAPTER THIRTEEN
THE AUTHORITY OF CHRIST OVER SIN

We are seeing the incredible extent of Jesus Christ's authority as the Son of God and second person of the Trinity. It reaches from the heights of heaven to the earth and below the earth into the realm of Satan and his demons.

In this chapter we are going to see that Christ's authority also reaches deep into the human heart, where sin resides and needs to be addressed. A classic story in the gospel of Mark provides us with an in-depth understanding of the authority Jesus Christ wields over sin and its consequences.

The incident is found in Mark 2:1–12. It is a well-known story because of the unusual way the paralyzed man was brought to Jesus for healing. We might have included this account in the earlier discussion of Christ's authority over disease, since this man definitely had a serious physical problem.

But much more was happening here than a miraculous healing. This encounter came fairly early in Jesus' ministry. He was gaining a lot of attention, so when He came back to His headquarters in Capernaum a huge crowd gathered (Mark 2:1–2).

Israel's religious leaders were also taking notice of this Rabbi from Nazareth, and Jesus was demonstrating His authority. In fact, according to Mark 1, Jesus had already shown His power over demons and disease. The case of the paralyzed man gave Him an opportunity to demonstrate His authority to forgive sins.

THE NEED FOR CHRIST'S AUTHORITY

The man who was carried to Jesus that day definitely needed a physical touch. He was unable to walk, being carried on a pallet or stretcher by four friends (Mark 2:3).

The house in which Jesus was teaching was so jam-packed with people that the four men had to take their sick friend up to the roof, dig a hole, and let him down through the roof (v. 4).

This is the part of the story most people remember, but we don't need to linger here. If you have ever seen drawings of houses in biblical days, you know that the roofs were flat. Because it was hot and the houses were small, the roof was used as a gathering place for family and guests. Usually an outside staircase on one wall led to the roof, so it was easy for these men to carry their friend to the roof.

The important thing is what happened when this man was lowered down to Jesus: "Jesus seeing their faith said to the paralytic, 'My son, your sins are forgiven'" (v. 5).

The Pervasive Presence of Sin

It's obvious that Jesus had a bigger agenda than the rest of the people in this story did. He dealt with the crippled man's soul before dealing with his useless legs. By pardoning the man's sins, Jesus put His authority on the line right up front.

Forgiveness did not seem to be this man's pressing need at the moment. But Jesus addressed his sins to underscore the fact that sin is at the root of all our problems, whether physical, emotional, environmental, or spiritual.

In fact, if Jesus had healed this man without addressing his spiritual need, this would have simply been a miraculous event whose deeper meaning would have been lost on the people watching and listening. Besides, Jesus did not want to leave the people He met in their sins without doing something about it.

Don't misunderstand. We are not saying this man's paralysis was the *direct* result of his own sins. We've already talked about that. I reject the theology which says that since physical health is always God's will for His people, if you are sick something is automatically wrong with you spiritually.

But having said that, we can say that sin is at the root of all human suffering. Before Adam and Eve sinned, they had no problems. And when we are ushered into heaven where no sin is allowed, we will be free of all pain and suffering.

But between Eden and heaven, we have nothing but problems because this world is under the curse of sin. The first tree that Adam ate from messed us up. The second tree that Jesus Christ died on fixed us up. And in heaven there will be a third tree, the tree of life (Revelation 22:2), that will keep us fixed up.

When you get your trees straight, you understand how badly sin has infected the human race and what it takes to remove it. Sin is pervasive; it's everywhere, especially in the human heart. Even those who have not sinned themselves, such as babies born addicted to crack or carrying the HIV virus, suffer from the pervasive presence of sin.

The Fallout of Sin

Like radiation from a nuclear blast, sin generates fallout that continues to spread contamination long after the initial explosion.

Sin's fallout can reach across generations. I can't tell you the number of people I have talked to over the years who were abused as children by relatives or someone else, and who are still battling the spiritual or emotional paralysis caused by someone else's sin.

A good example of sin's fallout is financial debt. Now don't get mad. I'm not saying all debt is sinful; I just want to make a point.

Most of us have felt the lingering effects of going into debt. We charge something on the "buy now, pay later" plan, only to discover we are still paying for it long after we had planned. One reason for this is that interest on a debt accrues. So you not only pay for what you purchase, you pay for the right to extend your payments over a period of time.

I heard recently that if you paid only the minimum amount due on a credit card debt of something like $1,500 at a certain level of monthly interest, it would take you years to pay off the bill and you would wind up paying almost three times the original debt.

Sin operates on a "buy now, pay later" plan. The problem

is the payments always come due, and the interest accrues. That's why one of the Greek words for sin in the New Testament is a word that means "a debt." The Lord's Prayer says, "Forgive us our debts, as we also have forgiven our debtors" (Matthew 6:12).

Sin not only pollutes individual lives; it can infect whole nations. "[If] My people who are called by My name humble themselves and pray, and seek My face and turn from their wicked ways, then I will . . . heal their land" (2 Chronicles 7:14).

The connection between sin and sickness is also evident in Scripture. During the year or so that David hid his sin with Bathsheba, he suffered terrible physical effects. His body "wasted away." He groaned "all day long" (Psalm 32:3).

In Psalm 103:3 David praised the Lord as the One "who pardons all your iniquities; who heals all your diseases." Sin's fallout often affects our physical bodies, and if we only seek physical healing, we may miss the ultimate solution.

Treating Sin as Sinful

But instead of admitting sin and seeking a solution, our world tries to deny and ignore sin. Sin is not a popular topic today. We have substituted other terms. People make mistakes. They show bad judgment. They have a problem. Liars are merely withholding part of their testimony. Adulterers have affairs, or even worse, just relationships.

But when we refuse to call sin what it is, we forfeit the chance to deal with the real problem. Suppose your doctor discovered you had cancer and said, "Take two aspirin and lie down." Suppose your house was on fire, and the firefighters stood by and said, "It will burn itself out after a while." Or imagine a police officer who saw two boys breaking into your house and said, "Well, you know, boys will be boys."

These are not the responses you want in critical situations. Cancer and fire destroy when left unchecked. Thieves can vandalize and strip your house bare if not dealt with. Sin can destroy a life, ruin a family, and send a person to hell. It's serious stuff, and unless it's taken seriously it can never be addressed properly.

Jesus' words to the paralytic in Mark 2, "My son, your sins are forgiven," seem to make a connection between the man's condition and his sin. We can't say for sure.

Some people are paralyzed physically because of sinful decisions they have made and sinful activity they have engaged in. Others are paralyzed emotionally because of sinful behavior patterns they have established.

But no matter what the consequences of a particular sin, we are all paralyzed by sin to some degree, and we need someone who can get to the root of the problem.

Jesus always treated sin as something very serious. From His perspective, it was more important for this man to be forgiven than it was for him to be healed. And Jesus had the authority necessary to forgive sin. So whatever help you are trying to get for whatever problem you may have, don't leave out Christ, because He's the only One who can address the root issue.

THE ACTIVATION OF CHRIST'S AUTHORITY

Jesus Christ's authority over sin was needed in that house in Capernaum. It was activated by the faith of the paralytic and the four friends who brought him.

We've talked about the "name it, claim it" theology that makes demands on God. The danger of denying this theology is that it makes us appear to deny the importance of faith. Mark 2 gives us a good balance point between these two errors.

Verse 5 says Jesus responded when He saw the faith of the sick man and his four friends. But it was their faith, not their demand, that moved Him.

Notice that Jesus *saw* their faith in action when a hole opened in the roof and this pallet came floating down. A lot of us have a good faith "rap." We say, "I'm trusting the Lord. I'm believing in God." But when it comes time to tear a hole in the roof, we back off.

The Importance of Cooperative Faith

At the heart of these men's faith was their decision to come to Jesus. The sick man said to his friends, "Take me to Jesus. He can help me." And they agreed to take him. The man was hanging around people who believed as he believed. These men exercised cooperative faith, and they tapped into Jesus' authority.

When you have been weakened in your faith, what you

need are other folk who know where Jesus is and can help you get to Him. Some people say, "But I'm so weak." That's an unacceptable excuse if there are other strong people around. That's why we need the body of Christ. Paul called it "bear[ing] one another's burdens" (Galatians 6:2). We need to come alongside each other so we can help each other get to Jesus.

This doesn't mean we or our fellow believers will always have perfect faith. Sometimes faith and doubt get mixed together in our minds.

You know the feeling. Part of you knows and believes God can do something, but another part of you wavers a little bit and you begin to doubt.

Well, let me give you good news about your doubt. A man once came to Jesus with his son who was in desperate need of healing. This father said to Jesus, "If You can do anything, take pity on us and help us!" (Mark 9:22).

Jesus challenged that statement. "'If You can!' All things are possible to him who believes" (v. 23). Then the man cried out, "I do believe; help my unbelief" (v. 24). In other words, "I believe, but I've got doubt too." And Jesus healed the boy.

So don't let doubt keep you from coming to Jesus. Don't just lie there with other paralyzed people who are saying, "I can't help you. I'm paralyzed too." You need to be around folk who are going to help take you where you need to go, not make you feel comfortable in your paralyzed state.

The Importance of Determined Faith

This paralyzed man and his friends also had determined faith. They said, "We are going to do whatever it takes to get you to Jesus." They did not let a room full of people stop them.

We need faith that isn't easily stopped. We need to be like Jacob, who wrestled with an angel all night and hung on, saying, "I will not let you go unless you bless me" (Genesis 32:26).

That sounds great, but you are not going to be determined in your faith unless you understand that Jesus Christ has authority over your problem. This paralyzed man and his pals realized that the solution to his physical need was in that house. What they got for their determination was the solution of his greater problem as well.

THE IMPLICATIONS OF
CHRIST'S AUTHORITY

Beginning with Mark 2:6 we get to the deeper issue Jesus had in mind here. By pronouncing the paralyzed man's sins forgiven, Jesus was making a deliberate statement of His deity. And He knew the response this was going to bring from the scribes sitting before Him.

Jesus' Claim to Be God

"But there were some of the scribes sitting there and reasoning in their hearts, 'Why does this man speak that way? He is blaspheming; who can forgive sins but God alone?'" (Mark 2:6–7).

Give these men credit; they understood completely the implication of what Jesus Christ had just said. They knew that by claiming the authority of God to forgive sins, Jesus was claiming to *be* God. The scribes were correct in saying that only God can forgive sin. And they were correct in reasoning that for a mere man to make this claim was blasphemy against God—a capital offense in Israel (Leviticus 24:16).

All this reasoning was going on in the minds of these scribes, but they didn't say anything. So Jesus demonstrated that He was God by telling them He knew what they were thinking (Mark 2:8). Then He offered them further, irrefutable proof of His divine authority and power.

Since no one can see a person's sins being forgiven, Jesus knew the scribes didn't believe Him. So He said, "'Which is easier, to say to the paralytic, "Your sins are forgiven"; or to say, "Arise, and take up your pallet and walk"? But in order that you may know that the Son of Man has authority on earth to forgive sins'—He said to the paralytic—'I say to you, rise, take up your pallet and go home'" (vv. 9–11).

Jesus' point was that for God, neither the forgiveness of sins nor a miraculous healing is hard to pull off. So He did the latter to prove the validity of the former. Jesus was saying, "If I can heal this man's disease, I can also forgive his sins, because both are coming from the same authority."

Jesus' Ability to Restore

In response to Jesus' authoritative command, the crippled man got up, folded up his pallet, and walked out in full view of everyone (Mark 2:12).

This is good news. Because Jesus can deal with the root of our problem, He can also deal with the symptoms.

Many people are going through pain in their lives that finds its root in sin at some level. Because Jesus is the only One who can forgive sin, He is the One we need to get serious with when the symptoms show up.

The scribes didn't come to that house in Capernaum because they had heard that Jesus could deal with the root problem of sin. They came, like their buddies the Pharisees, to see Jesus perform a miracle or two. They wanted to see the show. If they had been serious about fixing their problem, they would have come to Jesus to be forgiven too.

We have people who say, "My marriage isn't working." That's the symptom, but has this couple ever allowed Jesus' authority to deal with the cause of their conflict? Maybe if they get the sin issue straightened up, the symptom will fade away. The authority of Christ addresses the cause, which then frees Him up to address the symptom as He chooses.

Notice a key word Jesus used here. "Which is easier to *say?*" (v. 9, italics added). Because of who Jesus is, it doesn't matter whether the issue is the ability to forgive sins or the ability to bring about a physical healing.

Jesus can restore us internally and externally with just a word. The scribes were thinking, *It's easy for this Man to say He can forgive sins. Anyone can say that. But only God can do it.*

But Jesus countered their reasoning by telling them it was just as easy for Him to produce a verifiable result, healing, with the same word of authority. In fact, Jesus put the issue to them point-blank. If He could heal this man with a word of authority, then the scribes would have to admit that His authority to forgive sins was real too.

Jesus then turned around and healed the sick man. We aren't told what the scribes thought, but the people loved it (v. 12).

THE RESULTS OF CHRIST'S AUTHORITY

What was the result of this exercise of Jesus' authority over sin? I want to suggest two things.

A New Relationship with God

The paralyzed man received his healing. "He rose and immediately took up the pallet and went out in the sight of all" (Mark 2:12). That was wonderful. Thanks to Jesus' authority over disease, this man was cured.

But we are talking about Jesus' authority over sin. What this man received in addition to new legs was a new relationship with God. He was saved. His sins were forgiven. He became a child of God.

When Jesus addressed the man, He called him "My son" (v. 5). The man not only got up and walked physically, but Jesus raised him up from the paralysis of sin.

You see, God is free to release you from your paralysis when there is no more cause for judgment. If sin has judged you and paralyzed you, and then that sin is removed because you are forgiven, then you have no reason to lie around in your sin. God calls you His son or daughter. You are family now. You are free from the crushing burden of sin.

If I recall correctly, I have only intentionally stolen one thing in my life. It happened when I was in the eighth grade. They had those wonderful creations called sticky rolls in our cafeteria in Baltimore. Those things were good!

I didn't have any money that day and the rolls were warm and dripping. So I looked this way and that way, and when I thought no one was looking I helped myself to a sticky roll.

But lo and behold, one of the cafeteria ladies came over and confronted me by saying, "I saw what you just did."

I will never forget the terror that engulfed me. I was petrified. She sat me down and proceeded to give me a lesson on theft and its consequences. She explained how stealing a sticky roll will lead to stealing money, stealing money will lead to robbing banks, and robbing banks will land a person in jail. And if you happen to rob a bank and shoot someone, you could get the death penalty.

This dear, caring woman had me in the grave over a sticky roll! She scared me to death. But then she took that roll out of my hand and said, "I'm going to take this and put it back, and we are going to forget that this ever happened."

I will never forget the feeling of relief that came over me when that woman forgave me. Once she had dealt with the root problem, my dishonesty, she was free to relieve the symptom, the trouble I was in for stealing the roll.

When God forgives you and you come into relationship with Him, He takes your sins from you "as far as the east is from the west" (Psalm 103:12). You will never meet them again.

A husband and wife were arguing one time when the man said, "I'm tired of our arguments, because every time we argue you get historical."

His wife said, "You mean hysterical?"

"No, historical. You bring up everything I've ever done."

When God forgives you, He gets historical on you: He looks at the Cross in history, and He reckons you as forgiven.

New Strength for Living

Jesus told the man to get up, pick up his bed, and walk out of the house. The man couldn't get up until he had been healed. But he didn't know he had been healed until he obeyed Jesus, got up, and started walking.

Do you see where I'm going? Only Jesus can forgive and heal, but you must do the getting up and walking. Jesus didn't go over and lift this man off the pallet and help him out the door. Once Jesus has dealt with your problem, you must take responsibility for acting on what He's done. Once He has come in and taken care of the cause, you must move and claim the results.

Jesus healed this man to demonstrate His authority (Mark 2:10). That doesn't mean He didn't care about the man's condition and want to help him. That goes without saying. But the larger purpose of God in this healing was to show forth the identity and power and glory of His Son.

The people who saw the miracle got the idea, because Mark says they glorified God (2:12). They said, "We have never seen anything like this," which really means, "We have never seen Anyone like Jesus."

WHAT TO DO ABOUT CHRIST'S AUTHORITY

What paralysis has sin caused in your life? I'm talking about your sin, someone else's sin, or even the environment of sin in which you live. Sin may be causing you emotional, financial, marital, moral, or some other kind of trauma right now.

If the sin is yours and you can do something about it, get on the roof and start digging until you see Jesus. Forsake and confess your sin (1 John 1:9).

If someone else's sin is hurting you in a way you have no control over, take that sin to Jesus Christ, forgive the sinner, and pray, "Lord, help me to get past this sin. Move me forward."

And if you are suffering from the environment of sin— meaning simply the reality of the world in which we live— you can pray, "Lord, I believe You have power over the Evil One, and I commit myself to Your care and protection."

Whatever way you need to deal with sin, if you bring it to Jesus He will release you from it. Jesus may not always take away all of the symptoms of that sin, but many times He will. We have all seen God take care of financial concerns, grant a miraculous healing, or lift the stress and put our minds at ease. He is still in the restoring business.

It's something like parents setting up a trust fund for their children. The kids don't get the benefits of the trust when they want them or decide they need them, but when the parents decide the kids are ready to receive the trust.

God does the same thing. He decides when we receive the benefits. He will dispense the benefits to us according to His plan worked out in eternity. Some benefits may be delayed for a year, while others won't be released for five years. Still others may be delayed even longer—and the full benefits are going to be held in trust until eternity.

I'm not talking about the full benefits of salvation, because we receive those the moment we are saved. I'm talking about the lifting of the consequences of sin. This will be different for each of us, but all of us can experience the authority of Christ over sin *today*.

CHAPTER FOURTEEN

THE AUTHORITY OF CHRIST OVER CIRCUMSTANCES

The authority of Jesus Christ is a powerful and encouraging theme in the Scripture. As we move through this middle section of the book, I hope you are seeing how Christ's authority over every person and power that can be named is available to you where you are right now, if you are willing to bow to His lordship in your life and live in obedience to Him.

The reason for this is that, as I've said before and will say again, Jesus' authority is not diminished one iota today. The One who could command the wind and sea and conquer Satan and his demons is the same today.

The text before us in this chapter holds some of the most powerful, encouraging, and life-changing principles in all of the Bible. Our study centers on the only miracle of Jesus Christ that is recorded in all four Gospels: the so-called feeding of the five thousand.

Actually, it was probably closer to fifteen or twenty thousand people when the families were added in, because Mark 6:44 says the men alone numbered five thousand, and Matthew 14:21 says there were women and children besides.

This miracle came about two years into Jesus' ministry, when popular excitement over Him had reached a fever pitch. John 6:4 says the miracle occurred near the Jewish Passover, which helps explain Jesus' incredible popularity. You'll remember that the original Passover came on the night that God set Israel free from bondage in Egypt. The children of Israel put the blood of the lamb on their doorposts, and the death angel passed over their homes while striking dead the firstborn child in every Egyptian home.

So Passover was the feast during which the Jews celebrated their deliverance from Egypt. At the time of Jesus, Israel was under bondage again, this time to Rome. The people wanted to be free of Roman bondage as much as the Israelites under Moses wanted to be free from bondage to Egypt.

The Old Testament had prophesied that when Messiah came, He would bring in a new kingdom. Israel would be free of its oppressors when Messiah came. All things would be restored during Messiah's kingdom.

Messianic excitement was also at a fever pitch at this time, so when Jesus came doing miraculous things, the people began to flock to Him. They liked what they saw. But it was the goodies they were after, not the message Jesus came to deliver. As it turned out, they didn't want Him as their Messiah, their Lord, on His terms.

Are we bowing to His lordship? That's a question we need to ask as we study this miracle and learn what it teaches us about Christ's authority to overrule and change our circumstances.

CHRIST EMPATHIZES WITH OUR NEEDS

The events leading up to this miracle are important not only because they set the context, but because of what they reveal about the heart of Jesus Christ.

Jesus' Compassion

The twelve disciples had just returned from the ministry trip Jesus sent them on (Mark 6:7–13). They were telling Him all they had done, but the crowds were so great they couldn't get any time alone. So they tried to get away in a boat:

[But] the people saw them going, and many recognized them, and they ran there together on foot from all the cities, and got there ahead of them. And when He went ashore, He saw a great multitude, and He felt compassion for them because they were like sheep without a shepherd; and He began to teach them many things. (Mark 6:33–34)

Jesus saw all these spiritually lost and needy people coming to Him, many no doubt with crippled and broken bodies, and His heart went out to them. What a picture of Jesus Christ! He is not only a person of power, but He is a person of infinite compassion. The beauty of the Incarnation is that when God became a man, He felt the pain we feel.

This means that no matter what you may experience, from loneliness and rejection to fear and physical pain, Jesus Christ can identify with you. He experienced the full range of the human dilemma.

The Bible says Jesus had compassion on this huge crowd because the people "were like sheep without a shepherd." They were groping for direction. As we know, sheep left to themselves without a shepherd can stray away and get lost very easily, and they are totally defenseless against predators.

Things haven't changed much in two thousand years, have they? People today still don't know how to make the right choices. They are spiritually defenseless and directionless without Christ, vulnerable to the lures and attacks of the Enemy.

Jesus' Leadership

The job of the shepherd is to lead his sheep to safe pasture and then protect them. We often don't know which way to go and what decisions to make, but Jesus knows we are helpless and He leads us as our Great Shepherd. And He can lead us with authority, because no circumstance can thwart His word. Because Jesus Christ is man, He feels what we feel. Because He is God, He can do something about it.

That's why the old people could talk about Jesus as a lawyer in a courtroom, a doctor in a sickroom, a father to the fatherless, and a mother to the motherless. To the sick He was a balm in Gilead, to those who needed encouragement He was the Rose of Sharon, and to those who needed guidance He was the Bright and Morning Star.

We can empathize with people, but too many times we can't really do anything about their problem. Jesus doesn't have that limitation, as the feeding of the five thousand makes clear. He is Lord over any circumstance. Our need is to come to Him as our "merciful and faithful high priest" in our time of need (Hebrews 2:17; see 4:14–16).

CHRIST ACTS TO MEET OUR NEEDS

When you're facing a hungry crowd of fifteen to twenty thousand people, and it's getting close to dinnertime, you had better know where to turn for provisions. The disciples didn't know it yet, but Jesus was going to teach them that lesson. He had met the people's need for spiritual food by teaching them. Now He was going to meet their need for physical food.

The Disciples Identify the Need

As Jesus taught, the people gathered around Him, and as the day wore on, it became apparent to the disciples that something needed to be done if the crowd was going to make it home before it got too late.

So they came to Jesus and said, "The place is desolate and it is already quite late; send them away so that they may go into the surrounding countryside and villages and buy themselves something to eat" (Mark 6:35–36).

The disciples were basically saying, "Listen, Jesus, it's getting late. The markets will be closing pretty soon. Why don't You go ahead and pronounce the benediction so these people can make it to a town before everything closes?"

Remember that the disciples and Jesus had been trying to get some time alone to rest. Jesus' men were tired and wanted to go home. Besides, they didn't have anything to feed a crowd that large.

Jesus Challenges the Disciples

So you can imagine the disciples' surprise at what happened next. "But He answered and said to them, 'You give them something to eat!' And they said to Him, 'Shall we go and spend two hundred denarii on bread and give them something to eat?'" (v. 37).

John's account gives us more important details about this interesting conversation:

[Jesus] said to Philip, "Where are we to buy bread, that these may eat?" . . . Philip answered Him, "Two hundred denarii worth of bread is not sufficient for them, for everyone to receive a little." One of His disciples, Andrew,

Simon Peter's brother, said to Him, "There is a lad here who has five barley loaves and two fish, but what are these for so many people?" (John 6:5, 7–9)

The apostle John, who was there, said that Philip and Andrew were the ones involved in this conversation with Jesus. Jesus probably asked Philip to take care of the situation because Philip was from Bethsaida (John 1:44), the closest town in that area. So Jesus asked a "homeboy" who knew the region better than anyone else.

Jesus knew Philip didn't have enough money or time to buy food and feed all these people. This was, as they say on television or the radio, a test. "This He was saying to test him; for He Himself knew what He was intending to do" (John 6:6).

The Disciples Take the Test

When Jesus asks a question, it is not to gain new information. When Jesus inquires of you, it is to test you.

This was a test for Philip. Jesus reversed the roles. He was the One who could change water into wine and heal people. He was the One with supernatural power, yet He turned to Philip and asked, "What are we going to do?"

We can picture the look on Philip's face. It's the same look we would have if we were facing a seemingly impossible situation and, rather than Jesus meeting the need, He said to us, "What are you going to do?"

We would say, "But, Jesus, that's why I'm coming to You." And that's when the announcer interrupts the program and says, "This is a test." So Philip ran the numbers and panicked. A denarius was one day's wage for a laborer in that day. Two hundred denarii would have been about eight months' salary. Philip was saying, "You want to know how we are going to feed all these people? We can't. Pay attention now, Jesus. Let me get my calculator out here and show You something.

"Even if we had eight months' worth of wages, it wouldn't be enough for us to give everybody a few crumbs. Besides, we can't feed this crowd with crumbs. Some of these people are going to want a second helping. Jesus, we just don't have enough money in the budget to do this."

Philip was the logical one. "There's no way. This is impossible. It's too big. We can't afford it. Where are we going to find the money? Who are we going to get to do it?"

Have you ever said that about your impossible circumstance? Do you live with someone who says things like that?

Most of us know someone like Philip—people who face the insurmountable circumstances of life and see only how it can't be done. People who bring out the bank statement and show you down to the denarius why it can't be done. People who can give you every reason in the world why they can't get victory over their circumstance and why their case is unsolvable. That's Philip.

The Disciples Search for a Solution

Standing next to Philip was Andrew, Peter's brother. Andrew was a little more optimistic than "It can't be done" Philip. Andrew said, "There is a lad here who has five barley loaves and two fish, but what are these for so many people?" (John 6:9).

Barley loaves were small round cakes. This was poor people's food, and there wasn't a lot of it. It would be about the equivalent of our having sardines and crackers for dinner.

Philip saw no way the crowd could be fed. Andrew had a little more vision, except that his hope was punctuated by a big negative right in the middle. "Well, we have some food here, but it can't do much."

Philip saw nothing. Andrew saw something. But neither was looking in the right direction, at Jesus and His authority over any circumstance.

Andrew's response was like people who hold out something to you with one hand, then take it away with the other hand. "There's something here, *but* . . ."

In the early years of our church in Dallas, we heard from some Philips and Andrews. Our congregation faced impossible circumstances more than once. We had opportunities to purchase property when no one knew how the money was going to be provided. Some people said, "Forget it. It can't be done." Others said, "Well, I know the property is available, but . . ."

But you see, whether something can or cannot be done is never the question when God is in the formula. The only question is whether it is His will. God can always afford whatever He chooses to do. There is never a lack of resources with God.

This was true at the feeding of the five thousand. The other person involved in this miracle was the boy who gave his lunch to Jesus. Andrew had found the boy and brought him to Jesus, so we can be sure the boy was willing to let Jesus have what he had.

This boy didn't have much, because this was a poor person's meal. But the little that he had, he gave Jesus when he realized Jesus was asking for it.

The Danger of Holding Out on God

I don't know how old this boy was or what he was thinking. But I know how most boys are about food. We can imagine this boy saying to Andrew, "No, this is my lunch. My mama made it for me. It's all I have to eat. I'm not giving it to Jesus or anyone else. I wouldn't have anything to eat."

We could do a lot of theologizing here, but I think you get the point. This boy could have been like a lot of believers who talk a good game spiritually, but when it comes to letting go of what they have and making it available to Jesus, they want to keep it to themselves.

I need to ask you—as I need to ask myself regularly—are you holding something back from God? Jesus Christ has the power and authority just to take it from you, but He doesn't work that way. He wants you to bring it to Him willingly, whether it's your time or your skills or your resources.

Otherwise, if you hold out on God you lose, and others He could have blessed through you lose too. This boy could have eaten his lunch, but thousands of other people could have gone away hungry.

A young girl won three races at school and was awarded three blue ribbons. But then she saw another girl crying because she hadn't won anything. So the first girl took one of her ribbons and gave it to the girl who didn't have any.

Later, the girl who had won the ribbons was showing her two remaining ribbons to her mother. The mother said, "But I thought you won three races."

"I did, but I gave one of my ribbons to a girl who was crying because she lost every race."

Her mother said, "Why did you do that?"

"Because," the girl replied, "I don't need the decorations to know I won the races."

Too many people live for the decorations—the cars, the clothes, the job titles. But when you know who you are and whose you are, the decorations don't mean that much. Once Jesus has met your needs through His power and authority, you don't need to define yourself by the world's decorations anymore. You don't need to hold anything back from God.

CHRIST MEETS NEEDS
THROUGH HIS PEOPLE

In Mark 6:39–40, the Bible says that when Jesus got ready to feed the crowd, "He commanded them all to recline by groups on the green grass. And they reclined in companies of hundreds and of fifties."

Jesus got the crowd organized because He was about to use the disciples to carry the food to the people. Jesus mediated His authority through the disciples so the people would be fed and the disciples would learn a vital lesson.

Jesus Uses His Workers

Society is always benefited when God's people understand and tap into Christ's authority. It's because we often have such a weak view of Christ that the world sees such an anemic parody of Jesus.

When was the last time an unbeliever looked at you and decided that Christ must be real because of the power in your life? When was the last time a non-Christian saw the reality of Christ because that person saw you believe something that was impossible or insurmountable, and then saw Christ act in your behalf to meet the need?

Jesus was going to create the miracle of multiplying the bread and fish, but it was the disciples who were going to take the food to the multitude. The miracle was going to get to the people who needed it through their hands.

Jesus took the boy's lunch and gave thanks for it (John 6:11). There was a lesson here for the disciples too. I can imagine that when Jesus began to pray, Philip and Andrew were looking at each other saying, "Pray for what? For this?" But Jesus gave thanks for what He had.

One Saturday our family was going somewhere, and we were in a hurry. My wife didn't fix a big meal; she just boiled some hot dogs. We sat down and I said, "Let's give thanks." And from one of the kids came the remark, "Give thanks for hot dogs?" We proceeded to have a lesson on thankfulness.

Jesus gave thanks for what He had. Did He need more? Yes. Most of us would have started our prayer with, "Why do I have only five barley loaves and a couple of fish? Lord, You promised to meet my needs, and I need more than this."

Being thankful doesn't mean you have to pretend that you don't have any needs. You may need a more dependable car, but thank God you are not walking. You may want a house, but thank God your apartment has a roof. You may want steak, but thank God the hot dogs are there.

Jesus gave thanks because He had something and because He was anticipating more. He could give thanks for that small lunch because He was "looking up toward heaven" (Mark 6:41). Jesus' focus wasn't on the food but on His Father, the Provider of food. After Jesus prayed, He broke the loaves and divided the fish until all the people in that huge crowd had eaten and all were satisfied (vv. 41–42).

Jesus broke the bread and divided the fish, and the food just kept multiplying. It wasn't as if they passed around the barley loaves and a bunch of people broke off a little nibble until the bread was gone. Mark says the people ate until they couldn't hold another bite. And don't forget, this was a hungry crowd. They had been out there almost all day with nothing to eat.

Philip and Andrew, and probably the other ten disciples too, may have been weak in their faith and small in their vision, but when it was all over they were the ones God used to bring together the authority of Christ with the needs of the crowd. And when that happened, a miraculous provision occurred.

God still meets needs through His people. People are His method. But that means we have to be *what* He wants us to be and *where* He wants us to be so He can use us to the maximum. The good news is that God can do a lot with whatever we give Him, no matter how little it is. All through the Bible, we see God doing a lot with a little. A Hebrew baby crying in the Nile River is adopted by Pharaoh's daughter and becomes Israel's deliverer. A teenaged boy named David uses his sling to kill a giant of a warrior named Goliath and rout the Philistine army.

A widow with only one meal left to her name shares it with the prophet Elijah and has more food than she could ever eat for the rest of the famine (1 Kings 17) because when a little is given to God, He multiplies it and it becomes a lot.

Anything God has done with my life, it is because as an inner-city teenaged boy, I simply told God, "You can have my life." Whatever God has done through me is because of His multiplication table. And that's true of each of us.

Jesus Rewards His Workers

Jesus used the disciples to help meet the need for food, and then He taught them another important lesson. When everyone was full, Jesus told His disciples, "Gather up the leftover fragments that nothing may be lost" (John 6:12). The disciples gathered up twelve baskets of fragments.

Who do you think those twelve baskets of food were for? The disciples! They had been busy helping to organize and serve the crowd, and they had not eaten yet. They were hungry too.

But Jesus was teaching them this principle: "Take care of My business, and I'll take care of you. Invest in My kingdom, and you will not lose. My authority will reach to cover your needs too."

God always picks up the tab for His servants who are fulfilling His will. If you try to fulfill your own will, you get to pay the tab. Jesus worked through the disciples, and then He rewarded them. They had a basketful of food apiece.

CHRIST MEETS NEEDS
ACCORDING TO HIS AGENDA

Here's the final point I want you to see in this miraculous example of Christ's authority over circumstances. This story and the following events unfolded according to Jesus' agenda and no one else's. You and I cannot force Jesus to meet our needs whenever we feel like it.

No "Meal Ticket" Messiah

After Jesus had performed this great miracle in front of so many people, feeding the equivalent of a small city full of people with a poor boy's lunch, we shouldn't be surprised at what happened next:

> When therefore the people saw the sign which He had performed, they said, "This is of a truth the Prophet who is to come into the world." Jesus therefore perceiving that they were intending to come and take Him by force, to make Him king, withdrew again to the mountain by Himself alone. (John 6:14–15)

The people were saying about Jesus, "He is the Man! We have to grab this Man and make Him our King. Anyone who can take sardines and crackers and turn them into Moby Dick sandwiches ought to be king!" In other words, the people saw in Jesus their meal ticket, a miracle-worker who could keep them fed and satisfied.

But being the people's bread-making King was not on Jesus' agenda. The Cross was. So He withdrew before the crowd could take any action.

Jesus is not interested in being our "Sugar Daddy." He did not come to build a new welfare system, but to build the kingdom of God. Jesus has all the authority we will ever need for eternity, but it comes on His terms, as we have said before. Try to make Jesus function on your terms, and He will withdraw from you. He does not hang with people who only want His benefits.

It's fine to get up in the morning and say, "Lord, give me what I need today." But you need to get around to, "Lord, make me what You want me to be today."

Whose Authority?

It doesn't work to say, "Lord, I don't have time for the spiritual food You want me to have, but feed me with my daily bread anyway. Help me be successful at my job, but don't ask me to give You the glory in front of my co-workers. Give me more money, even though I'm not making any of my money available to Your kingdom."

God may bless you in spite of yourself, but over the long haul if you only want God's blessings with no real relationship, you won't see the power of His presence working in your life. Jesus came to exercise His authority as King of kings and Lord of lords, not to be a "meal ticket Messiah" who produced on command.

The question we need to answer is, Whose authority do we want operating in our circumstances? If we insist on having the final word, we won't see any insurmountable obstacles falling before us. But if we will bow to Christ's authority, there will be no need to panic even when a hungry crowd shows up.

CHAPTER FIFTEEN
THE AUTHORITY OF CHRIST OVER TRIALS

We should have put this notice at the end of the previous chapter: "To be continued. . . ."

That's because we are going to study "part two" of the biblical drama that began when Jesus miraculously fed five thousand men plus thousands of women and children. Things got a little heady after that, since the people decided they wanted Jesus to be their King (John 6:14–15).

The disciples may have thought they had arrived too, because if Jesus became King of Israel they would be on easy street themselves.

But if the Twelve had any illusion like that, it didn't last long. Not only did Jesus reject the people's superficial adulation (John 6:15), but He put the disciples into a boat and sent them out onto the Sea of Galilee . . . and head-on into one of the scariest trials they would ever face.

You say, "Well, that was Jesus and the disciples. He had to teach them some special lessons because they were going to be His apostles and the founders of the church."

Sorry, but that's not the case. The apostles definitely had some things they needed to learn. But we need to learn the same lessons—and one way God has chosen to teach us and strengthen our faith is through trials.

Let me give you a definition of trials. A trial is an adverse circumstance that God either allows or brings into the lives of His children in order to deepen their faith and commitment to Him. Trials are designed to make us grow, even though we may groan in the process.

Trials can come from any number of sources. Some of the things we experience are the result of living in a sinful, messed-up world. A thief may rob your home, or a war overseas may take a family member, because we all suffer the effects of the world's evil.

At other times we suffer because of our own sin. A bad choice or yielding to temptation can lead to a result that is difficult to bear. But even our sins and their consequences can become God-ordained trials that He uses to grow us if we will repent and learn from them.

God may also send a specific trial because He wants you to learn a specific lesson. And of course, trials can come about because you are under attack from your Enemy the devil.

It may help to pinpoint the source of a trial, especially if the source is a sin that needs to be eradicated. Generally, however, our focus needs to be not so much on where the trial is coming from, but on what to do with a trial when it shows up.

But in order to react properly to our trials, you and I need to understand something. Everything that happens to us is under the sovereign, total authority of Jesus Christ. There is no detail of any trial that He does not have firmly in His grip. Once you get this down, you can face any trial. Let's learn a few key principles about trials.

CHRIST CONTROLS
THE ARRIVAL OF OUR TRIALS

The situation we are going to consider is described most fully in Matthew 14:22–33, although we will also draw on some details from the gospels of Mark and John. Let's set the scene:

> And immediately He made the disciples get into the boat, and go ahead of Him to the other side, while He sent the multitudes away. And after He had sent the multitudes away, He went up to the mountain by Himself to pray; and when it was evening, He was there alone. But the boat was already many stadia away from the land, battered by the waves; for the wind was contrary. (vv. 22–24)

Trials Are God's Idea

Notice that the whole trip was Jesus' idea. He controlled the creation of this trial. It was at His authoritative word that the disciples set out on the sea. You'll recall that it was late in the day when Jesus fed the crowd, so by the time the storm hit it was dark.

Mark says the wind was so strong the disciples were "straining at the oars" (Mark 6:48). The harder they rowed, the more the wind pushed them backward.

I'm confident you have encountered storms like that in your life. No matter how hard you try to move ahead, when you look up you realize to your dismay that not only have you made no progress, but you are actually being pushed backward.

But even the most severe circumstances are subject to the authority of Christ. The Bible says Jesus "made" the disciples get into the boat. The implication is that they didn't want to go. After all, the people wanted to make Jesus their King. I can just hear the Twelve saying, "Jesus, we have been out here for several years telling these people that You are the King of the Jews. Now they finally have the picture. This is no time to leave!"

Jesus knew better, of course, since many of these same people would later cry out, "Crucify Him!" So He sent the disciples away and straight into a storm. There was a lesson waiting for them in the middle of the sea.

Trials Help Further God's Purpose

If you are a Christian, there is no such thing as a purposeless trial, no such thing as chance or a mistake. Those are all non-Christian terminology. God has a point for everything He allows us to experience. And Jesus' authority reigns even when you are in the middle of a storm and getting pushed backward.

When the disciples had left, Jesus sent the crowd away and went up to a mountain to pray. That seemed to complicate things for the disciples, since Jesus was not there when the storm engulfed them.

Do you ever feel like you're in a storm and Jesus is nowhere to be found? That's never true for us, because even when there's more water in the boat than there is in the sea, Jesus is firmly in control. He can even take our sin and failure and turn them to His glory.

This storm on the Sea of Galilee also proves that obedience to God does not necessarily remove obstacles. The disciples obeyed Jesus, and they still got rained on.

So don't buy this "television theology" that says the path of obedience is always the path of health and prosperity and so forth. The very act of obeying God may lead you into the teeth of a storm. He wants to take you to the next level of spiritual experience, and that often means going through trials.

Trials Are God's Tests

We used to take tests in school to help determine if we were ready to be promoted to the next grade or ready to graduate and move on to a higher level of education. Our teachers taught us what they wanted us to know, and then they tested us to see if we had learned the lessons.

Tests weren't usually fun, but it felt great when the test was over and we found out we had passed. The apostle James said, "Consider it all joy, my brethren, when you encounter various trials" (James 1:2).

Do we count the trial or test itself as a joy? No, the joy comes in knowing that God is doing something good through our trial. I remember final exams in seminary. I would thank God when each final was over, because I realized that once I passed that test, I could move on to the next course and my next year of training, with the goal of graduating.

God tests us to see if we have learned the material, to see whether the "amens" we said with our mouths on Sunday get transferred to our feet the rest of the week.

What happens when you fail a test? You must take it again. And if you fail enough tests, you have to repeat the whole course. So the idea in trials is to pass the test the first time, to learn what God is trying to teach us.

At the next level of spiritual growth, there will be more tests. But they will be of a different character because you are being tested at a higher level of maturity.

Mark's account removes any doubt that this storm was a

divinely designed test for the Twelve. When it was all over, Mark says that the disciples "had not gained any insight from the incident of the loaves, but their heart was hardened" (Mark 6:52). In other words, they still had a long way to go, and they were eligible for retesting on the same material.

CHRIST ENCOURAGES US IN OUR TRIALS

So the disciples were fighting a fierce storm, and it was now in the early hours of the morning. They were badly in need of Jesus' reassuring presence.

It was "the fourth watch of the night" when Jesus approached the boat, walking on the water (Matthew 14:25). That's from 3:00–6:00 A.M., so it was very dark. The disciples had been out there by themselves for a number of hours by now.

When I get to heaven, I want to see this one on a heavenly video. I want a playback on this one, because Jesus was not only walking on water, He was walking on stormy water.

Jesus Can Find You

Matthew continues, "And when the disciples saw Him walking on the sea, they were frightened, saying, 'It is a ghost!' And they cried out for fear. But immediately Jesus spoke to them, saying, 'Take courage, it is I; do not be afraid'" (vv. 26–27).

Jesus may not have come when the disciples wanted Him to come, but He came on time. God always shows up just in time. Jesus knew His disciples' predicament, even though they were several miles out on the sea engulfed in darkness and He was on a mountain somewhere else praying.

This kind of knowledge was no problem for Jesus, because as we have seen throughout this book, Jesus is God. In the same way, Jesus had no problem walking straight to their boat in the darkness.

God knows exactly where you are in your trial and what you're going through. And He is acutely interested in your predicament. In fact, since He either allowed or arranged the test you are in, He is the only person who can do something about it. God knows how to find you, even in the dark.

Jesus Can Calm You

Jesus showed up just when the disciples needed Him most, but at first they were anything but comforted and encouraged. The Greek text says they "stared intently" into the darkness when they saw this ghostlike figure coming toward them.

The Greek word for *ghost* in Matthew 14:26 is the word "phantom." The disciples thought that what they were seeing was a figment of their imaginations. The problem is all twelve of them saw it, so they figured they had a serious problem on their hands.

Isn't that the way trials so often progress? Your boat is about to capsize, you are in fear for your life, and a ghost shows up. But what the disciples thought was an added problem and cause of fear was actually their salvation.

When you are in the middle of a trial you can't always judge the situation by what you see, because what you see may not be all there is. The very thing that could look like your worst problem may be what Jesus uses to deliver you.

Jesus didn't let the disciples panic for long. He spoke to them "immediately" (v. 27). And when He said, "It is I," Jesus was using the Greek form of God's great statement of His deity to Moses, "I AM WHO I AM" (Exodus 3:14). Jesus answered their fear with a declaration of Deity.

Please note that the first thing Jesus did was calm the disciples on the inside, not calm their circumstances on the outside. He did not deal with the storm until after Peter tried walking on the water. Once Jesus calms you by His comforting and authoritative presence, it really doesn't matter if it's still raining and blowing hard.

Jesus walked on the water to demonstrate His power and His protection and to show the disciples there was no trial He could not penetrate. He walked *on* the problem to let them know He was bigger than the problem. When Jesus comes to you in your trial, He can walk on the mess you're in. He is the authoritative One.

Getting Up from Your Trials

I am a fan of the old *Rocky* films, the story of Rocky Balboa from inner-city Philadelphia who had nothing going for him but the ability to box and the heart to go with it.

Rocky fought his way to the top and became the heavy-weight champion, taking on tough opponents like Apollo Creed and the Russian fighter. But by the final film in the series, Rocky was getting older and his quickness was gone. Even though he was still the champ, he had been hurt, and he would risk his life to get back in the ring.

Rocky's wife told him, "Rocky, you can't fight anymore." He struggled with the decision, but finally decided to hang up his gloves.

Then a young fighter named Tommy Gunn came along. Tommy admired Rocky and wanted to be just like him. So Tommy asked Rocky to teach him everything he knew. Rocky saw an opportunity to relive his career through Tommy, so he trained Tommy to be a champion like him.

Tommy went into the ring and demolished everyone who came his way. But Tommy decided he didn't need Rocky Balboa anymore to be successful, so he launched out on his own. Tommy became the champion, and then he decided he needed to whip Rocky to prove what a big shot he was.

So this young fighter stood outside of Rocky's house, calling him names, and daring him to come out. Rocky went out to fight Tommy, and the younger man laid a bad whipping on Rocky. Rocky was bleeding and battered, and then Tommy threw a right cross that sent Rocky to the ground. He was lying in the street, bloodied and beaten down by his trial, unable to get up.

But that's when it happened. Rocky flashed back to an earlier fight, when he was lying beaten on the canvas and his old trainer named Mickey, who was now dead, called out to him, "Get up, you bum, Mickey loves you."

Those words had given Rocky the strength to get up before, and now they inspired him again. Rocky shook his head and that theme music started playing, and you knew Tommy was suddenly in trouble.

Having been changed on the inside, Rocky got up on the outside. Tommy was on his way back to his car when Rocky said, "Yo, Tommy. One more round."

Tommy came back over, and Rocky drew new strength from somewhere inside. He began punching, and pretty soon Tommy was the one lying in the street and Rocky was standing over his trial.

Mickey had told Rocky, "Get up." In other words, don't let

your trial control you. That's what Jesus is telling us. "Get up from your trial. I am Jesus. I love you, and I want you to get up and not let your trials control you."

The storm was just as fierce after Jesus spoke as it was before. The difference was that the disciples had heard His voice: "It is I; do not be afraid."

Special Encouragement for Peter

The disciples recognized Jesus' voice, because Peter said, "Lord, if it is You, command me to come to You on the water" (Matthew 14:28). The Greek word translated "if" here means "since." It's an expression of fact, not of doubt.

Peter was ready to step out of the boat and trust himself to Jesus, something no one else was willing to do. And when Peter heard Jesus' word, "Come!" (v. 29), he was ready to cast himself on Jesus' authority. Now you know why Peter was the leader of the Twelve. Even when he was making mistakes and saying the wrong thing, Peter's desire was always to be close to Jesus. Here Peter was willing to take a risk to get to Jesus.

But Peter didn't step out until He heard Jesus' word. What's the point? You don't have to go looking for trials. God will bring them your way—and don't worry, there will always be some with your name on them.

It took a lot of faith for Peter to step out into a raging sea. But when you are trusting Jesus and taking Him at His word, you can experience His power and authority to do what He does, which is walk on top of your trial.

Talk about encouragement in the middle of a storm. Peter figured it was better to be with Christ out in the storm than to be without Him in the boat.

CHRIST LOVES US IN OUR TRIALS

Peter started walking on the water toward Jesus, but then he hit a problem. "But seeing the wind, he became afraid, and beginning to sink, he cried out, saying, 'Lord, save me!'" (Matthew 14:30).

Peter started out great, trusting in Jesus and His authority over the water. But then Peter did something we all do at times. He took his eyes off of Jesus and started looking around. And when he did that, his trial started swallowing him up.

The interesting thing is that the circumstances had not changed for Peter. The sea was still raging, just as it had been when he was in the boat. The difference was in Peter. He began letting the trial control him, and he started going down.

At least Peter knew where to turn. His focus got shifted back to Jesus in a hurry when he cried out for help. When Peter turned back to Jesus and Jesus reached out to lift him up, Peter got back in the position he should have been in all along, which was walking on his trial and not under it.

The good part here is that Jesus loved Peter far too much to let him sink. "*Immediately* Jesus stretched out His hand and took hold of him, and said to him, 'O you of little faith, why did you doubt?'" (Matthew 14:31, italics added). In other words, "Peter, you know how much I love you. How could you think I would let you sink?"

Peter learned his lesson too. Years later, in 1 Peter 1:3–9 he told his scattered and persecuted readers that they were protected by the power of God, even though they were suffering temporarily under hard trials. Once you've begun to sink under a trial and Jesus has reached down to you in love, you are never the same.

CHRIST IS SOVEREIGN IN OUR TRIALS

Another important principle can be found in the last two verses of this story.

Jesus rescued Peter, and the two of them walked to the boat. "And when they got into the boat, the wind stopped. And those who were in the boat worshiped Him, saying, 'You are certainly God's Son!'" (Matthew 14:32–33). Everything was fine once Jesus got into the boat.

Jesus' Timetable

This raises several questions. Why didn't Jesus leave with the disciples in the first place? None of this trauma would have happened. Or, why didn't He come a lot earlier? He knew they were in trouble. Why did Jesus let the disciples twist in the wind for hours?

The only answer I can come up with is that Jesus came when He was ready. It was His prerogative all the way. He knew exactly how long to let the trial last, and when it was time to end it He came walking on the water.

Jesus' delay here was as much an expression of His sovereign authority as His arrival and calming of the storm— which, by the way, was another miracle that only Deity could perform.

I don't know if the disciples fussed and fumed during those hours of futile rowing. I don't know if they kept asking each other, "Where in the world is Jesus? Why doesn't He do something?"

But I do know this: If they did fuss and fume, it didn't hurry Jesus one bit. And guess what? Your fussing and fuming won't hurry Him either.

I hear people say, "I'm mad at God!" My response is, "Big deal." It's OK to be honest with God, but you have to understand that God is working His plan from the perspective of eternity, not your momentary emergency. Jesus is going to get into the boat when He's ready.

Reaching Their Destination

But the beautiful thing is that even if He is not in the boat with you, as long as He is in the vicinity you will be fine, because He can speak peace to you from the storm.

John's account of this trial includes an interesting detail. He wrote, "They [the disciples] were willing therefore to receive Him into the boat; and immediately the boat was at the land to which they were going" (John 6:21).

Matthew also said they crossed over and reached their destination (Matthew 14:34), but John said the arrival was dramatic. As soon as Jesus boarded, they were on land. The disciples thought the storm was taking them down, when it was actually taking them where they wanted to go.

What a great illustration of Romans 8:28, which tells us that "God causes all things to work together for good to those who love God, to those who are called according to His purpose."

Do you want to reach God's destination for your life? The fastest way to get there is to hang in there under trials, because if you are faithful Jesus has the authority to guarantee that you won't sink under the waves.

A New View of Him

The best thing of all that came from this trial was the way it changed the disciples' view of Jesus Christ. They saw Him for who He really was, and they worshiped Him.

These men had seen Jesus do miracles, but now it finally dawned on them, "You are really who You say You are. You are the Son of the living God!"

When you really discover who Jesus is, worship becomes a high priority. When you realize that He rules over all creation, that He wields the authority of God because He *is* God, and that He rules in authority in your life, you won't have any problem worshiping Jesus Christ.

As fast as the disciples could blink, they went from the middle of the Sea of Galilee in a raging storm to the calm of the other shore. They finally figured out that this Man who could find them in the dark, walk to them on the water, and instantly calm the storm and propel them to land without so much as a word was no ordinary Man. Nothing will change your perspective on your trials faster than worshiping God in the midst of them.

This does not mean the disciples had life all wired from there on out and never doubted or struggled again. We saw earlier that Mark included the disturbing note that the Twelve had not learned what God wanted them to learn from the feeding of the five thousand (Mark 6:52). This was one reason Jesus sent them into the storm for part two of the lesson.

Out there on the sea in the wee hours of the morning, the disciples forgot what Jesus had done the day before. So when He came and bailed them out of the storm, they were amazed that He could do something so miraculous.

We also tend to forget what God did for us yesterday, and last week, and last year. Worship helps to refresh our memories as we regularly praise God for who He is and what He has done and look to Him for what He is going to do in the future.

FLYING WITH GOD'S JET STREAM

The jet stream air currents were discovered after some airplanes began arriving at their destination far ahead of schedule. Scientists began to study this phenomenon after pilots discovered the jet stream, which propels a plane forward at a faster rate when the plane is flying in the same direction.

When you are in a trial, you need to learn how to use God's jet stream. You need to catch the "Jesus stream." When you catch the Jesus stream, He will propel you along to your destination faster than you could ever get there on your own.

But you have to be going in the same direction as Jesus to ride His jet stream. All the power, joy, and authority you need for any trial is in that stream. Get moving with Jesus by keeping your focus on Him, and He will carry you to your intended destination.

CHAPTER SIXTEEN

THE AUTHORITY OF CHRIST OVER DEATH

We're ready to wrap up this section of the book, in which we have been dealing with Jesus Christ's authority over any circumstance, trial, or attack of the Enemy we will ever face in this life. Since death is "the last enemy that will be abolished" (1 Corinthians 15:26), it's appropriate that we end this theme by talking about Christ's authority over death.

No chapter in the Bible brings this truth home more vividly than John 11, the story of Jesus' climactic miracle in raising His friend Lazarus from the dead. This miracle is climactic not only because it involves the conquest of death, but because this was the last miracle Jesus performed on His way to Jerusalem to die on the cross and be raised from the dead. So the apostle John used this miracle as an illustration of Jesus' power over death and His ability to make good on His promise of eternal life.

There is no question that death is an enemy. If you want to know how despicable sin is, look at death, because death is sin's reward (Romans 6:23). In Adam we all die (1 Corinthians 15:22).

But because Jesus Christ has exercised His authority over death, our last and greatest enemy need not hold any terrors for those who know Him. In this chapter I want to show you why we can make such a bold statement. Let's find out more about Jesus Christ's authority over death and what it means for us.

THE AUTHORITY OF CHRIST
GIVES PURPOSE TO DEATH

The first thing I want you to see in John 11 is that Christ's presence and authority give meaning or purpose to death, an event that would otherwise be full of meaninglessness and despair.

We are used to hearing that Christ gives us a purpose for life. The same is true of death. When Jesus is on the scene, death is not a random or meaningless event. That was true in the death of Lazarus. Jesus was firmly in command of the situation, as seen by His assurance to the disciples and to Martha that Lazarus would not remain in the grave (see John 11:4, 23).

Let's set the context of this story. Jesus was on His way to Jerusalem to be arrested, tried, and crucified. Bethany was a village only about two miles from Jerusalem (John 11:18), and it was the hometown of some of Jesus' favorite people— the sisters Mary and Martha and their brother Lazarus (John 11:1).

Their home was like a second home to Jesus. He was always welcome there. Jesus loved these three people very deeply, and they loved Him. In fact, when Lazarus became ill, the sisters' message to Jesus was, "Lord, behold, he whom You love is sick" (v. 3). John added, "Now Jesus loved Martha, and her sister, and Lazarus" (v. 5).

So we know right up front that Jesus was acting out of deep love for these three followers of His. And we can have the same assurance that He is acting out of love in our lives. But at first glance, Jesus' love for these people doesn't compute with His actions upon receiving word of Lazarus's illness. "When therefore [Jesus] heard that he was sick, He stayed then two days longer in the place where He was" (v. 6).

It's obvious this was not what Martha and Mary expected. They sent for Jesus in the hope that He would hurry to Bethany before Lazarus died. When Jesus did arrive, they both said the same thing: "Lord, if You had been here, my brother would not have died" (vv. 21, 32).

But Jesus intentionally delayed His coming to Bethany, even knowing that Lazarus was deathly ill. In fact, Jesus delayed long enough that Lazarus died (vv. 11–14).

To Bring Glory to God

Why did Jesus do this? He answered that question in John 11:4 when He said, "This sickness is not unto death, but for the glory of God, that the Son of God may be glorified by it."

We've already established that Jesus loved Lazarus, so a lack of love wasn't the issue. The issue is that God was operating with a bigger program in mind, and that program included the physical death of Lazarus.

This tells us that knowing God does not necessarily mean we will not suffer. God can love you and still let you be sick—and even die. We have talked about this before, but let me emphasize again that anyone who tells you that being a believer means always being healthy isn't giving you the whole story. People like that need to read John 11 carefully. Jesus loved Lazarus, but He stayed where He was until Lazarus took a turn for the worse and died.

Lazarus's sickness and death were in God's will, because God had a bigger purpose in view. Part of this purpose was so that Jesus would be glorified by raising a man from death. What a testimony to His deity this was, because only God can raise the dead.

We need to learn from this, because there are times when we are in desperate circumstances and call out to the Lord, and He delays. We know He loves us, and we send for Him in the hope that He will come with the solution right away.

But He doesn't come in the way we thought He would, the situation seems to get worse, and we wonder what's happening. A bigger program is at work. In the case of Lazarus, Jesus was going to get more glory by raising a dead man than by healing a sick man. Mary, Martha, and Lazarus did not know this, but Jesus knew it.

To Increase Our Faith

Here's another purpose God often has when the issue is death. He wants to use our situation to increase our faith. Jesus said to His disciples concerning Lazarus's death, "I am glad for your sakes that I was not there, so that you may believe; but let us go to him" (John 11:15).

When Jesus arrived in Bethany, He said to Martha, "I am

the resurrection and the life; he who believes in Me shall live even if he dies, and everyone who lives and believes in Me shall never die. Do you believe this?" (John 11:25–26). Martha's answer in verse 27 affirmed her faith in Jesus as "the Christ, the Son of God." Then at the grave Jesus said to Martha, "Did I not say to you, if you believe, you will see the glory of God?" (v. 40).

Another of Jesus' purposes in delaying His trip to Bethany was to strengthen the faith of everyone involved, including the disciples. Sometimes God doesn't do what you ask Him to do when you want Him to do it, so that you may learn to trust Him more. It's easy to trust God when you get what you are asking for. It's harder to trust God when you don't get your request.

To Save Sinners

We can see from the account in John 11 that God can also use death to bring sinners to salvation.

When Jesus prayed at Lazarus's tomb, He said, "I knew that Thou hearest Me always; but because of the people standing around I said it, that they may believe that Thou didst send Me" (John 11:42). After Lazarus came out of the grave, "Many therefore of the Jews, who had come to Mary and beheld what He had done, believed in Him" (v. 45).

Because of Jesus' delay and Lazarus's death, people got saved. I've conducted many funerals, and I don't know of any occasion when people are more receptive to the gospel, since they are face-to-face with eternity. God has used the deaths of many believers to bring unsaved relatives to Himself.

To Advance God's Prophetic Program

Another purpose for Jesus' delay was to further God's prophetic program in relation to His upcoming death. The miraculous resurrection of Lazarus stirred Jesus' enemies into action. Some of the Jews who witnessed the miracle went to Jerusalem and told the chief priests and Pharisees what Jesus had done (John 11:46).

These men got together in an emergency session to decide what to do about Jesus. One thing was not in doubt:

This man had to be killed. They were afraid if they let Jesus go on, the Romans would have all their heads (vv. 47–48).

Caiaphas, the high priest, told the others to relax. Then he made a remarkable prophecy: "It is expedient for you that one man should die for the people, and that the whole nation should not perish" (v. 50). Caiaphas was exactly right, but John added in verse 51 that Caiaphas made this prophecy in spite of himself.

Thus the decision was made. "So from that day on they planned together to kill Him" (v. 53). The order went out that "if anyone knew where [Jesus] was, he should report it, that they might seize Him" (v. 57).

In other words, the death and resurrection of Lazarus became part of God's larger plan because it moved Jesus' enemies to expedite their plans for His death. And since it was drawing near God's time for Jesus to die, these men's evil plans helped bring about the fulfillment of prophecy that Jesus Christ would die for the sins of the world.

No matter what happens, God is always in control. Whether He was facing the challenge of a dead body or a body of powerful people intent on destroying Him, Jesus remained firmly in charge of the situation. His authority was never in doubt. God always has something bigger in the works than what you and I can see. His plan may include illness and even death, but it's all part of His grand program and purpose.

It's easy to say this, but it takes faith to actually live it. Imagine Mary and Martha sitting at their dying brother's bedside, wondering why Jesus hadn't come yet. But this seemingly bad situation, which seemed to turn even worse when Lazarus died, was not meaningless, because Christ was in it.

THE AUTHORITY OF CHRIST
OVERCOMES THE FEAR OF DEATH

Our biggest problem with death is our fear of it. Death is the doorway to eternity, and that can be a sobering thought even for believers. The thought of death even brings panic to some people.

In one sense death is a fearful thing because it's unnatural. God created us to live, not to die. Death is part of the curse of sin, and so it brings fear and anxiety. But when you bring Christ into the equation, the sting of death is dismissed, because Christ has taken away our sins. As Paul said, "The sting of death is sin" (1 Corinthians 15:56). Remove the sin, and death loses its power to harm us.

This principle appears not in relation to Lazarus's death, but the impending death of Jesus. When Jesus announced He was going to Judea, the region of Bethany and Jerusalem, the disciples asked Him, "Rabbi, the Jews were just now seeking to stone You, and are You going there again?" (John 11:8). They couldn't understand why He would go into the backyard of the very people who were looking for Him. It was asking for a death sentence.

But Jesus said, "Are there not twelve hours in the day? If anyone walks in the day, he does not stumble, because he sees the light of this world. But if anyone walks in the night, he stumbles, because the light is not in him" (vv. 9–10).

Most of us aren't afraid to walk around in daylight, because we can see where we're going. But it's a different story at night, especially in that day when there were no lighting systems.

In the Bible, light and darkness often stand for the work of God and the work of the devil. Jesus was saying that He was not afraid to go back to Judea, because He was going there to do the will of God. Jesus did not fear death, because He was living in God's will, and He knew He would not die one second before God's appointed time (see John 7:30).

You only have to fear death if you are not in the will of God. Why? Because when you are in God's will, you won't die until God's appointed time for you. You see, people get all worried about dying before their time. The disciples were fearful for Jesus because the Jewish leaders were out to kill Him. But Jesus wasn't worried about that threat because He was walking in the light. The Pharisees were in danger of stumbling, not Him.

Since God has appointed our time of death, what about all the exercise and healthy eating? There's nothing wrong with trying to keep ourselves fit. Our bodies are part of our stewardship responsibility before God.

But these things affect the quality of life, not its length. God has ordained the time of our death. No one can touch you outside of God's will. Someone once said of believers that we are invincible in the will of God.

Death may seem ominous and beyond anyone's ability to

control, but that's not true. Jesus holds our last enemy firmly in His authority. That's why when Paul's death was near, he talked not about his fear of dying, but about the reward Jesus had waiting for him (2 Timothy 4:6–8). Death is only the next step in God's will for His children. That was true for Lazarus too, by the way.

The apostle Thomas also realized what Jesus was saying, because he said to the other disciples, "Let us also go, that we may die with Him" (John 11:16). Thomas stated that even if it was God's will for Jesus to go to Jerusalem and die, he was going to stick with Jesus.

This matter of fearing death reminds me of the little boy who was in a Sunday school play. He was supposed to come out and say what Christ said to the disciples when He came walking to them on the water: "It is I. Do not be afraid." But the little boy walked out on stage, saw all the people, and said, "It's me, and I'm scared to death."

If we had to face death alone, we would have a right to be scared to death. But because of Jesus' authority over death, we don't have to be afraid.

THE AUTHORITY OF CHRIST REDEFINES DEATH

Part of our problem in trying to cope with death is that it is sometimes hard to define. What constitutes death? To many unbelievers, death means the cessation of existence. They believe that people just lie down and die, and that's it. But the Bible teaches differently. Death is not the end of a person's existence. In fact, Jesus made an astounding promise to Martha concerning death. Let's go back to the story in John 11.

When Jesus arrived in Bethany, Martha came running up to Him and said, "Lord, if You had been here, my brother would not have died" (v. 21).

We have already quoted part of Jesus' reply, but I want to come back to it, because in the next few verses, Jesus redefines death on His terms:

Jesus said to her, "Your brother shall rise again." Martha said to Him, "I know that he will rise again in the resurrection on the last day." Jesus said to her, "I am the resurrection and the life; he who believes in Me shall live even if he dies, and everyone who lives and believes in Me shall never die." (vv. 23–26)

Temporary vs. Eternal Death

At this point in the story, Lazarus had already been dead four days. So how could Jesus promise Martha, "Everyone who lives and believes in Me shall never die"? Because Jesus does not define death the way we define it.

That's good news, because according to Jesus' authoritative definition of death, *you will never die* if you know Him as your Savior! Death is not in God's vocabulary. It is one of the things excluded from heaven (Revelation 21:4).

When people talk about death, they are referring to the temporary separation of the body from the soul and spirit, the immaterial part of a person. This is physical death, the kind Lazarus experienced and we will experience someday.

But as far as God is concerned, the only definition of death that matters is the eternal, spiritual separation of a person from God, which is hell. This is eternal death, which, unlike physical death, can never be reversed by resurrection.

When Jesus told Martha that Lazarus would rise again, He was acknowledging that Lazarus had died physically. But Jesus went on to promise that *eternal death* would never touch His people. He was about to taste death and hell for us. Therefore, our future is eternal life!

The Sleep of Death

So if death is not the end of existence or the final step for a believer, what is it? Jesus had said of Lazarus, "Our friend Lazarus has fallen asleep; but I go, that I may awaken him out of sleep" (John 11:11).

Jesus was talking about death, not slumber. Physical death is like going to sleep, because even when you are asleep and your body is inactive, the essential core of your being—your soul and spirit—are still functioning. Sleep doesn't change that fact. The soul is your self-consciousness.

The spirit is your God-consciousness. Both are just as alive when you sleep as they are when you awake. The only thing that sleeps is your body.

When you close your eyes in death, you will be as alive then as you ever were when you were walking around. The only difference is that your body will be asleep. It is the body that sleeps, not the soul or spirit. And one day, the body will be awakened in resurrection to be reunited with the soul and spirit. Then the entire person will enter either heaven or hell.

I'll stick with God's definition of death! Let me say it again: On the authority of Jesus Christ Himself, death will never touch you if you are His child.

In fact, even the moment of physical death is nothing, because Paul said to be absent from the body is to be at home with the Lord (2 Corinthians 5:8). Paul was eager to depart this earth because it meant being with Christ (Philippians 1:23).

We are going to get brand-new, perfect bodies after these imperfect, decaying bodies are laid in the ground. So why are we so worried about dying? You won't be at your funeral anyway! Everyone else will be there, but you will be with Christ faster than your eye can twinkle. What we call death is the sleep of the body in anticipation of the resurrection to eternal life.

THE AUTHORITY OF CHRIST
BRINGS COMFORT AT DEATH

What we just said above about death not really happening to a believer is not intended to ignore or minimize the sorrow and pain of physical death. Far from it. It hurts to be separated from friends and loved ones, even when we know we'll see them again someday.

Jesus did not minimize the pain Martha and Mary and the others were experiencing because Lazarus had died. On the contrary, He entered into their sorrow with them. When Mary learned Jesus had come, she ran and fell at His feet weeping (John 11:32). "When Jesus therefore saw her weeping, and the Jews who came with her, also weeping, He was deeply moved in spirit, and was troubled, and said, 'Where have you laid him?' They said to Him, 'Lord, come and see.' Jesus wept" (vv. 33–35).

There are at least three reasons Jesus wept. First of all, He saw Mary and Martha and all their friends crying, and

His heart went out to them in compassion. The Bible says Jesus sympathizes with our weaknesses (Hebrews 4:15). When you are hurting, Jesus hurts with you.

You might ask, "Well, if Jesus hurts with me, why doesn't He do something about my pain?" Because the plan of God is not governed by emotions, but by what is best for us. It's like a father who spanks his child, even though the spanking hurts the father emotionally more than it does the child. A father cannot allow his feelings to dictate the program of discipline that he needs to carry out with his child.

The second reason Jesus wept was because of His love for Lazarus (v. 36). This man was Jesus' dear friend.

The third reason Jesus cried and was "deeply moved" (vv. 33, 38) is that He was disturbed by seeing once again the pain and devastation that sin had caused. Death is an unnatural intruder into God's perfect creation. So the presence of death meant that Satan was at work again.

Christ was troubled in His spirit because He knows the work of Satan is a horrendous thing (John 10:10). Satan rules in the realm of death, and Jesus was face-to-face with the kingdom of death and darkness once again. This is not to ignore the fact that Lazarus was a believer. Jesus was stirred by another reminder of the reality of sin and death.

THE AUTHORITY OF CHRIST CONQUERS DEATH

But here's the best part of the story. Because He has supreme authority, Jesus can do something about the problem of death.

When He arrived at the grave of Lazarus, Jesus ordered the stone removed, prayed a prayer of gratitude and confidence to His Father, and then shouted "Lazarus, come forth" (vv. 39–43).

Martha was quick to remind Jesus that Lazarus had been dead four days. But Jesus is not limited to the laws of nature. In fact, it is incorrect to speak of the laws of nature. They are actually the laws of God that nature must obey. Jesus' authority is not subject to natural limitations. He can command a dead body to come out of the grave.

In response to Jesus' authoritative command, Lazarus came to life and walked out of his grave. He was still wearing his grave clothes and had to be untied. But Jesus' authority had conquered death once again.

Before we leave this chapter and this section, I want you to notice that Lazarus was resurrected by Christ, but he had to be untied and set free by others. Jesus didn't untie Lazarus. He told other people to do it.

There's a lesson here for us. If you know Jesus Christ, you have His new, resurrection life within you. But you may still be stumbling around in the grave clothes of your old life. If so, you need to be set free from those old clothes.

Jesus has given you life, but you need to shed those old ways of life that may still be binding you. You can't walk free and unhindered in your Christian life and still practice the walk and talk of the world. If you can't get unwrapped from those grave clothes yourself, let the body of Christ help you get free.

THE SHADOW OF DEATH

Death is real, and it can be frightening, but it is not the last word, thanks to the authority of Jesus Christ.

Donald Grey Barnhouse, a great pastor and preacher from the previous generation, experienced the death of his wife. He told about coming back from the funeral with his small children in the car. They were asking, "Why did Mommy have to die?"

Dr. Barnhouse did not know what to say. He was thinking about the question when they came to an intersection and had to wait for a train to pass by. As the shadow of the train passed over their car, a thought suddenly occurred to Barnhouse.

"Children," he asked, "would you rather be hit by that train, or by its shadow?" Of course, the children said they would rather be hit by the train's shadow.

Barnhouse then explained to his children that because their mother knew Jesus, she had only been struck by the shadow of death. They would see her again in heaven.

That's what the authority of Christ over death means for us too. The reality of death cannot hurt us when we belong to Him. *Not* to know Jesus is to be hit by the train, not its shadow. So my question to you is, When death comes for you, will just its shadow fall over you, or its reality?

PART THREE

THE PURSUIT
OF CHRIST

CHAPTER SEVENTEEN

EXALTING CHRIST

We're ready for the third and final portion of our study on the person and work of Jesus Christ. This section is the logical outgrowth and expression of what we have learned in the first two sections. Since Jesus Christ is the unique Son of God with all authority in heaven and on earth, the only response that makes any sense at all is to pursue Him with everything we have.

That's what I want to talk about in these remaining chapters. I want to try to answer the question, What does it mean to pursue Christ? What does it take to make Jesus Christ's lordship real in our lives? One way we can do this is by exalting Him, giving Him the place of preeminent power and authority in our hearts that He deserves. It's here that I want to begin.

We have a lot of help here, because an entire book of the Bible is devoted to the exaltation of Christ. The book of Colossians exalts Christ from beginning to end. It is a Christological book, in which Paul demonstrated that Jesus Christ reigns supreme by virtue of who He is and what He has done.

Colossians 1:18 says the goal of God's plan is that "[Christ] Himself might come to have first place in everything." This will happen on a global scale when Christ returns to establish His millennial kingdom on earth.

But for you and me as God's children, Christ is to have first place in everything right now, because He is "head of the body, the church." Colossians tells us how we are to exalt Christ, and I want to look with you at four major themes concerning how we can do that.

EXALTING CHRIST IN OUR FAITH

When I say that Christ is to be exalted in our faith, I'm talking about the attributes and the work of Christ that make Him worthy to reign supreme in our lives. We dealt with this material in detail in the opening chapters of the book, so what I want to say here is largely review. But it's important, and therefore worth reviewing.

Exalted Because of His Deity

When we were studying Christ's deity we referred to Colossians a number of times, because the book gives ample testimony to the truth that Jesus Christ is fully God. He is worthy to be exalted because of who He is.

Paul wrote that Jesus is "the image of the invisible God, the first-born of all creation" (Colossians 1:15). Jesus Christ is the "stamp," the exact likeness and representation of God, which means that His very essence and substance is full Deity.

God is invisible in His essence because He is spirit, but when Jesus Christ took on a human body in the manger of Bethlehem, God became visible (John 1:14, 18). That's why Paul could say that in Jesus, "all the fulness of Deity dwells in bodily form" (Colossians 2:9).

This is review, but don't move on too quickly. The next verse in Colossians says, "In Him you have been made complete" (2:10). If the fullness of Deity dwells in Christ and Christ dwells in us, it should be no problem for us to exalt Him in our daily lives. We need to get excited about who is within us and who wants to live His life through us, rather than getting excited about what is going on around us. There is no one else in the universe worthy of our praise except Jesus Christ.

Jesus is also worthy of exaltation because He is the originator of the created order. Again in Colossians, Paul said that Jesus is "the first-born of all creation. For by Him all things were created, both in the heavens and on earth" (1:15–16).

This is another tremendous statement of Deity. In order to be the Creator, Christ must be outside of creation Himself. That means Christ is uncreated, another way of saying He is eternal. And only one Being is eternal, God Himself. God the Father "made the world" through God the Son (Hebrews 1:2).

Exalted Because of His Position

Jesus is also worthy of our exaltation because of the unique position He holds.

Not only did He create everything, but Paul went on to say that everything points to Christ. "All things have been created by Him and for Him. And He is before all things, and in Him all things hold together" (Colossians 1:16b–17).

Notice that the "all things" here include "thrones," "dominions," "rulers," and "authorities" (v. 16). That covers any kind of human or demonic authority you could possibly imagine. Paul was saying that Jesus Christ is the moving force or cause behind all of it.

Let me give you a little theology that will show you why Jesus is to be exalted. Theologians refer to Him as the instrumental cause of Creation. That is, He is the agent of Creation, the One who made the process happen.

When God said, "Let there be . . ." Jesus went into action, because He is the Word of God. I realize it's difficult to grasp how the three persons of the Godhead work among themselves, but the Bible is clear that Jesus is responsible for Creation.

Jesus is also the final cause or the purpose of Creation, since Paul said everything was created for Him. When God spoke the world into being, He had the glory and exaltation of His Son in mind. Jesus is the reason God created the universe.

This universe is, as it were, a gift from God the Father to His Son. All of creation is designed to glorify and exalt Jesus Christ. He stands at the pinnacle of it all.

Exalted Because of His Work

Here is a third reason to exalt Christ in our faith: He is exalted for what He has done, and is doing, to sustain this universe and redeem us from sin.

First of all, Colossians 1:17 says Jesus is the One holding this outfit together. The reason the entire universe doesn't fly apart is that Christ is sustaining it by His power. His job is to hold the universe intact.

Is it any wonder, then, that Christ could stand up in a boat and command the wind and waves to be still (Mark 4:39)? The elements have no option but to obey Christ. When Jesus commanded Lazarus to come forth from the grave, death had no option but to release him. There was no negotiation here. The molecules of Lazarus's body could come back to life because Jesus holds the universe together.

Before we move on, I have a question for you—and for myself. If Jesus Christ can hold all the matter in the universe together, can He hold our lives together? Since Jesus is so good at holding things together, maybe we ought not to panic so quickly when things go wrong. Maybe we ought not to throw in the towel so easily. Maybe this same God who keeps universes intact can keep us together too!

Maybe what we need to be doing is exalting Christ by placing Him at the center of our lives and orienting everything else around Him. That's what it means to exalt Christ. It means that when you use His name, you put a period after it, because He is in a class by Himself.

Christ also deserves to be exalted because He sustains the church as our Head (Colossians 1:18). He is the source of spiritual life, both for individual believers and for the church as a whole. Jesus is also the "first-born from the dead," the first in line in the resurrection. And because He was raised from the dead, we will be raised someday with glorious bodies like His.

Of course, the supreme work of Christ for which He deserves our exaltation is His death on the cross to redeem us from sin. Christ has reconciled us to God, which He did when He "made peace through the blood of His cross" (Colossians 1:20). We would be lost for eternity without the Cross. Our faith would be worthless without the Cross. So it is only right that we exalt Christ in our faith.

EXALTING CHRIST IN OUR FOCUS

We also need to keep Jesus Christ at the center of our focus. "If then you have been raised up with Christ, keep seeking the things above, where Christ is, seated at the right hand of God. Set your mind on the things above, not on the things that are on earth. For you have died and your life is hidden with Christ in God" (Colossians 3:1–3).

If we are living spiritually where Christ is living, and if our lives are hidden with Him, guess where our focus should be! Some Christians are losing their way because they are looking in the wrong direction. You can't move forward while looking backward. Let me give several reasons for making Jesus our daily focus.

He Is Our Authority

Paul tells us that since we are heaven-oriented people, we need to view earthly things through heavenly glasses and make earthly decisions based on heavenly criteria. The only way we can function on earth from the standpoint of heaven is to keep Christ exalted in our focus.

The Bible says He is seated at the right hand of God the Father—the position of ultimate power and authority in the universe. That means Jesus Christ is the Sovereign of the universe, and therefore He commands the central place in our hearts.

He Is Our Life

Let me give you a practical, nonbiological definition of life. Life is whatever makes you come alive. For example, if you tell a child you are taking him to the toy store, he becomes alive with excitement. Tell a teenager you are taking him to get his driver's license tomorrow, and he comes alive. A person who has met Mr. or Miss Right will gladly tell you all about this dream person and show you all kinds of pictures. In other words, the new relationship is all it takes to bring this person to life.

Do you know what made the apostle Paul come to life? "For to me, to live is Christ" (Philippians 1:21). If you can't say that right now, the problem could be one of focus. Maybe your spiritual glasses have become a little fogged by circumstances or the things of this life, so that you are not seeing Christ as clearly as you should.

When that happens, you won't feel alive spiritually, because God wants to bring you to the place where Christ is more important than your race, religious status, citizenship, social or economic status, or anything else. God wants us to be able to say, "Christ is all, and in all" (Colossians 3:11).

He Is Our Provision

When Christ holds this place of supremacy in your focus, some good things happen in your life. You begin to reap some incredible benefits. Let's look at three of them.

First, "the peace of Christ [will] rule in your hearts" (Colossians 3:15). That word *rule* refers to an umpire or a referee in a sporting event. This is the person who calls the shots in the game, who determines what's legitimate and what isn't. The umpire keeps the game moving and keeps the peace (most of the time!) by rendering the decisions.

Paul said when Christ is your focus, when He is your all in all, God will place His peace in your heart to give you direction and help you in making the right calls in life. God's peace will dominate when you are going the way He wants you to go—and when you begin heading in the wrong direction, you will know it, because God's peace will no longer be the ruling force.

One of the best ways to keep your focus on Christ is through prayer, and the Bible has a promise of God's peace for those who pray about everything instead of worrying about everything (Philippians 4:6–7).

Worry is the great peace stealer, but when you pray, God's peace will "guard" or do sentry duty in your heart (v. 7). This is a calmness of spirit God gives you when your focus is on Christ.

A second benefit of keeping your focus on Christ is that "the word of Christ [will] richly dwell within you" (Colossians 3:16). The word *dwell* means to make yourself at home. God did not intend for the Word to be a guest, kept in the "front parlor" of our lives. He wants us to allow His Word to rummage around in the attic, to open the drawers and the closets, to have total access to every part of us.

We tell our guests to make themselves at home, but we usually don't literally mean it. We don't want them going back to our bedroom, or sitting down at our desk and going through our personal papers and the checkbook.

What we really mean when we tell visitors to make themselves at home is, "I am going to lead you into this room called a den, and I want you to have a seat here and to relax while you're here." Our focus is much narrower than the entire house.

But when Christ is our focus, His Word is free to make itself at home within us. And when the Word starts rummaging around in our lives, it helps us locate and get rid of the junk we have accumulated and don't need and the spiritual toxins that can make us sick. That's why we need to let the Word be at home within us. It will do any housecleaning needed.

We can let the Word of God make itself at home within us by "teaching and admonishing one another with psalms and hymns and spiritual songs, singing with thankfulness in [our] hearts to God" (Colossians 3:16b).

Notice the prominent place that gratitude plays in the Christian life. The more you keep your focus on Christ, the more of a grateful believer you will become. That's crucial, because the Bible teaches that one of the signature qualities of a Christian is thankfulness (see also v. 17b).

The third benefit of keeping our focus on Christ is that we have the privilege of acting in His name. "And whatever you do in word or deed, do all in the name of the Lord Jesus" (Colossians 3:17).

In the Bible, a name meant two things: identification and authority. We are identified with Christ through redemption. His name is already upon us. When our focus is on Him, we will see every decision and action in life in terms of how it affects our identification with Him. And we will act in the authority He has given us.

EXALTING CHRIST IN OUR FAMILY

The exaltation of Christ also extends to the way we conduct our family life as believers. Christ is glorified when our homes reflect His priorities, and the Bible has specific instructions to each member of a Christian family.

The Submission of Wives

Paul wrote in Colossians 3:18, "Wives, be subject to your husbands, as is fitting in the Lord." This is a controversial statement these days, mostly because it is so often misunderstood and misapplied.

I want to clarify right away that this command does not address a woman's intrinsic worth as a person and a child of

God. A wife is equal in value to her husband. Peter said the wife is a "fellow heir of the grace of life" (1 Peter 3:7).

A wife's submission has to do with function, not value. Just as Jesus Christ is functionally subordinate to the Father, yet equal with the Father, so a wife is functionally subordinate to her husband, yet equal to him.

It is "fitting in the Lord" that a wife should defer to her husband's authority. The idea is that it is proper and becoming for a wife to conduct herself this way, because this is what God asks of her and what exalts Christ in her life and in the home.

A wife who separates her relationship with her husband from her relationship with Christ will not relate to her husband properly. She will resist and rebel against his God-given authority, and thus separate herself from God's hand on her life.

The matriarch Sarah is a good example of a woman being in submission to her husband and receiving a blessing from God.

Abraham was far from perfect. He lied about Sarah to protect himself, but the Bible says Sarah honored Abraham by calling him "lord," a title of respect (1 Peter 3:6). She may not always have agreed with his person, but she honored his position as head of the home. And she got a miracle, the birth of Isaac when she was old and barren.

So a wife exalts Christ in her home by honoring her husband and placing herself under his leadership. We'll see later that this does not give a husband permission to be a demanding tyrant. The qualifying phrase "as is fitting in the Lord" means a husband can't demand anything of his wife that would cause her to displease God.

A husband can't just say, "I am the husband and you do what I say, period." There is another equation here, what is fitting and pleasing to God.

The Love of Husbands

Paul also addressed husbands. "Husbands, love your wives, and do not be embittered against them" (Colossians 3:19). This is the self-sacrificing, *agape* love that Christ displayed when He loved and gave Himself for the church (Ephesians 5:25).

A husband ought to ask himself regularly, "What have I given up for my wife lately? What has it cost me to be her husband? What sacrifices have I made to enhance her well-being?" Christ loved the church so much He made the ultimate sacrifice for her. That's the model of a husband's love.

Many men have the idea that being a husband means being "the boss." But Christ demonstrated sacrificial, servant love. To put it simply, a husband should be outserving his wife.

One way a husband can test his servanthood is to list all the things his wife does for him and all the things he does for her, and see which list is longer. Christ is exalted when we husbands demonstrate His love in our marriages.

It would be a major revelation to some husbands to discover that their wives were not put on earth to serve them. A wife is there to love, help, and support her husband, but his love should outserve hers because a husband's love is commanded in Scripture. The wife is never commanded to love her husband.

The Bible also tells husbands not to become bitter toward their wives. The reason is that what you see is what you created. A wife is a mirror that reflects back to her husband what she is receiving from him, because a woman was made to respond.

That does not mean that everything wrong in a woman's life is her husband's fault. She may have brought a lot of baggage into the marriage. But if Christ's actions toward the church are an example of a husband's actions toward his wife, perhaps part of a husband's job is to sanctify his wife (Ephesians 5:25–26), to help fix what's wrong.

God created woman as a "weaker vessel" (1 Peter 3:7), not weaker in character but more fragile in spirit, needing tender, loving care and nurturing lest she be crushed. A husband's love can cause his wife to open and bloom like a flower with new life.

The Relationship of Parents and Children

The other important relationship in the home is that between the children and parents.

God has a word here too, a way that we can exalt Christ in our families. "Children, be obedient to your parents in all things, for this is well-pleasing to the Lord. Fathers, do not exasperate your children, that they may not lose heart" (Colossians 3:20–21).

The Bible views disobedience to parents as rebellion against God. We parents need to teach our children that their number one responsibility under God, as long as they are under our authority, is to honor us by their obedience. But let's also teach them that they can bring the Lord great honor and glory by their obedience.

Parents have a responsibility too. It involves encouraging and building up their children rather than exasperating and frustrating them with criticism. Parents have to correct wrong, but the dominant thing children should be able to remember about their parents is the encouragement they received, not the criticism. Children need an environment of encouragement.

EXALTING CHRIST IN OUR FIELD

The fourth and last area is what I'm calling our field, our place of employment, our behavior in the marketplace.

The dominant marketplace relationship in Paul's day was slaves and their masters, which translates most closely to employees and employers in our day. The bottom line is that Christ is to be exalted in the workplace.

The Responsibilities of Employees

The basic command to those who work for someone else is to serve their employers as if they were serving Christ Himself:

> Slaves, in all things obey those who are your masters on earth, not with external service, as those who merely please men, but with sincerity of heart, fearing the Lord. Whatever you do, do your work heartily, as for the Lord rather than for men; knowing that from the Lord you will receive the reward of the inheritance. It is the Lord Christ whom you serve. (Colossians 3:22–24)

A passage like this raises the question, Why didn't Paul just command the immediate and complete eradication of the institution of slavery in the early church?

The answer is he didn't have to. He did something better,

more lasting, and more effective. He Christianized the institution of slavery by commanding slaves to obey their masters and give them an honest day's work and commanding masters to treat their slaves with justice, compassion, and fairness.

In other words, Paul commanded slaves and masters to exalt Christ in their relationship. When that began to happen, the institution of slavery collapsed of its own weight.

The book of Philemon illustrates this revolution in action, as Paul urged Philemon to receive back Onesimus, his slave who stole from him and then ran away. Onesimus met Paul and got saved, and Paul told him, "You need to go back to Philemon and make things right."

Then Paul wrote to Philemon to say, "You need to receive Onesimus, but not just as a runaway slave. He is now your brother in Christ, and I want you to receive him as you would receive me." Onesimus had the same job description, but his relationship to Philemon was totally different because they were now brothers in the Lord.

The key to exalting Christ in our field of employment is to work as if He were our employer—because, in the final analysis, He is. It is Christ we are serving, not just the boss.

If a lot of Christians would make one simple adjustment in their thinking about their jobs, it would revolutionize their work life—beginning tomorrow morning.

The adjustment in thinking is this: Instead of focusing on the job and what they like or don't like about it, instead of focusing on the boss or their co-workers, many Christians need to bow their heads at their desks or workstations and say, "Lord, for the next eight hours it will be my joy and delight to serve and exalt You by the work I have to do today."

That prayer works whether you are a vice president or a janitor. It doesn't matter whether you are designing rockets or typing letters. If you determine to exalt Christ and do your work for Him, it will revolutionize your ability to function properly and joyfully on your job.

You see, joy comes from the inside, not the outside. So if you are lacking joy in your work, it is not because you are in miserable circumstances, but because you are not working for the right person. Exalt Christ on the job, and watch what happens.

You may be asking, "What *will* happen? What good will it do for me to work with this attitude?"

Paul said you will receive a reward from the Lord. It may not be a pay raise or a promotion, but make no mistake. Jesus Christ is not a stingy, tightfisted Employer. He is not going to let His faithful employees go under while serving and exalting Him on the job.

The Responsibilities of Employers

Even if you own the company, even if you are the CEO or chairman of the board, you are under the authority of a Master who owns the entire world, including the ground your company occupies. Paul wrote, "Masters, grant to your slaves justice and fairness, knowing that you too have a Master in heaven" (Colossians 4:1).

Employers are to be equitable in their dealings with their employees. They are to be fair in paying employees what their work is worth, just as employers would want the Lord to deal fairly with them.

Employers have a great opportunity to demonstrate a Christlike attitude on the job, because their employees are looking to them for guidance and direction. Exalting Christ as a master or employer means that your love for Him shows up in your work, both in the quality of what you do and in the way you treat the people under your direction. If you are an employer, working for you should be like working for the Lord Jesus.

KEEP EXALTING CHRIST

Exalting Christ in every area of life will cost you something. It will require selfless commitment on your part. But you will come out far ahead when you make the exaltation of Christ your life's passion.

In the words of James 4:10, "Humble yourselves in the presence of the Lord, and He will exalt you." The higher you exalt Christ, the higher Christ will exalt you. Exalt Him in your faith, your focus, your family, and your field of employment. He deserves your praise and your exaltation, for He is Lord of lords.

CHAPTER EIGHTEEN

LOVING CHRIST

We're talking about our response to who Jesus is and what He has done. The fact is that He is worth pursuing with everything we have. Jesus Christ is worthy of the devotion of our entire lives, and He is worthy of our complete, unreserved love.

I want to talk about the importance of loving Christ, and I want to put some "skin" on our study by looking at the life of a man who claimed to love Jesus more than anyone else, a man who vowed he would stay true to the Lord no matter what anyone else did—but then failed Jesus at the moment of truth. You may know that I'm referring to Simon Peter.

There is no doubt that Peter loved Jesus, but Peter's love needed to be tested and purified because, like an impure metal, it had a lot of junk in it. Our love for Christ needs the same testing and purifying, so we can learn a lot from Peter's failure at the crucifixion of Jesus and his restoration by Jesus. I want to draw three principles about our love for Christ from the story of Peter's denial and restoration.

LOVE IS TESTED BY OPPOSITION

The night Jesus was crucified, Peter discovered something we need to realize too. The test of our love for Christ is not what we say and do when we're in safe surroundings, but what we say and do when we run into opposition.

It's easy to declare our devotion to Christ at church or in

our prayer circle. I'm not minimizing this at all, but pointing out that staying true to Christ is a lot tougher out there in the world where people don't share our commitment. When it gets tough, we can be intimidated. For example, I know people who say their grace at mealtime in silence if non-Christians show up.

Peter faced very stiff opposition the night Jesus was arrested, tried, and sentenced to death. The leader of the twelve apostles became so fearful of Jesus' enemies that he denied he even knew the Lord.

Let's review the familiar story of Peter's denial, because it has a lot to teach us about how to keep our love for Christ strong so it will stand the test when opposition comes.

Beware of Overconfidence

One thing we can learn from Peter's denial is the danger of becoming self-assured and boastful about our spiritual strength and ability to handle anything that comes our way.

This was Peter's problem. In the Upper Room before He was arrested, Jesus told Peter, "Simon, Simon, behold, Satan has demanded permission to sift you like wheat; but I have prayed for you, that your faith may not fail; and you, when once you have turned again, strengthen your brothers" (Luke 22:31–32).

Instead of heeding this warning, Peter answered, "Lord, with You I am ready to go both to prison and to death!" Then Jesus told him, "Peter, the cock will not crow today until you have denied three times that you know Me" (vv. 33–34).

Peter was the leader of the disciples, the spokesman for the group. His name was always first on the list when the Twelve were named. He was the one who made the great confession of Christ's deity on which the church is founded (Matthew 16:16–18).

But Peter allowed himself to become overconfident. He started to brag about his ability to hang in there with Jesus when things got hot. Peter wanted Jesus to know that no one loved Him the way he did.

Peter miscalculated on a couple of things, however. He miscalculated his own spiritual condition. Jesus had told Peter that the devil was demanding permission to put him to the test, but Peter thought he was spiritually mature enough to handle it. He forgot how evil and deceptive the human heart is (Jeremiah 17:9).

Peter also miscalculated the devil's power. He was about to come under attack from hell itself. It takes more than human determination to cope with the devil. There has never been a man or woman alive who can compete with Satan.

So Peter overestimated his strength, underestimated his weaknesses, and thus became proud of what he could do. But the Bible warns us, "Let him who thinks he stands take heed lest he fall" (1 Corinthians 10:12).

Peter's love for Christ was sincere. He meant well, but he had a huge lesson to learn about spiritual strength and weakness and where a believer's power for living really lies.

We tend to do the same thing Peter did. We overestimate ourselves spiritually. We mean well. We tell ourselves we won't fall into the traps we see other people falling into. We'd be better off to say, "Let him who boasts boast of this, that he understands and knows Me, that I am the Lord" (Jeremiah 9:24).

In your desire to demonstrate your love for Christ, don't forget that the power for that love comes from Him. The flesh has no capacity for the kind of faithfulness Peter was bragging about.

Stay on Your Knees

If we want our love for Christ to stand the test of opposition, we had better be on our knees.

Peter followed up his confident statement by going with Jesus to the Garden of Gethsemane and falling asleep while Jesus was praying in agony (Luke 22:39–46). Jesus was praying with such fervency and passion that His sweat "became like drops of blood" (v. 44). He was facing the Cross, so this was serious prayer.

But when Jesus came to the disciples, He found them asleep. This happened three times (Matthew 26:44), and finally Jesus said to them, "Why are you sleeping? Rise and pray that you may not enter into temptation" (Luke 22:46).

Peter needed to be praying, because he was about to be tempted. But as long as we think we can do the job, we won't see any real need to talk to God about it. Prayer is necessary because of our weaknesses. It is proof of our dependency.

We tend to forget that prayer is work, not recreation. Sometimes, prayer is the last thing we want to do. Some people don't pray until bedtime. Before they know it, they are falling asleep. Why is fervent, serious prayer so hard for so many believers to do?

The answer is that when we pray, we enter into a different spiritual realm. Prayer lifts us into the presence of God, and when a believer comes into God's presence through prayer, things start getting done. So Satan does everything he can to block our access to God in prayer.

Satan doesn't mind too much when we shoot up a little prayer like, "Now I lay me down to sleep . . ." But when we decide to get serious about prayer, the Enemy gets serious about hindering us. That's why we need to learn to pray fervently, with passion. We need to be like Jacob, who wrestled with God all night and said, "I will not let you go unless you bless me" (Genesis 32:26).

We can empathize a little with the disciples, because Luke says they were sleeping from sorrow (Luke 22:45). They were in the midst of a long and emotionally draining night. Their beloved Master was leaving them.

But it's often at the time when we feel most vulnerable and spiritually sleepy that we need to rouse ourselves, get awake, and pray. You know what it's like to be awakened in the middle of the night by a burden or problem that's pressing on your mind. That may be God's call to prayer. When something is that important, you need to grab hold of God.

Jesus told Peter to stay alert and pray, and Peter never forgot the lesson. Years later he wrote to the church, "Be of sober spirit, be on the alert. Your adversary, the devil, prowls about like a roaring lion, seeking someone to devour" (1 Peter 5:8). Peter was speaking from experience.

Make Sure You Are Acting in God's Will

We can learn a third lesson from Peter's experience. When the soldiers and crowd arrived to arrest Jesus, Peter decided to take things into his own hands.

After Judas had betrayed Jesus with a kiss, the disciples were ready to fight. "When those who were around Him saw what was going to happen, they said, 'Lord, shall we strike with the sword?' And a certain one of them struck the slave of the high priest and cut off his right ear" (Luke 22:49–50). This was Peter, of course (John 18:10).

This was a perfect example of Peter's impetuous nature. The other disciples asked if they should draw their swords, but Peter didn't wait for an answer.

Peter was acting out of love for Jesus. "You aren't taking my Lord" was his attitude. But he acted too quickly, and he was outside the will of God. We know this because Jesus told Peter, "Stop! No more of this." Then He healed the slave's ear (Luke 22:51). According to John, Jesus said, "The cup which the Father has given Me, shall I not drink it?" (John 18:11).

Having a fervent love for Jesus is one thing. Stepping outside of God's will in a misguided attempt to help accomplish God's program is something else entirely. Before you act, make sure you are in concert with God's will. Peter lost sight of God's purpose for Jesus to go to the cross.

Jesus doesn't need our human efforts to help Him accomplish God's divine will. Besides, when we pull out our swords and start slashing away before we get the real picture, someone around us is usually going to get hurt.

Stay Close to Jesus

It's hard to keep your love strong when you're pulling away from the person you love. Peter made this mistake in reacting to the opposition he encountered as he tried to express his love for Christ. He moved away from Jesus, following Him from far away. "Having arrested [Jesus], they led Him away . . . ; but Peter was following at a distance" (Luke 22:54).

Once it became obvious that Jesus was going to be arrested and taken away, Peter pulled back. He was up next to Jesus, ready to defend the Lord. But when he saw how things were going, when he realized this was going to be done God's way and not his way, Peter faded into the background.

This might not seem so bad, because Jesus had basically told Peter to stay out of it. The problem is that as Peter pulled back from following Jesus closely, he was drawn to the enemy camp. While Jesus was being questioned in the high priest's house, Peter was in the courtyard enjoying the fire (Luke 22:55).

Psalm 1:1 says, "How blessed is the man who does not walk in the counsel of the wicked, nor stand in the path of sinners, nor sit in the seat of scoffers!" Why? Because the cozier you get with wicked people, the more you wind up thinking and acting like them.

Peter fell into this pattern. He started hanging with Jesus' enemies, and pretty soon he was acting like he didn't care either. The longer the night wore on, the more vehemently he denied Jesus, until he wound up denying the Lord with cursing and swearing (Matthew 26:74).

If you want to keep your love for Jesus fervent, keep the relationship intimate. We can't love the Lord from a distance.

LOVE REQUIRES BROKENNESS

Most people don't enjoy being humbled and broken, but that is on the agenda for those of us who want to love Jesus Christ with all our hearts, minds, souls, and strength.

Brokenness is a term we are hearing more these days as people talk about revival and what it takes for a great movement of God among His people. Being broken before the Lord means being emptied of the pride and self-sufficiency that keep so many Christians from loving and following Christ the way He desires.

Brokenness may or may not include a setback, such as a physical or financial problem. Some people require that kind of intervention to get back on track. But whatever the case, a genuine love for Jesus Christ is a tested love, a purified love. Given our tendency to rely on our own efforts, we need the Lord to empty us of ourselves so we can be filled with Him.

Peter needed to be broken of his self-sufficiency before he could become useful to God once again. Peter's brokenness, and restoration, occurred one day at the seashore, an amazing story told in John 21.

Peter's Confrontation with Jesus

After his three denials of Jesus, Peter sank pretty low. He wept bitterly over his failure (Luke 22:62), and apparently he thought his discipleship was over. According to John 21:2–3, Peter and six other disciples were sitting around when Peter said, "I am going fishing." The others decided to follow him.

Peter was a fisherman when Jesus first called him (Luke 5:1–11), so he was going back to what he knew best. According to John 21:3–6, the same thing happened this day that happened the first time Peter met Jesus. That is, they fished all night and caught nothing, then Jesus showed up and gave them a miracle catch of fish.

Jesus had said to Peter that first time, *"From now on* you will be catching men" (Luke 5:10, italics added). But Peter had failed the Lord he loved and had lost his vision for his calling. He was saying, "God can't use me. I might as well go back to fishing."

But then Jesus showed up. After the nets filled with fish, John said to Peter, "It is the Lord" (John 21:7). Peter immediately dove into the water and did an Olympic freestyle swim straight to Jesus.

Verses 8–14 describe an amazing scene, with Jesus serving breakfast to this group of disciples. We're going to leave these verses for a while and go down to verse 15, because this is the reason the resurrected Christ appeared to Peter that day. Peter needed to be broken before he could be restored.

Peter's Brokenness Before Jesus

Once the meal was over and the dishes were done, Jesus got down to business. He turned to Peter and said, "Simon, son of John, do you love Me more than these?" (v. 15a).

This is the heart of what we are talking about. Peter loved Jesus and had been trying to demonstrate that love in all the wrong ways. He needed to see what love for Jesus involved.

Jesus' question must have reminded Peter that he had bragged to the Lord, "Even if the other disciples forsake You, I won't. I'm going to stick with You. You count on me. I love You more than these other guys do" (see Matthew 26:33). So now Jesus was asking Peter, "Is it really true, Peter? Do you love Me more than My other disciples?"

Peter answered, "Yes, Lord; You know that I love You" (John 21:15b).

Jesus asked this three times, and Peter answered three times. To understand this exchange, you need to know that two different Greek verbs for love are being used: *agapao* and *phileo*. The former is God's sacrificial love, the love that seeks the highest good of the one loved. It's John 3:16 love. The latter is the term for "brotherly love," a word of affection.

Let me plug these words into the narrative and show you what's happening here.

Jesus said, "Simon, son of John, do you *agapao* Me more than these?" Peter answered, "Yes, Lord; You know that I *phileo* You." Jesus was asking, "Peter, do you love Me sacrificially? Do you love Me supremely?" But Peter said, "Yes, You know that I like You. I am fond of You."

What happened here? Well, reality had set in for Peter. He found out that he wasn't as spiritual as he thought he was. His love for Jesus wasn't as rock solid as he thought it was.

Peter was saying to Jesus, "I can't say that I love You supremely. I would never have denied You if I really loved You like that. So the best I can say is that I like You. I'm not going out on that limb again."

Once you say you will never do something, but then you go ahead and do it, you are never going to say never again. Why? Because you've learned that in the flesh, you are capable of failing at any time.

In order for us to understand how to love Christ, we need to be broken—to be cleansed of our pride and self-sufficiency. Peter needed to face his failure and allow himself to be broken by the reality of what he had done. Jesus didn't want to break Peter to humiliate and destroy him, but to restore and use him.

Every man or woman in the Bible whom God used greatly, He humbled first. Moses is a prime example. He tried to liberate the Israelites on his own, and he had to run for his life. It took forty years of herding sheep in the desert for Moses to come to the place where he was ready to hear from God. And even then, he protested that he couldn't do the job of going to Egypt and leading Israel out.

God had to literally break Jacob before this schemer was of any use. God threw Jacob's hip out of joint and gave him a limp (Genesis 32:25, 31) that Jacob had the rest of his life. But that limp was a blessing, because it was then that God changed Jacob's name to Israel, "the one whom the Lord helps."

Pain can be one of the greatest blessings in your life if it breaks you of your independence and teaches you to be dependent upon God. Jacob was broken and restored, and now Peter was in the process of restoration because he was coming face-to-face with his failure. He was being humbled, that he might be lifted up.

Let's go back to John 21 and Jesus' second question. "[Jesus] said to [Peter] again a second time, 'Simon, son of John, do you *agapao* Me?' He said to Him, 'Yes, Lord; You know that I *phileo* You'" (v. 16).

This time, Jesus dropped the reference to the other disciples. He simply wanted to know if Peter loved Him. But Peter gave Him the same answer. "Lord, I like You, but I am not going to stick my neck out again and say I love You supremely."

In the third exchange (John 21:17), things changed. "[Jesus] said to him the third time, 'Simon, son of John, do you *phileo* Me?' Peter was grieved because He said to him the third time, 'Do you love Me?' And he said to Him, 'Lord, You know all things; You know that I *phileo* You.'"

Now they were both speaking the same language. Guess what Jesus did? He came down to where Peter was. Peter was saying, "Lord, I'm not at *agapao* yet. I'm struggling. I'm in pain. I'm broken. I'm still at *phileo*." So Jesus came down to meet Simon.

Peter was hurt when Jesus asked him the third time if he loved Him. But those questions reminded him of the three times he had denied Jesus. If we are going to love Christ the way we need to love Him, we must face ourselves and be broken before Him.

The greatest need in our lives today is brokenness. We have too many self-sufficient Christians. Jesus had told His disciples, including Peter, "Apart from Me you can do nothing" (John 15:5).

But Peter had said to Jesus, "No, Lord, You don't know me very well. I can stay true to You on my own." Once you learn that you can do nothing without Christ, you are ready to be used by Christ. Let's see how Jesus restored Peter to usefulness.

LOVE IS POSSIBLE BECAUSE OF GRACE

The third principle I want to lay down concerning our love for Jesus Christ is this: The reason we can love Him in the first place, and commit ourselves to Him, is because of His grace to us.

To see this provision of grace in Peter's life, we need to go back to John 21. This time we will pick up some of the earlier verses in the chapter and talk about Jesus' statements to Peter concerning the care of His sheep.

Jesus Comes Looking for Us

Peter was saved and made an apostle by the grace of God. Jesus came after Peter that first time in Galilee (Luke 5). After he denied Jesus, Peter went back to his fishing.

Then Jesus showed up on the beach (John 21:4). Peter may have gone back to the sea for fish, but Jesus went back for Peter. That is called grace. Grace is when we mess up, but He still comes looking for us. Grace is when we walk out on Jesus, but He doesn't let us go.

If we got what we deserved from God as sinners in rebellion against Him, I wouldn't be here to write this book—and you wouldn't be here to read it. We are only here because Jesus came looking for us even after we blew it.

Jesus asked the disciples, "You do not have any fish, do you?" (v. 5). The answer was no, they were having no success at all. That's what Peter deserved. But what did he get? A miraculous haul of fish that was so huge the net should have torn. But it didn't tear (v. 11), and Peter and his companions pulled in their net full of blessing.

That's what grace does. Even after we have messed up, Jesus is ready to bless us if we will come to Him in brokenness and repentance.

We read earlier that as soon as Peter realized it was Jesus on the shore, he dove into the water and started swimming. Why? Because Peter really did love the Lord. It wasn't that Peter had stopped loving Jesus. But he was afraid he had gone too far, and maybe Jesus didn't want him anymore.

But Jesus had showed up, and Peter knew that meant Jesus still loved him. Just knowing that was enough to make Peter hit the water and head for Jesus. Understanding God's grace to us ought to make us hurry to Jesus too.

Jesus Provides for Us

When Peter and the other disciples got to shore, Jesus had a breakfast of fish and bread ready for them, and He invited them to eat (John 21:12). Jesus had done some fishing of His own. He already had some fish cooking on the fire when they arrived. He then served it to each of them (v. 13), which must have reminded them of the miraculous feedings of the five thousand and four thousand. Jesus had graciously provided food for those hungry crowds, and now He was inviting the disciples to feast on His grace.

Notice one other important detail about this. John noted that Jesus' meal was being cooked over a charcoal fire (John 21:9). It was over a charcoal fire that Peter had denied Jesus (18:18). Jesus was taking Peter back to his place of sin in order to lead him to the place of forgiveness. Jesus was preparing Peter to receive grace.

All of the disciples needed grace, not just Peter. In one way or another, they had all deserted Jesus at the cross. But here He was, providing for their needs because He is a gracious, forgiving Savior.

Grace is God giving us what we *don't* deserve. The disciples were fearful and doubting and wavering. But Jesus was meeting them in their need, feeding them as an act of grace.

Jesus Reaches down to Us

One reason I dealt with the events of John 21 in reverse order to the text is so you could see the grace in Jesus' exchange with Peter.

Twice Jesus asked Peter to declare his supreme love. But Peter couldn't get beyond a statement of affection or fondness. So the third time, Jesus reached down to Peter's level. "Peter, if that is all you can do right now, I will accept it." The grace of God means that when you can't come up, He will reach down and help lift you up.

You see, Peter didn't stay at the *phileo* level. He loved Jesus with *agapao* love, and he proved it by the rest of his life. Don't confuse grace with self-indulgence. Grace doesn't leave us where it finds us. Grace reaches down to lift us up where God wants us to be.

Jesus Restores Us

The last thing I want you to notice about this passage is the gracious way that Jesus brought Peter along and put him back on the track.

Peter may have thought Jesus was through with him, but Jesus knew He wasn't through with Peter. Before the Cross, when Jesus warned Peter that Satan was seeking him, He had said, "But I have prayed for you, that your faith may not fail; and you, when once you have turned again, strengthen your brothers" (Luke 22:32).

Not only did Jesus not give up on Peter, He had plans for Peter to minister His grace to others. Now in John 21, Jesus revealed in broad outlines what He wanted Peter to do now that he was being restored to service.

"Tend My lambs" Jesus told Peter (v. 15). The second time, Jesus said, "Shepherd My sheep" (v. 16). Peter loved Jesus, and Jesus knew He could do something with Peter because His grace was going to take over.

God does not want us to sin and fail. But when we do, we need to understand that our failure does not cancel God's grace. If you love Jesus Christ and want to be used by Him, He can do something wonderful with you.

By God's grace, Peter made the most of his second chance. His love for Jesus grew and blossomed into mature, committed love, and the story does not end with his denials.

You don't get the full picture on Peter until you turn to Acts 2 and find Peter leading the way on the Day of Pentecost. The denier was now the declarer, boldly preaching Christ.

Peter's love for Christ was severely tested by opposition, and out of his brokenness he discovered a new dimension of God's protecting grace. Peter was a fearless witness for Christ the rest of his life.

CHAPTER NINETEEN

FOLLOWING CHRIST

When I was a boy we used to play the popular children's game "Simon Says."

I'm sure you remember how the game is played. You must do whatever the person playing Simon says. "Simon says stand up," so you stand up. "Simon says sit down," so you sit down. "Simon says raise your right hand," so you raise your right hand.

Then the leader would say, "Raise your left hand." Of course, if you raised your left hand you were out of the game, because Simon didn't say it. You had to be listening for what Simon had to say, so you could follow Simon's instructions.

That was a child's game, but as Christians we need to be engaged in a very real and serious lifelong activity called "Jesus Says." That is, we need to be following Him. This is what I want to talk about in this chapter, as we consider three things about the important task of following Christ.

FOLLOWING CHRIST IS
A PERSONAL DECISION

The first thing I want you to see about following Christ is that it is a personal decision each of us must make for ourselves.

In the previous chapter we spent a lot of time in John 21, looking at the restoration of Peter. We ended with verse 17, in which Jesus told Peter to tend His sheep. But the discussion between Christ and Peter did not end there. Jesus said to

Peter, "When you were younger, you used to gird yourself, and walk wherever you wished; but when you grow old, you will stretch out your hands, and someone else will gird you, and bring you where you do not wish to go" (John 21:18).

Notice verse 19. "This He said, signifying by what kind of death he would glorify God. And when He had spoken this, He said to him, 'Follow Me!'"

This should have been enough for Peter. He had just been forgiven for his denials, and Jesus had prophesied what he could expect in the future. Then Jesus gave Peter the all-important command to follow Him, a repeat of Peter's original call to discipleship. In other words, Jesus was restoring Peter to his place as an apostle.

But Peter still had enough of the old Peter in him that when he saw John, he couldn't resist asking Jesus, "Lord, and what about this man?" (v. 21). Jesus basically told Peter to mind his own business and said again, "You follow Me!" (v. 22).

Jesus couldn't have made it much clearer. Following Christ is a personal decision. You can't follow Him for someone else, and no one else can follow Him for you.

God's Plan for You

Too many believers don't get around to following Christ because they are too busy watching other people, worrying about what they are doing or where they are going. But Jesus made the matter intensely personal. "You follow Me!"

It's OK to follow other people as they follow Christ. Paul told the Corinthians to imitate him as he imitated Christ (1 Corinthians 11:1). But that's far different from letting someone else become the focus of your attention.

Someone might say, "I would be a better follower of Christ's if that person weren't in my life." But that person is not keeping us from following Christ. If a human being can lead us away from the King of kings and Lord of lords, He doesn't have much influence in our lives.

A Person, Not a Program

When Jesus says to us, "Follow Me," He is calling us to connect to Him, a person, not just submit to a program.

You see, we can go to church each Sunday without following Christ. We can have devotions every day and yet not follow Christ. When we reduce our Christian faith to a program and lose sight of the relationship Jesus wants to have with us, we lose sight of what it means to truly follow Him.

Married couples know what it's like for a marriage to go from an intensely personal, love relationship to a program to be carried out. Of course, cooking and cleaning and other routine things have to be done in a marriage. But when the routine overshadows the people involved, the marriage becomes a sterile institution, not a dynamic relationship.

That's why I often tell young couples not to date in order to marry, but to marry in order to date. In other words, don't lose the joy and thrill of the relationship that made you want to get married in the first place. Keep the romance and the relationship alive so boredom won't set in. That happens when two people lose sight of the reason they got married.

The same is true of our Christianity. Watch out for institutionalized Christianity, a sterile faith in which we do what we ought to do simply because we know we ought to do it. Jesus wants us to follow *Him*, not just a program.

Quit Worrying About Others

If we would spend our time focusing on following Christ instead of listening to and watching other people, we would get a lot farther in our Christian lives.

I'm reminded of the old man and the young boy who were walking along the road leading a donkey. Someone said, "Look at that foolish old man, walking when he could be riding on that donkey." So the old man got on the donkey, and they continued their journey.

But a little farther down the road someone else said, "Look at that cruel man riding on that donkey while he makes the little boy walk." The man and boy looked at each other, and the boy got on the donkey while the old man got off and walked. And they continued on down the road.

But then another person said, "Look at that selfish boy, making that old man walk." So they decided that both of them would ride on the donkey.

But after they had gone a little farther, somebody said, "Look at that cruel man and boy, overloading that poor donkey." So both the man and the boy got off the donkey again. The next time someone saw them, the man and the boy were carrying the donkey. If you live your life focusing on everybody else, you'll wind up carrying an impossible load.

Jesus had to tell Peter not to worry about John. Jesus' plan for John was not His plan for Peter, and Peter had enough to deal with in his own life. Jesus actually prophesied that Peter would die as a martyr, whereas He told Peter it was none of his business if His plan was that John would live to a ripe old age—which is what happened. But Jesus' message was that He wanted Peter to follow Him no matter what.

To follow Christ means that He must become to you what the sun is to our solar system—the center around which everything else revolves. The good news is that when the Son is at the center, all the other parts of your life stay in their intended orbit. It's only when someone or something else takes Christ's place that things start to spin out of control.

I don't know how a camera works, but I know this: If you want something to show up in your picture, it must be framed within that little square box you squint through. If your subject does not appear in the viewfinder, it doesn't matter how expensive your camera is, you won't get the right picture.

But if you frame the picture correctly, the camera is designed to take care of everything else. Get Jesus framed in the center of the square, and He'll take care of everything else.

A Non-Negotiated Trip

There's something else you need to know about following Christ: The agenda for the trip is not up for negotiation. By that I mean you can't follow Christ the way you choose your meal at a cafeteria, taking this piece over here because it looks good, but rejecting that item over there because you don't feel like having it today.

Following Christ does not work that way. We can't say,

"Jesus, I'll do this, but not that. I want this part of You, but not that part. Why don't You lay out the smorgasbord of choices for me, and I'll show You what I like and what I don't like."

Jesus Christ is not negotiating on His program. He said to Peter, "Follow Me." Period. End of statement. Too many Christians want to negotiate with God. You'd think Peter would want to do a little bargaining after Jesus predicted his martyrdom. But Jesus made it clear that what He did with His followers was His choice and His business. Peter's only responsibility was to follow Christ. That was a personal decision he had to make. We have to make it too.

FOLLOWING CHRIST IS
A PROGRESSIVE DECISION

Following Christ is also a progressive decision. By this I mean it's a decision you have to make every day. It's not a commitment you make one time and that takes care of it for the rest of your life.

Paul brought this out in a powerful way in Philippians 3:7–8. He was discussing his own life and commitment to Christ in this chapter, and in these two verses he talked about a decision he made once and had to keep on making.

A Decision in the Past

In verses 5–6 Paul talked about his impressive background. He was well educated, had a good family background, and was held in high esteem by his peers.

Then in verse 7, Paul said concerning these human accomplishments, "But whatever things were gain to me, those things I have counted as loss for the sake of Christ." Notice that the verb *count* here is in the past tense. Paul had made a decision in the past to discard all of his human pedigree and count it as nothing in order to follow Christ.

A Decision in the Present

But the apostle didn't stop there. He went on to say, "More than that, I count all things to be loss in view of the surpassing value of knowing Christ Jesus my Lord, for whom

I have suffered the loss of all things, and count them but rubbish in order that I may gain Christ" (Philippians 3:8).

Here the verb *count* is in the present tense. Paul was still making the decision to count everything else as rubbish in order that he might know and follow Christ. So when Paul got saved, he counted all things as loss. But as a saved person in the present, he kept on counting all things as loss. His decision to follow Christ was a progressive one.

Consider Paul's decision. When he took all of his human accomplishments and pedigrees and placed them next to Jesus Christ, they paled into insignificance and appeared to him as garbage.

That is a great description of what it means to follow Christ. Unless our commitment to Christ supersedes every other commitment in our lives, we are not following Him.

Let's make it practical. Unless Christ means more to us than our career, our relationships, our money, or anything else we can name, we are not following Him according to a biblical definition. Following Christ requires a passionate commitment that makes everything else in life fade into insignificance by comparison.

A Daily Walk of Faith

So if you want to follow Jesus Christ, I want to ask you a question: Is anything more important in your life than your relationship with Him? Only you can answer that question for yourself, but I encourage you to answer it.

This is a question you and I need to ask ourselves often because following Christ is progressive. It's a daily walk of faith. Paul said he wanted to be found in Christ, "not having a righteousness of my own derived from the Law, but that which is through faith in Christ" (Philippians 3:9).

The problem with too many of us is that we have not learned to walk by faith. Instead, we walk by sight. So we are limited in following Christ because we are too tied to the information we receive through our five senses.

Paul said, "I want to be a man of faith more than anything." The reason he considered everything else as rubbish was so that he could know Christ (see Philippians 3:7–10). Paul had a passion to know Christ. David said, "As the deer pants for the water brooks, so my soul pants for Thee, O

God" (Psalm 42:1). Moses prayed to the Lord, "Show me Thy glory" (Exodus 33:18).

When will you and I know what it is like to follow the Lord with this kind of passion? When we want it bad enough. It boils down to that.

Let's face it. When most of us want something badly enough, we will find a way to make it happen. We will even make a way where there is no way if we are passionate about the thing we are pursuing.

When a man really wants to get a woman's attention, he will find a way. He'll come up with words he didn't even know were in the dictionary to charm her, because he wants a relationship.

People like Paul and David and Moses were hungry for God. You say, "I don't feel hungry. What should I do?" You need to hang around good spiritual cooks. If you're not hungry to follow Christ, get around people who are. Get with people who are really cooking spiritually, and you'll develop a hunger to know and follow Christ.

The End of the Journey

If following Christ is a progressive decision, when do we reach the end of the journey? When we leave this earth and go to be with Him—and not a day earlier.

Go back to Philippians 3, where Paul said, "Not that I have already obtained it, or have already become perfect, but I press on in order that I may lay hold of that for which also I was laid hold of by Christ Jesus. . . . Reaching forward to what lies ahead, I press on toward the goal for the prize of the upward call of God in Christ Jesus" (vv. 12–14).

Why did Christ lay hold of Paul? So that Paul might know Him. Why did Christ lay hold of you? So that you might know Christ.

God did not save me to preach or lead a national ministry or write books. Those are bonuses. He saved me that I might know Him. He saved me to have a relationship with Him.

Many wives have told their husbands, "I didn't marry you so I could eat dinner alone at night while you are down at the office making money and building a company. I married you because I want to be with you." A wife who says that is pleading with her husband not to let other things get in the way of their relationship. We need to be on guard against the same thing happening to us as believers, because following Christ is what we should be about.

Paul knew he had not yet achieved the goal he wanted to attain, so he kept pressing on. He understood that we can't live today off yesterday's spiritual victories. If you are having a great day with God today, that's wonderful. But don't forget that tomorrow morning you must get up and follow Him again. And as you do that, you'll find that a week or a month or a year from now, you are following Christ more closely than you are following Him today.

Our journey won't be complete until we are in Christ's presence—and even in eternity, we will still follow Christ. A million years from now, you and I will be following Him.

I remember one time when our family was driving home from California. As we crossed the Texas line and our children saw the sign saying, "Welcome to Texas," they started cheering. "Yeah, we're almost home!" Well, it takes about eight to ten hours of driving to get from West Texas to Dallas. But the kids thought another thirty minutes or so and we'd be pulling up in our driveway.

If you have just started out on the journey of following Christ, don't get discouraged, because you will arrive someday. And if you have been following Christ for many years and you feel like you're almost home, don't give up yet because you still have a way to go. Don't be satisfied to follow Christ almost to the end. I'm not talking about salvation, but faithfulness to Christ.

As we follow Him, Jesus Christ wants to take us to higher heights than we have ever known before. He wants to show us "things which eye has not seen and ear has not heard, and which have not entered the heart of man" (1 Corinthians 2:9). So don't quit now. The best is still ahead of you, because following Christ is a progressive way of life.

FOLLOWING CHRIST IS A PRIORITY DECISION

The third and final principle I want you to understand is that following Christ must be a priority decision.

This truth is illustrated in a powerful way in Luke 9:57–62, in which three would-be disciples came to Jesus in rapid-fire succession. In Jesus' response to each one we learn what it takes to follow Him.

The "Rapping" Disciple

The first "disciple candidate" who came up to Jesus said to Him, "I will follow You wherever You go" (Luke 9:57). You can almost hear the confidence in this man's voice. He had a good rap going. He was ready not just to follow Jesus, but to follow Him anywhere.

But Jesus' response put the issue in a different light. "The foxes have holes, and the birds of the air have nests, but the Son of Man has nowhere to lay His head" (v. 58).

Why did Jesus say that? Because He wanted this man to understand that if he became a follower, he would have to do so without any assurance of even a place to sleep at night, other than on the ground with a rock for a pillow.

This man's problem was that he thought following Christ included a few guarantees, such as three squares every day and reservations at the local Holiday Inn every night.

A lot of people still have this problem today. Its most extreme form is known as prosperity theology, the teaching that says being a Christian guarantees paid-up bills, a nice roof over your head, and a nice car in the garage.

I would never deny that God blesses His servants. But when blessing—particularly material blessing—becomes your motivation for following Christ, you are in serious error. Jesus told this potential disciple that the animals He created were better off than He was when it came to accommodations. Jesus did not rebuke the man for wanting to become His disciple. But He knew the man was not ready to follow Him, and the clear implication of the text is that he did not become one of Jesus' disciples.

The Procrastinating Disciple

The second man who approached Jesus is what I call the procrastinating disciple. Notice that Jesus called this man the same way He called Peter and the other disciples: "Follow Me." But the response was "Permit me first to go and bury my father" (Luke 9:59).

It seems like a reasonable request, but Jesus said no.

"Allow the dead to bury their own dead; but as for you, go and proclaim everywhere the kingdom of God" (v. 60).

At first it seems that Jesus was being harsh here. But the fact is the man's father was not dead. The Jews buried their dead within twenty-four hours. So if his father had just died, this man wouldn't have been there talking with Jesus at all. He would have been home seeing to the funeral.

Jesus' statement is a second indication that the father was not dead. "Allow the dead to bury their own dead," He said. When was the last time you saw dead people burying another dead person? Jesus' statement makes no sense if He was talking about an impending funeral.

The best understanding is that Jesus was telling this man to let the spiritually dead—those who refused to follow Him—stay home and bury those who died physically. This idea is reinforced by the Lord's instruction to this would-be follower to go and preach the kingdom of God.

This man wanted to put off following Jesus until after his father had died and the family estate was settled—which could have been months or even years later. In other words, he wanted to make sure that he got his share of the inheritance.

Maybe this guy had heard Jesus tell the first man that following Him was a no-guarantee deal. Maybe he wanted to be sure he had some money in his pocket first, so that if Jesus went some place and had to sleep on the ground, he could get a room at the local inn. Maybe this man wanted to make sure his future was secure before risking his security by following Jesus.

Whatever the reason, he wanted to put off following Jesus. Again, the text implies that he never got around to answering Jesus' call.

We have procrastinating disciples today. They say things like, "When I get a better job, I'll follow Jesus." "When I get a mate, I'll follow Jesus." "When I get out of this apartment and get my family settled in a home, I'll follow Jesus."

The problem with putting off obedience to Jesus is that there will always be one more thing you want to take care of before you start taking Him seriously. The devil will make sure you never get all your ducks in a row.

The choice is clear. We are either agents of spiritual death or agents of spiritual life. When we follow Him we become involved in life.

Too many Christians are still hanging out with the spiritually dead folk. We're still back home helping to dig graves rather than following Jesus and helping people find spiritual life. Don't put off following Jesus until something else happens, because you may be waiting a long time.

The Undecided Disciple

The third man who offered to follow Jesus wasn't sure he wanted this deal. He said, "I will follow You, Lord; but first permit me to say good-bye to those at home" (Luke 9:61). Jesus' response was, "No one, after putting his hand to the plow and looking back, is fit for the kingdom of God" (v. 62).

Even non-farmers understand that a farmer can't plow a straight furrow while looking back over his shoulder. This man was being very indecisive, and Jesus challenged him on it because this was not simply a matter of the man dropping by home on the way out of town to tell Mom and Dad good-bye.

The idea behind this request was more along this line: "Jesus, I'm pretty sure I want to follow You, but let me go back home first and discuss this one more time with the family. And the folks will probably want to throw me a farewell party."

Jesus knew what would happen if this man went back home. First of all, farewell parties in those days didn't last a few hours. That thing could have gone on for days.

Second, if the man went back home he would be vulnerable to the family's pleas not to leave. Mama would be in tears, saying, "You're going to leave me to follow Jesus?" Daddy would be saying, "Look, Son, I was counting on you to take over the family business. I need you here at home."

You get the idea. For this man, going back home meant plowing a crooked furrow when it came to following Jesus. Some of us have started following Jesus, but like Israel in the wilderness we keep looking back at Egypt and saying, "Boy, we sure had it nice when we were in Egypt."

Jesus says, "Follow Me. Don't look back, because if you do, you will change your mind." Following Jesus must be a priority decision.

Making the Right Decision

Those are three ways not to make following Christ your priority. Now let me show you some people who made the right decision. These men put Jesus first.

I'm talking about our friend Simon Peter again, along with his fishing partners. The story of their response to Jesus' call to discipleship is found in Luke 5:1–11.

Jesus already knew Peter, because He had been a guest in Peter's home in Capernaum (Luke 4:38). So one day as Jesus was teaching by the Sea of Galilee (the "lake of Gennesaret," Luke 5:1) and was being pressed by the crowd, He got into Peter's boat and asked him to launch out a little way so Jesus would have room to teach (vv. 1–3).

When He was finished, Jesus made an unusual request of Peter: "Put out into the deep water and let down your nets for a catch." Simon answered and said, "Master, we worked hard all night and caught nothing, but at Your bidding I will let down the nets" (vv. 4–5).

Why did Peter say this? Because he was the professional fisherman. He had been fishing that lake for years. He knew the fish came close to the surface at night to feed, which meant that if they hadn't caught any fish that night, they certainly were not going to have any luck in the daytime.

Peter was drawing on his own feelings, knowledge, and experience—in other words, his self-sufficiency—to enlighten Jesus about the intricacies of the fishing business. Jesus still has a lot of followers who are trying to explain things to Him. They say, "Jesus, I know what the Bible says, but I know what I'm doing. I've been doing it this way for years."

Men are especially vulnerable to this approach. We don't want anyone telling us how to do our jobs or run our families. We don't want to be stripped of our sense of self-sufficiency.

But that's the price of following Jesus. We have already discussed the fact that love for Jesus requires brokenness. Peter was about to be relieved of his self-sufficiency in two ways: first, in the area of his profession, and then in the area of his personal life.

Why is brokenness necessary? Because when we do things our way, we work all night and catch nothing. A lot of Christians live their whole lives that way. They are doing everything they know to make life work, but it still won't work. They are trying everything to make the marriage work or get the career on track, and they are coming up empty.

It's painful to be stripped of your self-sufficiency. I won't lie to you. It's painful, but when you allow Jesus to become your sufficiency, you wind up with a boat full of fish.

Simon Peter did obey Jesus and put down his nets, but you know what he was thinking. "Jesus, my feelings say this is a waste of time. My knowledge of this lake says nothing is going to happen. My professional experience tells me the fish simply aren't out there right now. But I'll do it anyway."

Sometimes, following Jesus Christ requires rejecting your feelings, ignoring your knowledge, and setting aside your experience. Why? Because Jesus doesn't operate by our human agendas.

Peter and the other man on his boat let down their nets, and we know what happened next. They enclosed such a huge catch of fish they had to call for James and John to come out in their boat and help them (Luke 5:6–7).

There's something you need to know about Jesus. If you will allow Him to break you of your limited self-sufficiency, He will replace it with His super-abundant sufficiency! But as long as you insist on doing it your way, He will let you sweat and toil all night and catch nothing. As long as you think you can do it without Him, Jesus will let you do it your way and get nowhere.

By now, some of us ought to be tired of working all night for nothing. We ought to be weary of trying life our way. We need to come to the point that we respond the way Peter responded. "When Simon Peter saw that, he fell down at Jesus' feet, saying, 'Depart from me, for I am a sinful man, O Lord!' For amazement had seized him and all his companions because of the catch of fish which they had taken" (Luke 5:8–9).

That's what Jesus wants. He wants us to fall on our knees and confess, "Lord, there is no One like You. You are in a class by Yourself. I am not worthy to be in Your presence, but I will follow You." That's what Peter, James, and John did when they finally reached the shore. "They left everything and followed Him" (v. 11).

If you are not saying that yet, if you are not leaving everything else behind to follow Jesus, maybe it's because you haven't encountered Him the way Simon Peter encountered Him. After seeing this miracle, Peter couldn't help but make following Jesus his top priority.

Think about the decision Peter and his partners made. They had just hauled in the biggest catch of their fishing careers. This was the most successful day of their lives. There was a lot of money flopping around in those nets. Yet they walked away from all of it to follow Jesus.

People talk about "blind faith," as if trusting yourself to Jesus Christ is like leaping blindfolded off a cliff into the darkness. But faith isn't blind when you know who you are following.

Have you ever taken a medical prescription you couldn't even read to a pharmacist you didn't know, and then ingested the medicine given to you? Of course you have. Did you take that medicine on blind faith? No, you took it because the person who gave it to you had the title M.D. after his or her name. That physician was qualified to prescribe the medicine you were given.

Jesus has a title after His name. It's not M.D., but L.O.R.D. He is Lord, and that means you can follow Him with perfect confidence. You may not always understand what He tells you to do, but you can obey it because you know who you are following.

A little blind girl was trapped in a fire. She was at a window, and the firemen were waiting below to catch her. A fireman yelled to her, "Darling, jump!"

But the little girl said, "I can't jump. I'm too scared. I can't see."

The fireman yelled, "It's OK. We'll catch you. Jump!"

But again the girl said, "I'm too scared!"

But then another voice called to the little girl, "Jump, darling! It's all right. I'm here." The girl began to smile, and she jumped out of that window to safety. The difference was that the second voice was that of her father.

It makes all the difference in the world whose voice you are listening to. When Jesus says, "Follow Me," you can trust His voice. To follow Him means safety, security, and spiritual success. Is there anything keeping you from following Him? He's calling you to jump!

CHAPTER TWENTY
OBEYING CHRIST

One of the challenges, and often one of the problems, in writing a book like this is the necessity of taking concepts that are closely related and dividing them into chapters. This makes it appear that they are separate ideas that exist in isolation from one another.

That's not the case, however, as you can see from the chapters in this section of the book. Exalting Christ, loving Him, and following Him are all aspects of the same reality, which is our need to know Christ fully.

The subject of this chapter, obeying Christ, also fits on this continuum. One way we can know the Lord as He desires us to know Him is to obey Him.

I'm talking about radical obedience, which is the hardest kind of obedience to carry out. It's pretty easy to obey Christ in areas where you are comfortable. But to follow Him with dogged obedience no matter what else happens is the real challenge of the Christian life.

Obedience like this requires a solid foundation, it produces close fellowship with Christ, and it results in a fruitful life. I want to consider each of these principles, beginning with the foundation of obedience.

THE FOUNDATION OF OBEDIENCE

At the end of the Sermon on the Mount, Jesus told a familiar story about two men who decided to build themselves houses:

Therefore everyone who hears these words of Mine, and acts upon them, may be compared to a wise man, who built his house upon the rock. And the rain descended, and the floods came, and the winds blew, and burst against that house; and yet it did not fall, for it had been founded upon the rock. And everyone who hears these words of Mine, and does not act upon them, will be like a foolish man, who built his house upon the sand. And rain descended, and the floods came, and the winds blew, and burst against that house; and it fell, and great was its fall. (Matthew 7:24–27)

Since He grew up in the home of the carpenter Joseph, Jesus knew what was required to build a home that would stand up to the weather. It was natural for Him to use the analogy of a building to talk about the importance of the way we construct our lives.

Jesus says there are only two ways to build our lives— wisely or foolishly. He does not allow for any middle ground or offer us five or six options. That's because of the nature of obedience. We are either obeying Christ, or we are not obeying. There are only two ways to go. The men in Jesus' story illustrate this.

The Difference in Foundations

These two hypothetical home builders had a lot in common. Both undertook to build a house. I assume their homes were in the same vicinity, since when the rain came it beat against both of their houses. We could also assume that externally, both houses looked solid. They were probably similar in style. It would have been hard to see any difference between them.

To put this in our terms today, we are talking about two men who may go to the same church, belong to the same organizations, live on the same side of town, have children of the same ages, and work in similar professions.

In other words, Jesus told of two people whose lives appeared to be identical. Any difference was not externally apparent because it had to do with the foundation upon which they had constructed their lives. But there was a vast difference between them: One man was obedient to Jesus Christ, and the other was not.

If you were to look at the home sales advertisements in your newspaper, I can pretty much guarantee that you would not see ads focusing on the quality of a home's foundation. People who go house hunting don't usually check out the foundation first. It may be a concern, but it's not the first thing on most people's list of features they want in a home. They tend to look at the externals of size and arrangement and location and things like that.

But if you were living in our part of the country, you would be aware of a house's foundation. The soil in the Dallas area expands and contracts so much that it can crack a house's foundation and literally break the house apart. If you were buying a house down here, you would want to know all about its foundation.

Two Kinds of Foundations

The Greek word Jesus used for "rock" in Matthew 7:24 means a large expanse of bedrock. The wise man dug down deep for his foundation, while the foolish man built his house on the sand.

You couldn't ask for a greater contrast between these foundations. Bedrock is solid, while sand is unstable and loose. When you build a sand castle, you don't expect it to last very long.

These two men had radically different perspectives on life. The man who built his house on the rock was taking the long-term view. In spiritual terms, which is the real point of Jesus' story, he was building with God and eternity in mind.

But the foolish man took the short view. All he cared about was the externals, how the house looked. He just wanted to throw something together so he could get on with living. The foundation didn't matter to him.

After the homes were built, however, Jesus says they were pounded by the torrential rains that tend to come in that part of the world. Many of the homes in the Middle East are built in valleys. During the dry season all is well, but when the rains come the water can really rise. That's what happened to these two houses.

The quality of our lives is not tested when the weather is good. Until it rained, the foolish man's house looked as good as the wise man's. It wasn't until a storm started blowing against their lives that their obedience, or lack thereof, became apparent.

It's when the rains come and the wind blows that we find out whether our life's foundations will hold. What is the rock that Jesus says we are to build upon? It is Him and His Word, heard and *obeyed*. That's the difference between a life that withstands the storm and one that is swept away.

Notice that in Jesus' story both men heard His words. The only difference was what they did with those words. One man obeyed, and the other didn't. One man understood that Jesus knew more about building a solid life than he did, and he allowed Jesus to be the architect of his house. The second man refused to follow Jesus' blueprint.

This difference is so important because one thing is sure: The rains and floods are coming against your life. Anyone who tells you that after you accept Christ it no longer rains is lying. Jesus said the obedient man still got rained on and flooded. But what mattered was that his house withstood the storm because he had the right foundation.

Paul said that as a "wise master builder" he had laid a foundation for God's people, that foundation being Christ and no other (1 Corinthians 3:10–11). Paul laid out the truth of God, and it was up to believers to build their lives on the foundation of the truth concerning Christ.

The foolish man, however, had spent all of his time and energy and resources building a life that would not last because it had the wrong foundation. And when it fell, it fell hard (Matthew 7:27).

If you are enjoying sunny days right now, make the most of them, because it is going to rain again. Make sure you are living in obedience to the Lord while the sun is shining, because obedience will stabilize your life when the rain and floods come.

The foundation of obedience to Christ made the difference in the two houses Jesus described in Matthew 7. It's not enough to hear what Jesus says. We need to do something about what we have heard.

Laying Your Foundation

When you and I begin obeying Jesus, we begin laying a deep foundation for our lives. If you have ever seen a skyscraper being built, you know how far builders dig down to lay the foundation and how long it takes. The hole for that foundation goes deep.

In fact, the higher the building reaches into the sky, the deeper the foundation must go. If you want a "skyscraper" spiritual life that soars into the heavens, don't lay it on the foundation of a chicken coop. If you do that, your life may look OK for a while. But when the rains come it will be clear that there was not much underneath.

Here's another thing you need to know about laying a foundation of obedience. It's best to lay it on the sunny days, because stormy weather is not the time to try to pour a foundation. Any builder will tell you that you can't pour concrete when the weather is too cold or too wet. If your life is going to withstand the storms, your foundation has to be in place before the rains hit. To wait until then to lay your foundation is foolish. And all the other stuff won't matter if the foundation is washed away.

One of the finest biblical examples of a person with the right foundation in place was Abraham. God asked Abraham to do the hardest thing any believer has ever been asked to do: sacrifice his son Isaac, the son of promise (Genesis 22:1–2).

The astounding thing is that Abraham got up the next morning and proceeded to obey God. Where did he get that kind of spiritual strength? Abraham was already a man of obedience. He had left his home and his people in the upscale city of Ur to journey to a forsaken-looking stretch of desert called Palestine, simply because God told him to (see Hebrews 11:8). Abraham had obeyed God and had seen God honor that obedience, and he knew that God knew what He was doing in Isaac's case (see Hebrews 11:17).

We don't know what God will call us to do or the tests He might send our way. But if we have built a good foundation, it won't really matter.

THE FELLOWSHIP OF OBEDIENCE

A second principle of obeying Christ is what I call the fellowship of obedience. Jesus said in John 14:15, "If you love Me, you will keep My commandments."

Obedience to Christ is, and always has been, the acid test of our love for Him. Obeying the Lord is a response of love, not just a duty. Jesus said it was incongruent to claim to love Him and then not obey Him.

Obedience Brings Jesus Close

Later in John 14, Jesus added another dimension to the relationship between love and obedience when He said, "He who has My commandments and keeps them, he it is who loves Me; and he who loves Me shall be loved by My Father, and I will love him, and will disclose Myself to him" (v. 21). Now notice verse 23: "If anyone loves Me, he will keep My word; and My Father will love him, and We will come to him, and make Our abode with him."

Look at the promises Jesus made to His obedient followers. Not only will we experience His love, but we will be loved by the Father—because the Father responds to those who respond to the Son. Jesus said He will "disclose" Himself to obedient people, and also that He and the Father will make Themselves at home in the hearts of the obedient.

Now don't misunderstand. We are not talking about salvation here. This is an issue of fellowship. Jesus says to lukewarm believers, "Behold, I stand at the door and knock; if anyone hears My voice and opens the door, I will come in to him, and will dine with him, and he with Me" (Revelation 3:20).

This is Jesus talking to the church. He wants to enjoy close fellowship with His people. If we are willing to obey Him, He will enter into a new level of intimacy with us.

Many of us pray, "Dear Jesus, draw me closer to You. Help me to know You more fully." Part of the answer to that prayer lies with us, in the form of our commitment to radical obedience.

Let me show you how this works. We quoted John 14:15 above, in which Jesus said those who love Him are the ones who obey Him. Now look at verse 16. "And I will ask the

Father, and He will give you another Helper, that He may be with you forever."

This promise of the Holy Spirit comes in the context of obedience. Jesus is saying, "If you love Me, you will obey Me. And if you will obey Me, I will ask the Father to give you a Helper." In other words, the sequence is crucial. We often get it backward. We pray, "Lord, help me to obey You," when what we should be saying is, "Lord, I am obeying You the best way I know how. Please help me obey You more completely by the power of my Helper, the Holy Spirit."

The Holy Spirit's job is to enable us as we obey, not to make us obey. As I have often said, the Spirit is not going to move our feet in the way we should go. But if our deepest desire is to follow the Lord in obedience, we can expect the Spirit to empower us.

Later on in the Upper Room, Jesus told His disciples, "If you keep My commandments, you will abide in My love" (John 15:10). Do you want to experience more of the love of Jesus in your life? Obey Him, and you'll be living in the environment of His love.

Here's another way to bring Jesus close. All of us long to see God answer prayer in our lives. Jesus said in John 15:7, "If you abide in Me, and My words abide in you, ask whatever you wish, and it shall be done for you." Abiding is the state of intimate fellowship we achieve when we are obeying Christ.

Jesus was saying that when we draw close to Him through loving obedience, His Father is ready to answer our requests. If you want a more potent prayer life, make obedience your focus. Otherwise, God does not feel obligated to respond to you. Remember, He responds to those who respond to His Son.

We are talking about the fellowship of obedience. This is all about cultivating our relationship with Christ. It is possible for us to be on our way to heaven and yet not really know the One with whom we are going to share heaven for eternity.

Taking Fellowship to a Higher Level

If you want to know Jesus Christ in a way you have never known Him before, if you want to love Him in a way you have never loved Him before, then the apostle John has a great word for you:

> By this we know that we have come to know Him, if we keep His commandments. The one who says, "I have come to know Him," and does not keep His commandments, is a liar, and the truth is not in him; but whoever keeps His word, in him the love of God has truly been perfected. By this we know that we are in Him. (1 John 2:3–5)

Let me clarify again that the knowledge of God we are talking about here is not knowing God in salvation, but in fellowship. John has the same message as Jesus. If you want to know Him, keep His commandments. In fact, verse 4 establishes the fact that without the proof of obedience, our profession of love for Christ amounts to a lie. Again, obedience is key to fellowship. But there is another level of fellowship with Christ we can attain by our obedience, and these verses spell it out.

I want to point out two phrases in particular. In verse 3 John said we have come to know Christ if we keep His commandments. But then in verse 5, our love is "perfected" by keeping His word. Perfection is a synonym for maturity or completeness. When we keep God's Word, we display a mature love that helps us know we are "in Him."

What's the difference between these two concepts? What is this higher level of obedience that causes our love for Christ, and His love for us, to be perfected? The difference is in a slight nuance of meaning between *commandment* and *word*. They are not exactly the same.

You can obey Christ for a number of reasons. For example, you can obey Him because you have to. We all have things in life we do out of a sense of obligation, not because we enjoy doing them.

You may tell your child to wash the dishes. He drags himself over to the sink and starts washing. He is keeping your commandment, but there isn't much heart in it. If he had a choice, he'd be out the door. It's possible to obey Christ at this level. Another reason to obey Christ is because you feel the need. That is, you know that there are certain blessings and benefits tied to obedience. But the heart's desire to obey God still isn't quite there. A lot of people get up and go to work every day because they need that paycheck to pay the bills.

You can obey a commandment without wanting to obey or feeling like obeying. But you do it because it's a command. Remember Peter in Luke 5? "Jesus, You don't really know fishing the way I do. I can tell You there are no fish down there. But since You told me to let down my net, I'll do it."

I am not suggesting there is no value in this kind of obedience. On the contrary, when Peter obeyed Jesus he got a miracle. In the words of John 14:21, Jesus disclosed Himself to Peter in a new way. Peter obeyed even though he didn't see any sense in throwing out his net, and his net filled with fish.

Follow the progression. When Peter saw Jesus disclose Himself at this deeper level because he obeyed Jesus' command, Peter was ready for the next level of fellowship. Jesus called Peter and his partners to follow Him and become fishers of men, and they dropped everything on the spot and followed Jesus (Luke 5:10–11).

In other words, Peter obeyed Jesus' command just because it was Jesus saying so. But then he joyfully obeyed Jesus' word, "Follow Me."

Let's go back to our dish-washing example. When your children obey your command to do the dishes even though they do not feel like it, something happens in the level of your fellowship with them.

First of all, your heart is inclined toward them more because you realize they could have made a big scene or even rebelled against you and refused to do the dishes. But they obeyed you and did what you asked them to do, so you express your gratitude for that obedience.

Something also happens to the kids when they obey. They sense that they have pleased you, and that sense of satisfaction may result in a more joyful obedience next time. Eventually, you may not even have to command them to do the dishes. A simple word may do the job.

I know what you're thinking. "Tony, on what planet do you find children like this?" I realize the example is idealized, but you get the point. Our goal as Christians should be to come to the point where just knowing what Christ wants is enough to motivate us to do it.

This is taking our fellowship with Christ to an entirely new level, and it happens through obedience to Him. This is the fellowship of obedience, and it's available to you. When you obey Christ's commandments, He is free to disclose Himself to you that He might unleash His Word in your life. Then you come to the place where you "walk in the same manner as He walked" (1 John 2:6). You are so much like Jesus you start walking the way He does! Obedience is the process that brings you to this point.

It's like the little boy who was running away from home. He just kept riding his bicycle around the block, all the time rearranging a bulky bag he was carrying over his shoulder, until finally a police officer stopped him and said, "Son, I've been watching you riding your bicycle around the block. What are you doing?"

"I'm running away from home."

"Well," the officer replied, "if you're running away from home, why do you keep circling the block?"

"Because my mommy told me not to cross the street!" When you learn to love Jesus Christ until His Word becomes part of you, your intimacy with Him keeps you close even when you feel like pulling away.

THE FRUITFULNESS OF OBEDIENCE

We're ready for the third and final principle in this matter of obeying Jesus Christ. The foundation of obedience has to do with your own life. The fellowship of obedience focuses on your relationship with Christ. And now we need to talk about the fruitfulness of obedience, which involves the overflow of your life into the lives of other people.

According to the apostle James, when we "receive the word implanted," not being a "forgetful hearer but an effectual doer," we will be "blessed in what [we do]" (James 1:21, 25). That is, our lives will be fruitful.

Did you see the importance of obedience in this process? It's the hinge on which the whole thing turns. Let's go to James 1 and find out how we can nourish the implanted seed of God's Word until we reap the ripe fruit of His blessing.

Cultivating the Seed

If you are a believer, God's Word is already implanted in you. You are one of the "brethren" (James 1:2). So we need to point out one more time that James is not discussing how a person gets saved. He's talking about our response to Christ. The seed is there, and it's good. Our responsibility is to cultivate it so it can grow.

How do we cultivate the Word implanted in us? James gives us this well-known formula: "Be quick to hear, slow to speak and slow to anger" (1:19). Then he tells us to put aside "all filthiness and all that remains of wickedness," and receive the Word "in humility" (v. 21).

Being "quick to hear" means your priority and passion is to take in the Word of God. A good illustration of this eagerness is a new mother who is incredibly sensitive to the cries and even the slightest movements of her baby. Her priority is to receive and act upon the messages her baby is sending out. We're to be like that when God speaks through His Word.

Being "slow to speak" has nothing to do with whether you are a talkative person. The idea is, don't argue with the Word you hear from God. Let God speak before you start interrupting with your thoughts and your ideas.

Have your children ever cut you off and interrupted you when you were trying to tell them something? We usually tell children, "I am talking. Wait until I finish." We want them to hear what we have to say before they venture their opinion.

Why? Because they have things backward. We are the parents, and we are speaking from a perspective they don't possess. It's not that we never allow our kids to express their ideas and opinions. Most kids don't have any problem there. But they need to learn to listen before they speak. They do not have as much knowledge as we do.

In the same way, God has already anticipated what we are going to say. If we would just slow down and not be so quick to interject our ideas, we would understand better what He is saying to us, and we would see His Word begin to grow in us.

We're also told to be "slow to anger." Why would we be angry with the Word? Because we don't like what it is telling us. We want to go ahead and get that divorce, but God says stay together. We want to marry that non-Christian or enter a business partnership with an unbeliever, but God tells us not to be unequally yoked (2 Corinthians 6:14).

Are you impressed when your children throw temper

tantrums? Do you say, "Oh my, baby is upset. Better do what he wants right away so he will stop crying"? I hope not.

God is not impressed with our temper tantrums either. He is not going to change His Word because we don't agree with it or feel like obeying it. Our anger will not get us anywhere with God (see James 1:20).

If the implanted seed of the Word is going to bear fruit in our lives, we have to cultivate it God's way.

Doing the Word

James 1:22 brings us full circle to the point at which we began this chapter. That is, if you are going to get anywhere in your Christian life, you have to hear *and* obey what Jesus says. Otherwise, you are building your life on sand. Or as James says, "Prove yourselves doers of the word, and not merely hearers who delude themselves" (James 1:22).

If you are not ready to obey the Word, you are wasting your time. It's like looking in the mirror but not doing anything about what you see there.

James uses this illustration in verses 23–24, and the word he uses for "man" is the specific word for a male. He wants to drive home his point, because we know most women don't just glance in a mirror and then hurry on. Men tend to give it one quick glance and say, "Looks OK to me." But most women look, and then look some more.

At least it works this way in my house. Lois is always sending me back to the mirror to fix my hair or straighten my tie. The difference is that I spent five minutes in front of the mirror while Lois spent—well, let's just say more than five minutes!

James says we need to look intently "at the perfect law . . . of liberty" (James 1:25a), the way we would stare into a mirror to check ourselves out and fix what's wrong. He's talking about the kind of obedience that results in fruitfulness.

The Reward of Consistent Cultivation

Any farmer will tell you a seed doesn't sprout the first time he waters it. He doesn't give up on the seed because it doesn't produce the first day it is planted. A farmer has to cultivate that seed consistently to reap its fruit.

We need that same consistency, that same kind of commitment. If you set your heart to obey Christ, don't expect things to change overnight. Don't say, "Lord, I am going to obey You this one time. But if I don't see the results I want, I'm giving up." No, obedience has to be cultivated until it is a way of life. And when it is God's proper time, you will be blessed and God's hand will be on you.

You will see Jesus Christ at work in your life. You will see Him answering prayer and dealing with people and situations you thought were impossible. And you will see Him changing you into His image.

Have you ever decided you were going to start exercising? If you have, you know that about the only thing that happens the first time is that you are so tired and sore you want to quit and never do that again.

But you know you have to exercise again and again to see any benefit. And sure enough, as you become an "effectual" exerciser you begin to see the fruit of your consistent commitment.

So let me leave you with this challenge, in the form of a prayer. If you want to cultivate a life of obedience to Christ that results in a firm foundation under you, intimate fellowship with Him, and fruit in your life, wake up each morning with this prayer on your lips:

"Lord Jesus, show me what You want me to do today in response to Your Word, and I will obey, trusting the Holy Spirit to help me. Dear Jesus, please disclose Yourself to me in a new way today, so that I will become more sensitive to Your Word and enjoy the fruit of Your blessing in my life."

CHAPTER TWENTY-ONE
SHARING CHRIST

Suppose you were a world-famous physician who had undertaken to find the cure for a deadly virus that had infected the entire human race. Every man, woman, boy, and girl on the planet was infected with this dread disease—including you. And it was fatal in every single case.

So you put your medical skills to work, and you come up with a vaccine that you believe will bring about a cure. You decide to test it on yourself first. You inject yourself with the potential cure—and it works! The deadly virus disappears from your bloodstream. You are now completely healed.

At this point, do you suppose you would tell anyone else about your incredible discovery? Would you be eager to share your precious vaccine with the people who mean the most to you? Would you be willing to give the formula for the vaccine to others so it could be produced and used on a worldwide scale, saving millions or billions of lives?

I would hope the answer to each of these questions would be yes. You would want to do all of those things. In fact, you would have a moral obligation not to withhold from dying people the cure for their fatal illness.

This scenario is imaginary, but it addresses a real problem. A disease *has* infected the entire human race, and it is terminal in every case. That disease is sin. However, there is a cure, an antidote—the blood of Jesus Christ.

We who have received the cure for sin, who have been forgiven and cleansed by the blood of Christ, have the privilege and holy obligation of sharing the cure with others. As we pursue Christ in our own lives, we need to be ready to give the good news of His love to others.

THE MESSAGE ABOUT CHRIST
WE HAVE TO TELL

We have already established that Jesus Christ is the unique figure in all of history. What puts Him in a class by Himself is His person as the God-man and His work as the Savior of the world. This is the message about Christ that we have to tell to a needy world.

Paul gave us the heart of the gospel, its irreducible minimum, in 1 Corinthians 15:1–6. I want to look at this critical passage as we flesh out the message God has given us concerning Jesus Christ.

The apostle began with a word of reminder. "Now I make known to you, brethren, the gospel which I preached to you, which also you received, in which also you stand, by which also you are saved, if you hold fast the word which I preached to you, unless you believed in vain" (1 Corinthians 15:1–2).

First, notice the interplay between the past and present tense of the verbs Paul used in these opening verses. The reason for this is that the book of 1 Corinthians was written around A.D. 55, approximately five years after he had first come to Corinth to preach the gospel.

Paul wanted these believers to know that the message about Christ he had preached to them five years earlier, which they had received and believed resulting in their salvation, had not changed at all. What he was about to write was the same message he had preached back then.

In fact, the gospel is so constant and so unchangeable that Paul could confidently tell the Corinthians they were still standing in its truth. The verb "stand" at the end of verse 1 is in the perfect tense, which in Greek denotes an action completed in the past that has abiding results in the present.

In other words, Paul didn't have a new or different message for these people. His message was still Christ:

For I delivered to you as of first importance what I also received, that Christ died for our sins according to the Scriptures, and that He was buried, and that He was raised on the third day according to the Scriptures, and that He appeared to Cephas, then to the twelve. After that He appeared to more than five hundred brethren at one time, most of whom remain until now, but some have fallen asleep. (1 Corinthians 15:3–6)

The message we have to tell is the good news of the death, burial, and resurrection of Jesus Christ for our sins.

Christ's Death for Our Sins

Paul was careful to say that Jesus Christ died *for* our sins. He did not die simply to set a good example, to show us how to die. He did not die as a martyr because He was misunderstood. Christ died in our place, as our Substitute, for our sins.

This is important because sin is the great disease that separates us from God and causes us to die physically and eternally. It is sin that brings the eternal judgment of God upon us. Only Christ can deal with sin—and He has done so by His death for us. The substitutionary death of Jesus Christ is the centerpiece of the gospel.

This event, the greatest of history, is not a spiritual fairy tale. Paul said Jesus died "according to the Scriptures" (v. 3). In other words, Jesus' death was well prophesied in the Old Testament, the Scriptures that were available to the people of Paul's day. He was appealing to the written record of God's Word as his authority.

We don't have the space for a full study of Old Testament prophecy related to Christ's death, so let me mention two key passages.

As far back as Genesis 3:15, just before God drove Adam and Eve out of Eden for their sin, He gave them a message of hope. Someone would come one day and crush Satan, but not before being wounded by Satan.

Bible teachers have long held this to be a prophecy of Christ's death on the cross, when Satan appeared to have won the victory before being crushed by the Resurrection. Genesis 3:15 is thus the first mention of a Savior in the Bible, the gospel in a nutshell, so to speak.

Then, six hundred years before Jesus Christ was born, the prophet Isaiah wrote of God's suffering Servant, the Messiah, who would be "pierced through for our transgressions [and] crushed for our iniquities" (Isaiah 53:5).

It is not difficult to establish the fact that Jesus Christ died according to the Scriptures.

Christ's Burial as Proof of Death

We don't usually think of Christ's burial as a seminal part of the gospel, but Paul included it here for a very important reason: Jesus' burial is proof that He died.

That may seem unnecessary even to mention, but think about it. One of the heresies about Christ's resurrection is that He did not actually die, but merely fainted and was revived by the cold and dampness of the tomb.

But if Jesus did not die, then He did not rise from the dead—and our faith is useless (1 Corinthians 15:14). However, even Jesus' enemies testified to the fact that He was dead (Mark 15:44–45). And more important was Jesus' own dismissal of His spirit (Matthew 27:50). No one who was involved in the crucifixion and burial of Jesus doubted that He was dead.

But praise God, the burial of Jesus Christ is not the end of the gospel message! Several years ago, I took my family to see a magnificent Christmas pageant at the Radio City Music Hall in New York City. It told the story of Jesus' birth, including live animals.

Toward the end of the play, a statement about Jesus Christ appeared on the screen, touting His uniqueness and saying there is nobody like Him. Then the play ended with Him dying on the cross. The audience stood to its feet and erupted in applause.

I was clapping too, but my daughter Priscilla pulled on my shirt sleeve and said, "But, Dad, something's missing."

"What do you mean?" I asked her.

"The program ended with Jesus still in the grave." I stopped applauding and sat down, because my daughter was right. The story ended with Jesus in the grave. And a dead Savior can do nothing for anyone.

Christ's Resurrection as God's "Receipt"

Jesus was "raised on the third day according to the Scriptures" (1 Corinthians 15:4). The gospel must include Jesus' resurrection, because the Resurrection is our "receipt" from

God the Father that He accepted His Son's payment for sin on the cross.

When you buy something, the clerk accepts your money and gives you a receipt confirming that the bill was paid in full. If there is ever a dispute about whether payment was made, all you have to do is produce your receipt.

When Jesus cried "It is finished!" (John 19:30), He uttered the Greek word *tetelestai,* which means "Paid in full." The payment for sin that God demanded had been paid, and the empty tomb is proof that the payment was received and the debt satisfied.

This means you and I no longer have to face the penalty for our sins. Jesus paid a debt He did not owe because we owed a debt we could not pay. Who else but Jesus Christ is worthy of our praise and total commitment?

Paul said the Scripture testified to Jesus' resurrection. We devoted an earlier chapter to the subject of the Resurrection, but I want to show you briefly how the Old Testament prophesied Jesus' resurrection.

In Psalm 16:10, David wrote, "Thou wilt not abandon my soul to Sheol; neither wilt Thou allow Thy Holy One to undergo decay." The question is whether David was speaking of himself or someone else.

That question was answered by the apostle Peter in his sermon on the Day of Pentecost. Speaking of Jesus Christ, Peter told his listeners that although "godless men" crucified Jesus, "God raised Him up again, putting an end to the agony of death, since it was impossible for Him to be held in its power" (Acts 2:23–24). Then, to prove his assertion, Peter quoted Psalm 16:8–11.

To make sure his audience understood that he was not talking about David's body being preserved from decay and rising from the dead, Peter added, "Brethren, I may confidently say to you regarding the patriarch David that he both died and was buried, and his tomb is with us to this day" (Acts 2:29).

In other words they could verify that David was still dead and buried. David wasn't writing about himself, Peter said. Instead, "Because [David] was a prophet . . . he looked ahead and spoke of the resurrection of the Christ" (vv. 30–31).

So Paul said in 1 Corinthians 15:4 that there was biblical evidence for Jesus' resurrection. There was also empirical evidence. The risen Christ appeared to Peter and the other apostles and to more than five hundred witnesses at one time (vv. 5–6). Paul himself also saw Christ (v. 8). Peter and Paul could say, "We know the Resurrection is true. We saw Christ."

This verification is important, because if just one person or only a handful of people saw Jesus just once, someone could argue that the appearance was a figment of their over-active imaginations—a case of people wanting to believe something. But when hundreds of witnesses could be called to testify, the truth of the Resurrection was beyond dispute.

The Importance of a Decision

Before we go on to the next point, let me mention another element that is important to our message. This has to do not with the content of the gospel, but with the *intent* behind our presentation of it. We have not fully presented the gospel until we have called for a decision on the part of the hearer.

In other words, it is not enough just to tell someone, "Jesus died for your sins and rose again. Think about it." To borrow from our opening illustration, that's like a doctor showing a patient a syringe with the antidote for that person's fatal disease and saying, "I have good news. The cure for your disease is in this syringe. Think about whether you want it."

Peter's listeners at Pentecost were convicted by his message and asked what they should do. His answer was "Repent" (Acts 2:38). Jesus told His disciples He would make them fishers of men, not throwers of fishing lines. There's a big difference between throwing out a line and putting bait on it.

Once you have told people they have an eternally fatal disease for which the only cure is repentance and faith in Jesus Christ, you have not completed your responsibility until you have called for them to make a decision about Christ. Our intent in giving the message of Christ must be to convert the hearer to faith in Christ.

In 1 Corinthians 9:19 Paul said, "Though I am free from all men, I have made myself a slave to all, that I might win the more." Then he added in verse 22, "I have become all things to all men, that I may by all means save some."

What did Paul mean by saying he wanted to "win" and "save" as many people as possible? He wasn't claiming to be the Savior. Only the Holy Spirit can convict sinners of their sin and their need to be saved.

Paul was saying that we have a part to play in salvation by presenting the gospel and calling for a decision. Paul's intent was that the people who heard him would make a decision for Christ.

The one reaction we don't want from people when we explain the gospel is indifference or neutrality. We need to make it clear that Christ calls for a decision. I can assure you, a young man who is deeply in love with a young woman is not content just to announce his desire to marry her. He wants a decision from her!

OUR MOTIVATION FOR
TELLING ABOUT CHRIST

We've already touched briefly on this aspect of telling others about Christ. The fact that people are terminally ill with the disease of sin, and we have the antidote, should motivate us to share the cure with them.

Actually, the Bible gives us several motives for introducing people to the Christ we love and serve. I want to examine three motives we find in another seminal passage on the gospel, 2 Corinthians 5:10–21. Paul wrote:

> For we must all appear before the judgment seat of Christ, that each one may be recompensed for his deeds in the body, according to what he has done, whether good or bad. Therefore knowing the fear of the Lord, we persuade men. (vv. 10–11)

One motivation for witnessing of the gospel is what Paul called the fear of Christ.

The Fear of Christ

The fear of Christ is a two-edged sword. For Paul, and for all believers, it is not a terror at the prospect of eternal judgment. God judged Christ on the cross for us. But we should feel a sense of deep awe in the knowledge that we will have to stand before Christ someday and give an account of our lives. We'll talk about that later.

But for unbelievers, the fear of God is the fear of His wrath and judgment. We have not told people the whole truth about the gospel until we explain clearly that God is a God of judgment as well as a God of love.

In fact, God's wrath is as complete and perfect as His love. If it were not, He would be less than God. If heaven lasts forever, then hell lasts forever. The eternal torment of hell is as real as the eternal bliss of heaven.

God has extended His offer of love and forgiveness to sinners, but He cannot and will not ignore His wrath for those who refuse the offer of salvation. Christ endured God's wrath on the cross, which freed God up to show His love. But those who reject Christ's payment must endure God's wrath themselves.

The fear of Christ motivated Paul to please Him, not people (see 2 Corinthians 5:9). Let me say something about trying to please people: You'll never be able to do it, so don't even try. You can't worry about making folk happy when you are explaining the gospel, because the Cross is an offense to many people's sense of self-righteousness. They don't see themselves as lost sinners under God's decree of eternal punishment.

I'm not talking about being nice or kind to people. I'm talking about holding back on our responsibility to communicate the gospel for fear of how people will react.

Here's another reason that trying to please people won't do us any good. When we appear before the judgment seat of Christ, each of us will stand before Him alone. Those people we tried so hard to please will not be present. They can't help you in receiving your reward from Christ, and they can't hurt you.

God wants us to love people, but not to the extent that it overshadows our fear of Christ and our desire to please Him. When that happens, what we have isn't love but the fear of men.

Because the fear of Christ was Paul's motivation, he could say he had a clear conscience before people (2 Corinthians 5:11–12). That does not mean that everybody understood or appreciated Paul's motives and ministry. Some of his critics said he was beside himself (v. 13). Their attitude was, "Paul, you are crazy. You have gone off the deep end with this Jesus thing."

Well, if we are going to be thought of as out of whack, we might as well go overboard on the Lord, because He's the One we have to stand before. So don't feel bad if someone says you're crazy. They said the same thing about Paul and Jesus (see Mark 3:21). That's pretty good company!

The fear of Christ is a strong motivation. Peter wrote, "It is time for judgment to begin with the household of God; and if it begins with us first, what will be the outcome for those who do not obey the gospel of God? And if it is with difficulty that the righteous is saved, what will become of the godless man and the sinner?" (1 Peter 4:17–18).

The gospel is serious business. We must persuade people to believe in the fear of Christ, because "Our God is a consuming fire" (Hebrews 12:29).

Our Love for Christ

A second motivation we should have for passing on the message of Christ is found in 2 Corinthians 5:14. "The love of Christ controls us, having concluded this, that one died for all."

Here is the balance again between God's wrath and love. Romans 11:22 speaks of "the kindness and severity of God." Both are perfect aspects of His character.

How does the love of Christ motivate us? The answer is, "We love, because He first loved us" (1 John 4:19). John is talking about what Jesus did for us on the cross. Jesus Himself said, "Greater love has no one than this, that one lay down his life for his friends" (John 15:13).

The fact is that the more we are in love with Jesus Christ, the more we will want to tell others about Him. Show me a person who witnesses about Christ regularly, and I'll show you a person who's in love.

When we're in love, we do things we wouldn't normally do. We show pictures of our beloved to strangers, we talk about the object of our love to anyone who will listen—and even to people who don't want to hear it. Quiet people become talkative when they fall in love. Love dominates their conversation.

So if we are failing to talk about Christ, it is evidence of a lack of love for Him. Pursuing a passionate, intimate relationship with Jesus Christ will automatically increase our evangelistic outreach.

There's another reason that Christ's love should control and motivate us. Let's finish Paul's thought on this subject: "He died for all, that they who live should no longer live for themselves, but for Him who died and rose again on their behalf" (2 Corinthians 5:15).

Jesus died for us and saved us that we might live for Him. He has the right to expect our full commitment, because where would we be without His sacrifice on the cross? We would be under a death sentence. We need to understand the priority call Jesus has on our lives, because we are living in the "me" generation that values personal fulfillment and happiness above all else.

"Am I happy?" and "Does this fulfill me?" are the big questions of the day. Unfortunately, people can use this as an excuse for sin, as in this line: "I'm not happy anymore in my marriage, and God doesn't want me to be unhappy. Therefore, I'm quitting."

I hope it is not news to you that God's priority desire for His children is not to make us happy, but to make us holy. We are not saved so we can live in our own world.

Don't misunderstand. I'm not saying God's will is that we be miserable. But if we will get beyond the issue of our own happiness and begin living for Christ, we will find a happiness we cannot even imagine. Christ Himself will become our joy and our happiness. Living for His glory will be our greatest delight. But the only people who find this level of true happiness are those who are controlled by the love of Christ.

Our New Relationship with Christ

This is the third motivation for witnessing of Christ. We are to share His message because we have entered into a new relationship with Him that changes everything for us and for everyone around us. Stay with me on this one, because it's rich.

We're still in 2 Corinthians 5, looking at verses 16–17: "Therefore from now on we recognize no man according to the flesh; even though we have known Christ according to the flesh, yet now we know Him thus no longer. Therefore if any man is in Christ, he is a new creature; the old things passed away; behold, new things have come."

Do you see the radical change in our relationships here? Paul said we are not to evaluate people any longer based on external criteria.

Obviously, that does not mean we are supposed to ignore people's identity or pretend we don't know them. Paul was saying that when it comes to how we relate to people, whether a person is black, white, brown, or red, Democrat or Republican, poor or rich, male or female, doesn't matter anymore. We must relate to people based on whether they are in Christ or outside of Him.

In other words, we are back to the need to tell others of Christ, because those who are outside of Him are still carrying the spiritually fatal virus of sin that will plunge them into the eternal abyss unless they receive the cure.

Paul said he even related to Jesus Christ in a different way now. Paul may have met or heard Jesus before he was saved. In his days of unbelief, Paul probably considered Jesus to be just another man—maybe even a dangerous man, because Paul felt the need to persecute and kill Jesus' followers.

But now that Paul belonged to Christ, all of that had changed. Paul had experienced the new birth that made him an entirely new person. All of his old life was gone. He had a new relationship with Christ that radically changed his perspective on life.

This sounds wonderful, but the reality is that there are a lot of Christians who refuse to see all of life from the radical perspective of their relationship to Christ. They want to look at things according to the flesh.

That's why the church of Jesus Christ is still plagued with things like racism, classism, culturalism, and materialism. When believers view life according to the flesh, things break down.

Paul went on to say, "Now all these things [the new things of the Christian life] are from God" (2 Corinthians 5:18a). He is the standard in this realm. Paul described this new relationship with Christ that changes everything as being reconciled with God. "[God] reconciled us to Himself through Christ, and gave us the ministry of reconciliation" (v. 18b).

To reconcile means to restore harmony or peace, to bring two hostile parties into peace and agreement with each other by removing the reason for their hostility. Here is a tremendous picture of what Christ has done for us. "God was in Christ reconciling the world to Himself, not counting their trespasses against them" (v. 19a).

Paul went on to say we have been given this wonderful message of reconciliation to share with others (vv. 19b–20).

But before we can tell this good news effectively, we need to understand exactly what God has done for us by reconciling us to Himself through Christ.

Notice a couple of things about this reconciliation. First, God took the initiative. He reached out to us with the offer of peace, not the other way around. That's significant because God is the offended party in this deal. He was the innocent party. We offended Him and broke fellowship with Him by our sin. Whether people are upset at God or not is irrelevant. The only thing that matters is His attitude toward us.

The "sticking point" that kept God from simply overlooking our sins and reaching across the table to us is the aspect of His nature we talked about earlier—His justice and wrath. God could not ignore sin and remain a perfect and holy God. His justice demanded that sin be atoned for with blood.

Enter Jesus Christ! God knew we could not satisfy His demand for sinlessness, so because He loves us He let the penalty stroke of death fall on His own Son. Christ's death removed the reason for God's hostility toward sinners by satisfying God's judgment against sin.

To put it in everyday terms, God isn't mad at us anymore! He is free to reach out to us with the offer of peace. He has reconciled the world to Himself. He isn't counting our sins against us, because He has already counted them against Christ. I told you this was good stuff!

This does raise a question, however. If the whole world has been reconciled to God, why isn't everyone saved? Because people can refuse God's offer of reconciliation. They can say no to Christ.

Make no mistake. People who go to hell do so not because God is cruel, but because they refuse to believe in Christ (see John 16:9).

Let me deal with one more issue here, because it often comes up when we are telling others about Christ. The work of Christ in paying for sin and reconciling the world to God is effective for those who cannot choose Christ for themselves—including infants and small children and the mentally handicapped. That's because Christ's death removes the penalty of original sin (John 1:9; Romans 5:18), the only kind of sin these individuals carry and are morally responsible for.

We should be motivated to tell of Christ because of our new relationship with Him. That includes our commission to tell others the wonderful news that in reconciliation, God is reaching out His hand to sinners.

That's good news because most people think they need to reach out their hand to God. Most people think they can earn God's favor by their feeble good works, which is the definition of every man-based religion. They don't understand that there is nothing they can do by themselves to please God. The pleasing, so to speak, has already been done by Christ.

The world needs to hear the message of reconciliation, because most people you will meet are trying to work their way to heaven. They need someone commissioned by heaven to tell them the truth.

That someone is you and me. We are Christ's ambassadors to this lost world, "begging" people to be reconciled to God. In reconciliation God has charged our sins to Christ and credited Christ's perfect righteousness to us (2 Corinthians 5:21). That's the best deal in history!

OUR METHOD FOR
PASSING ON THE MESSAGE

We have a message to be passed on and more than enough motivation to tell it. The Bible also tells us how to present the message of Christ.

I'm not talking about mechanical steps in evangelism here, but the framework or mind-set we need to have as we tell others about Christ. Let me show you what I mean.

We Need to Verbalize the Message

This takes us all the way back to John 1:1, where we read that Jesus is the Word of God. We could say that Jesus is the verbalization of God. According to Hebrews 1:2, "[God] has spoken to us in His Son." Jesus is the very Word of God. At Jesus' transfiguration God the Father said, "This is My beloved Son, with whom I am well-pleased; listen to Him!" (Matthew 17:5).

We have a message to pass on, but it doesn't get communicated by osmosis. We need to tell people the good news of the gospel.

We Need to Visualize the Message

In John 1:14 we read, "And the Word became flesh, and dwelt among us, and we beheld His glory." Jesus was also the visible representation of God. People could see Him, could observe His life as well as hear His words.

We need to live out the gospel too, even as we are speaking it. People should hear and see the Word through us. It's a matter of both/and, not either/or.

Some people think it's enough to "live the life" before the world. They believe people will see Christ in us and want Him. It's true that our lives should reinforce our witness, but a silent witness is an oxymoron.

A CLOSING CHALLENGE

One of the most challenging passages of Scripture in regard to telling about Christ occurs at the end of John 1.

One day John the Baptist pointed two of his disciples to Jesus. They followed Him, spent some time with Him, and went away convinced that Jesus was the Messiah (John 1:35–40).

One of these men was Andrew, who immediately went to his brother Peter and brought him to the Lord (vv. 41–42). The next day Jesus met Philip and called Him to become His disciple. Philip took off and brought back Nathanael, who also believed and followed Christ (vv. 43–51).

That's how the ministry of witnessing about Christ is supposed to work. Someone has said that evangelism is simply one beggar telling another beggar where to find bread. When you are pursuing Christ in an intimate, committed relationship of love and obedience, you won't need anyone to cajole or browbeat you to tell others about Him.

So my question to you is, How much do you love Jesus Christ? If your answer is, "With all my heart, soul, and strength," then I want to ask you, Have you brought anyone else to Him lately? We have a great Savior and a great message to pass on!

CHAPTER TWENTY-TWO

SERVING CHRIST

We can't dive into a subject like pursuing Christ without talking about what it means to serve Him. The Bible says that Jesus came to serve (Mark 10:45), and it's clear that we are saved to serve.

I say that because if God did not have anything for us to do after we got saved, He would have taken us to heaven on the spot. He left us here to glorify Him and make a difference for Jesus Christ in the lives of other people by serving Christ.

We hear a lot of talk about serving Christ—but a lot of what passes for service to Him does not meet the biblical criteria. The question we have to ask, and the question I want to explore in this chapter, is this: Are we serving Him in the ways He wants to be served and the ways He has explicitly told us in His Word to serve Him?

We know it's possible to serve haphazardly and sloppily, but that does not do justice or honor to the person we are serving. I am convinced you want to honor Jesus Christ in every area of your life. If not, you probably would not be reading this book. So let's find out what is involved in serving Christ. I want to suggest seven ways that we should serve Him, seven attitudes that will help us honor and please the Lord in our Christian service.

WE SHOULD SERVE
CHRIST SACRIFICIALLY

We know that Christ's service was sacrificial, because it took Him to the Cross. His goal is that our service be sacrificial too. As Jesus looked toward the Cross, He made this statement:

Truly, truly, I say to you, unless a grain of wheat falls into the earth and dies, it remains by itself alone; but if it dies, it bears much fruit. He who loves his life loses it; and he who hates his life in this world shall keep it to life eternal. If anyone serves Me, let him follow Me; and where I am, there shall My servant also be; if anyone serves Me, the Father will honor him. (John 12:24–26)

Jesus used an illustration from agriculture, which was very familiar to His listeners, to explain what He meant by an attitude of sacrificial service.

We Must Die in Order to Live

Just as the grain of wheat planted in the ground must burst open and thus "die" to produce a harvest, so death was the means of a great harvest—both for Him and for His followers. Here is a biblical principle that seems like a paradox: We must die in order to live.

Jesus was speaking first of His own death, because it is by His death that we have life. If Jesus had not died, we would be spiritually dead. But the same principle is true for His servants. If we try to hold on to our individual "grain," our lives, by living for ourselves, we will eventually lose our lives. But if we are willing to die to ourselves and our agenda in service to Christ, we will produce all manner of bountiful spiritual fruit.

This is the paradox of sacrifice. Jesus said anyone who wants to serve Him must follow Him. Where was He going when He said that? To the cross to die.

You say, "Well, that was Christ. It was God's will that Jesus take up His cross and sacrifice His life." That's true, but guess what? It's God's will for us too. Jesus said, "If anyone wishes to come after Me, let him deny himself, and take up his cross *daily,* and follow Me" (Luke 9:23, italics added).

God has a calling on each of our lives, which will vary in

the details from person to person. But all of us have been called to take up our cross. The cross means death—and if there is no death, there will be no life. You can't serve the way Jesus served if you are too busy trying to look out for yourself.

The Bible describes the life we have in Christ as eternal life. When you hear that, you may think of heaven. But eternal life refers to more than the length of life. It has to do with the quality of our existence here on earth. Eternal life begins the moment we receive Christ as Savior, and He intends that we experience a quality of life now whereby we grow in Him, find His purpose, and produce a full harvest of spiritual fruit.

The Nature of Our Death

Paul gave us a clear picture of what it means to die in order that we might live, to serve Christ in such a sacrificial way that we give up our lives for Him.

The verse I want to examine is a familiar one. Because it is so familiar we may miss its full impact:

> I have been crucified with Christ; and it is no longer I who live, but Christ lives in me; and the life which I now live in the flesh I live by faith in the Son of God, who loved me, and delivered Himself up for me. (Galatians 2:20)

It is obvious that Paul was very much alive when he wrote this potent verse—and yet he had experienced a crucifixion. So he was not talking about physical death.

Instead, Paul died to his own identity—his rights, plans, goals, desires, and dreams. They were subjected to Christ so completely it was as if Paul were dead. His life was so immersed in sacrificial service to the Lord that he could say, "Christ lives in me."

In other words, Paul gave Christ the freedom to live out His life through him. Paul's hands became Jesus' hands. Paul's feet walked where Jesus told them to go. Paul's mind operated in concert with the mind of Christ.

That's what it means to die to self. Jesus demands this of His servants, and He is the great example who prayed in the Garden of Gethsemane, "Not as I will, but as Thou wilt" (Matthew 26:39).

In Galatians 2:20 Paul also said he now lived "by faith in

the Son of God." His life was a daily faith walk. So is ours. As Christ's servants we may not always know where He is going to lead us—but that's not really our concern. After all, a servant doesn't tell his master what to do and where to go. All we need to know is that we have entrusted our lives to Christ, and we can trust Him to take us where we need to be.

This may sound easy to some people, but the fact is that it is hard for us to trust someone else this completely. It flies in the face of human nature, especially if we have been burned by trusting other people.

That's why being Christ's servant requires dying to the old life with its old prejudices and fears and worries. Jesus had to go to Calvary to fulfill His sacrificial service to God. Our job is to follow Him to the Cross. The words of martyred missionary Jim Elliot are still true: "He is no fool who gives what he cannot keep to gain what he cannot lose."

A Daily Commitment

Notice how the Cross keeps showing up in Galatians 2:20. Paul ended the verse by referring to Christ's sacrificial death for us on the cross. It was the Cross that motivated Paul to give himself in sacrificial service. It is because so many Christians don't fully understand the meaning of the Cross that they still live for themselves.

Jesus said in Luke 9:23 that we must take up our cross "daily." This isn't a onetime deal. We must renew our commitment to Christ each day. We should begin our day with this prayer: "Lord Jesus, I present myself to You today as Your servant. I die to myself and deliver all of myself to You for Your will to be done in me today."

This is the prayer of a person who is willing to die daily for Christ, who understands that a seed has to die to produce its harvest.

You say, "Tony, death sounds like a costly commitment." It is, but here's the good news: When you die to yourself for the sake of Jesus Christ, you will start living more fully than you have ever lived before. Remember, the person who loses his life for Christ is the one who finds it again.

When God called Moses to deliver the Israelites from Egypt, Moses objected. So God asked him, "What is that in your hand?" (Exodus 4:2). Moses was holding his shepherd's staff, so God told him, "Throw it on the ground" (v. 3). Moses did so, and it became a serpent.

Then God ordered Moses, "Stretch out your hand and grasp it by its tail" (v. 4). Moses obeyed, and the serpent became his staff again. But now, instead of being the staff of Moses, it was the staff of God.

Now that stick could be used to turn the waters of Egypt into blood, eat up the snakes of Egyptian magicians, and open the Red Sea. That ordinary shepherd's staff was charged with life because Moses gave it up to God.

So allow me to ask you, What is it God wants from you that you are still holding on to? Jesus said following Him means giving up our lives to Him. But when we do that, we will get them back charged with new life.

WE SHOULD SERVE
CHRIST AUTHENTICALLY

Our service for Christ also needs to be authentic. None of us serves Christ perfectly, but all of us can serve Christ authentically.

In Acts 20 we have a great picture of authentic service. Paul was on his way to Jerusalem when he called for the elders of the church at Ephesus to tell them good-bye and give them a final charge.

He began by reminding them, "You yourselves know, from the first day that I set foot in Asia, how I was with you the whole time, serving the Lord with all humility and with tears . . . [and] how I did not shrink from declaring to you anything that was profitable" (Acts 20:18–20).

Paul served Christ with authenticity. He didn't try to pretend he was a spiritual superman. The Ephesians knew his heart. They knew his strengths and weaknesses. Later he also told these elders that he had not coveted anyone's money or possessions (v. 33).

To another church Paul wrote, "We never came with flattering speech, as you know, nor with a pretext for greed—God is witness—nor did we seek glory from men. . . . But we proved to be gentle among you, as a nursing mother tenderly cares for her own children" (1 Thessalonians 2:5–7).

Paul's ministry was the real deal. We are not to serve Jesus Christ because of what we can get out of it. Our service should not be designed to advance ourselves and our agenda. As I said, authentic service doesn't mean perfect service. That's impossible. It means we are real.

So I need to ask you, Are you serving Christ authentically, or do you have another agenda working?

WE SHOULD SERVE CHRIST ENTHUSIASTICALLY

The psalmist wrote, "Shout joyfully to the Lord, all the earth. Serve the Lord with gladness; come before Him with joyful singing" (Psalm 100:1–2). That's enthusiastic, joyful ministry.

Paul repeated this concept when he told us that when it comes to serving Christ, we should "not [be] lagging behind in diligence, fervent in spirit, serving the Lord" (Romans 12:11). In other words, there should be some pep in your step as you serve the Lord!

Let's be honest. If most of us were serving someone who was paying us enough money, we would find a wellspring of energy and enthusiasm we didn't know we had! We would hop, skip, and jump to the job if the reward were great enough. Or if a person of great fame or power or stature called and asked us to serve on his or her staff, we would probably accept and serve with energy.

Well, the most important person in the universe has called us to serve Him, and He asks us to serve Him fervently, with some fire.

What would keep us from serving Jesus Christ that way? I think it can happen for several reasons. For example, when we forget whom we are serving we begin to perform in a perfunctory, routine way, just punching the Christian time clock every day as we go to work. We need to remember we are working for the King of kings and Lord of lords.

Our enthusiasm and energy for service can also drop when we serve others and they don't treat us right. But we never have to worry about that when we serve Jesus Christ.

A third reason our enthusiasm for service can sag is when our service gets ignored, taken for granted, or unrewarded. Again, no problem there when we serve the Lord. He said even a cold cup of water given in His name will bring His reward (Mark 9:41). When you serve Christ, it doesn't matter what anyone else does. He is the determiner of our reward.

The Bible gives us a revolutionary approach to our work, whatever type it is. "Whatever you do, do your work heartily [or enthusiastically], as for the Lord rather than for men" (Colossians 3:23). Take that attitude with you to work tomorrow or next week and see what it does for your service. Tell the Lord, "I am going to make this widget, type that letter, or deal with those clients for Your sake, since I am serving You."

At least two things will happen when you do that. First, it will change your outlook, which is half the battle anyway. And second, it gives the Lord the chance to be your Boss and determine your reward. And He is not a miserly Employer. He honors our fervent, enthusiastic service for Him.

WE SHOULD SERVE CHRIST RELATIONALLY

This is the fourth aspect of our service for Jesus Christ. By serving Him relationally I mean that we need to make sure our service for Him doesn't outpace our walk with Him. In other words, service is not meant to replace relationship.

The Importance of Our First Love

When Christ wrote His letter to the church at Ephesus (Revelation 2:1–7), He said, "I know your deeds and your toil and perseverance" (v. 2). These people were servants *par excellence.*

But there was a problem. "I have this against you, that you have left your first love" (v. 4). This church was full of hardworking Christians, but their service had become a substitute for their love for Him.

All of us know how easily that can happen. We can become so busy doing things for Christ that we have no time to spend with Him. The result is the loss of that intimacy Jesus desires to have with us.

We need to have balance. We can't use relationships as an excuse for failing to fulfill our responsibilities. A man can't legitimately say, for example, "I can't go to work because I don't want to leave my wife." He is going to have to leave his honey sometime to make some money! On the other hand, responsibilities are real, but they should not be allowed to overwhelm the relationship.

Putting Things in Perspective

One of the classic biblical examples of this principle is the familiar story of Jesus' visit to the home of Mary and Martha for dinner (Luke 10:38–42).

You may recall the scene. Jesus and the disciples dropped by for a meal at the house in Bethany. It was one of His favorite places, because He loved Mary and Martha and their brother Lazarus. Mary sat down at Jesus' feet to hear His words, while Martha was sweating and steaming in the kitchen.

Finally, Martha blew a fuse and came storming up to Jesus. "Lord, do You not care that my sister has left me to do all the serving alone? Then tell her to help me" (v. 40). This woman was steamed.

But Jesus answered, "Martha, Martha, you are worried and bothered about so many things; but only a few things are necessary, really only one, for Mary has chosen the good part, which shall not be taken away from her" (vv. 41–42).

I know exactly what was happening. Martha was cooking some fried chicken for Jesus and the disciples. (It had to be fried chicken because Jesus was a preacher!) She also had potato salad, green beans, nice hot bread, and iced tea going at the same time because she had a bunch of preachers to feed that day.

But as she was running around in the kitchen it suddenly dawned on Martha that the last time she remembered, she *and* Mary had invited Jesus for dinner, not just her. But now, Mary was nowhere to be found. So Martha became evangelically ticked off. She was very upset and vented her frustration on Jesus.

In other words, Martha's service for Jesus had not only spoiled her attitude toward Mary, at whom she was very angry, but it had soured her relationship with Jesus. She chewed Him out, accusing Him of not caring. This woman was not having fun.

Let me tell you, that's what happens when service overrules relationship. The service loses its joy. It isn't fun anymore.

The problem was not that Jesus didn't care about the situation. The problem was that Martha wasn't around Him long enough that day to find out that He did care. In fact, Jesus cared so much I'm sure He would have been happy with just a casserole, if that's what it took to get her out of the kitchen and sitting with Him where Mary was.

You see, the solution to this mess was not to send Mary into the kitchen too. Then there would have been two frustrated women in the house. The solution was to have Martha scale down the menu to one dish if necessary so she would be free to spend time with the Lord. That's what He wanted, not a big meal.

Jesus didn't tell Martha to forget the dinner and sit down. It was OK for her to do something, but it was not OK for that something to push the Lord out of the picture. After all, this meal was supposed to be in His honor.

How many times have we told ourselves we'll spend more time with Jesus next week, after the big project at work is done and the pressure is off? Or next month, when things settle down at home. Somehow, next week or next month never comes. And in the meantime the pressure inside us is building up as our relationship with Christ goes south.

When some believers feel this pressure, they try to compensate for it by redoubling the intensity of their service. But that only makes things worse, and eventually they explode.

So the principle is, don't allow your service for Christ to overwhelm your relationship with Him. Make time to be in His presence, sitting at His feet, listening to His Word.

WE SHOULD SERVE
CHRIST EXPECTANTLY

What does it mean to serve Christ expectantly? Jesus explained this in Luke 12:35–38:

> Be dressed in readiness, and keep your lamps alight. And be like men who are waiting for their master when he returns from the wedding feast, so that they may immediately open the door to him when he comes and knocks. Blessed are those slaves whom the master shall find on the alert when he comes; truly I say to you, that he will gird himself to serve, and have them recline at table, and will come up and wait on them. Whether he comes in the

second watch, or even in the third, and finds them so, blessed are those slaves.

This is an incredible passage of Scripture. It is a complete reversal of roles for a master to wait on his servants. But that's what Jesus promises to His servants who watch eagerly for Him to return, no matter how late He may come.

In Jesus' day a bridegroom had dinner with his friends, then went to the home of his bride to claim her before returning to his own house. So it could be late when he arrived, even the wee hours of the morning. But his servants needed to be ready to let him and his bride in and wait on them.

This is a picture of Jesus our Bridegroom, who is coming back someday. We are told to expect Him at any time. Serving Christ expectantly means serving with one eye on the sky and one ear listening for the trumpet.

In other words, the point is to be ready. This can also apply to our own home going. Whether we meet Jesus "here, there, or in the air," as the saying goes, we should be ready.

So the question is, Are you ready to meet the Lord? I'm not talking about your salvation, but your service. Are there things you need to settle between you and the Lord, or between you and someone else? Are important things left undone, or are you looking expectantly for Jesus?

Jesus' promise for His alert and expectant servants is that they will be served by their Master. This is referring to the great kingdom rewards awaiting those who serve Christ faithfully.

This has nothing to do with your earthly status, by the way. If you live every day in the light of Jesus' coming, you are in for a grand reward in eternity whether or not you receive honor here in history.

WE SHOULD SERVE
CHRIST DEPENDENTLY

This principle may sound redundant, since by definition a servant is a dependent person. But it's important that we understand what the Bible means by dependent service.

The apostle Peter wrote, "As each one has received a special gift, employ it in serving one another, as good stewards of the manifold grace of God" (1 Peter 4:10). Notice one of the ways Peter applied this truth. "Whoever serves, let him do so as by the strength which God supplies; so that in all things God may be glorified through Jesus Christ" (v. 11).

Peter said that as we serve one another, which is actually serving Christ, we need to do so leaning on the strength God supplies. I would remind you that Jesus said, "Apart from Me you can do nothing" (John 15:5).

What does it mean to serve in God's strength? Peter gives us the key at the end of verse 10. The key is to live a life based on grace.

Grace is God's unmerited favor. It is God doing for us what we couldn't do for ourselves. Grace is recognizing our total dependence on the Lord to pull off any service He asks us to perform.

Most Christians do not really understand grace, so they feel this tension between law and grace. We know God has rules He wants us to obey. Yet grace is the foundation that gives us the power and motivation to obey.

Many times as we try to serve Christ we have to come to Him and confess, "Lord, I don't want to do what You want me to do." Or, "Lord, You know I don't have the strength to do what You want me to do."

But then because of His grace we can say, "Despite how I feel, I will depend on You to give me what I don't have on my own so I can accomplish Your will." When you lean on God's strength—which is to say, His grace—you discover His supply. That's why Peter's desire for believers is, "May grace . . . be yours in fullest measure" (1 Peter 1:2).

So if we are going to serve Christ, we need to serve Him in the strength He supplies. And I can tell you, there is nothing like seeing God give you the ability to do something you could not possibly have done without Him.

WE SHOULD SERVE
CHRIST SELFLESSLY

The seventh and final principle I want to talk about is the selflessness of serving Christ. This brings us back full circle to the concept of sacrificial service, but here I want to look at it from a slightly different perspective.

A Grab for Honor

The discussion of selfless service came up among Jesus and the disciples one day when the mother of James and John approached Jesus with a request. "Command that in Your kingdom these two sons of mine may sit, one on Your right and one on Your left" (Matthew 20:21).

Mrs. Zebedee was looking out for her boys. She wanted to make sure they had the places of honor in the kingdom. "But Jesus answered and said, 'You do not know what you are asking for. Are you able to drink the cup that I am about to drink?' They said to Him, 'We are able.' He said to them, 'My cup you shall drink; but to sit on My right and on My left, this is not Mine to give, but it is for those for whom it has been prepared by My Father'" (vv. 22–23).

The Priority of Service

This is the background to the part of the story I want to focus on. The other ten disciples got mad at James and John when they heard this request, probably because they wished they had thought of it first. So there was anger among the Twelve when Jesus called them together for a lesson in selfless service:

> You know that the rulers of the Gentiles lord it over them, and their great men exercise authority over them. It is not so among you, but whoever wishes to become great among you shall be your servant, and whoever wishes to be first among you shall be your slave; just as the Son of Man did not come to be served, but to serve, and to give His life a ransom for many. (vv. 25–28)

What Jesus did here was turn the world's idea of greatness on its head. If you want to soar high in His kingdom, you do so by going low. If you want the first place in line at His table, you go to the back of the line. You don't exalt yourself by lording it over others. You serve them as their slave and wait for God to exalt you.

So the question is, Whom have you served lately? What have you done for others to better them, help them, and encourage them—even to your own hurt, if necessary? When you are a truly selfless servant, Jesus Christ takes note of it. As we saw earlier, He will make sure you are served.

We need to practice selfless service in our marriages and families. Here's a good exercise for a family or a married couple: Have a contest to see who can outserve the other person. If some husbands and wives would start having a contest like this, we would see some wounded marriages starting to heal. The reason is that in most troubled marriages, the problem is either one or two selfish people who want their own way.

What I am saying is make every day a day in which you seek at least one opportunity to do something for someone else, without expecting anything in return. Do this as unto the Lord, and your clout will grow in the kingdom.

The Greatest Example of Selfless Service

I want to close this chapter with a prime illustration of selfless service.

Jesus and the disciples were in the Upper Room, preparing for their last Passover together before Jesus would be crucified. Early in the evening, Jesus did an extraordinary thing:

> Jesus, knowing that the Father had given all things into His hands, and that He had come forth from God, and was going back to God, rose from supper, and laid aside His garments; and taking a towel, He girded Himself about. Then He poured water into the basin, and began to wash the disciples' feet, and to wipe them with the towel with which He was girded. (John 13:3–5)

Here was Jesus, the Lord of creation, doing the job a slave normally did in that day. It was the custom that when dinner guests arrived, a servant would be at the door with a basin of water and a towel to wash their feet after their walk through the dusty or muddy streets of Palestine in open sandals.

But there was no servant present in that room, and none of the Twelve was volunteering to do the job. So Jesus took the place of a servant (see Philippians 2:7).

How could Jesus do that? Because He knew who He was, and therefore His identity or worth was not threatened by doing the most menial of a servant's tasks. Also, the disciples

desperately needed the lesson He was about to teach them.
All was quiet until He came to Peter:

> And so He came to Simon Peter. He said to Him, "Lord,
> do You wash my feet?" Jesus answered and said to him,
> "What I do you do not realize now, but you shall under-
> stand hereafter." Peter said to Him, "Never shall You wash
> my feet!" Jesus answered him, "If I do not wash you, you
> have no part with Me." Simon Peter said to Him, "Lord,
> not my feet only, but also my hands and my head." Jesus
> said to him, "He who has bathed needs only to wash his
> feet, but is completely clean." (John 13:6–10)

Since we are focusing primarily on Jesus' selfless act of
service here, let me summarize the exchange between Him
and Peter.

Peter's objection was based on the fact that this was all
backward. Jesus was the Lord; He wasn't supposed to be
doing this. Peter was saying, "Jesus, You don't have to do
this. This isn't Your job. I'm not going to let You embarrass
Yourself by washing my feet."

But Jesus' answer startled Peter, and he promptly asked
for a bath! Jesus said a bath was not necessary because spiritually speaking, Peter was already clean, already saved. But
what he needed to do was let Jesus cleanse his daily walk,
which is what feet are a symbol of.

There's a great lesson for us here. We walk in a dirty world
every day, and some of the dirt rubs off on us. We need to let
Jesus get close enough to us so He can keep our lives clean.

When Jesus had finished His task and taken His place at
the table again, He brought home the lesson of servanthood:

> Do you know what I have done to you? You call Me
> Teacher and Lord; and you are right, for so I am. If I then,
> the Lord and the Teacher, washed your feet, you also ought
> to wash one another's feet. For I gave you an example that
> you also should do as I did to you. (John 13:12–15)

The logic of Jesus' point is inescapable. If He was willing
to humble Himself to perform an act of selfless service for us,
how can we refuse to serve a brother or sister in the same
way? Answer: We can't, not if we want to be like Jesus.

We must be willing to serve each other. And by the way, when you wash someone else's feet—that is, when you serve another person—don't let the water be too hot or too cold. If you wash a fellow believer with boiling water, you are going to scald that person. Some of us do that in our service. We serve, but we don't like it. We do it grudgingly and with lots of grumbling. We can also serve with the water too cold—with an attitude of indifference.

Jesus' Offer to Judas

Jesus performed one other act of selfless service that evening at the Last Supper.

Later in the meal He predicted His betrayal by one of the Twelve. While they were wondering who it was, John asked, "Lord, who is it?" (John 13:25).

Jesus said, "'That is the one for whom I shall dip the morsel and give it to him.' So when He had dipped the morsel, He took and gave it to Judas, the son of Simon Iscariot. And after the morsel, Satan then entered into him. Jesus therefore said to him, 'What you do, do quickly'" (vv. 26–27). This is one of the great acts of servanthood in the Bible. Let me summarize it.

The morsel Jesus prepared for Judas was a piece of the Passover lamb wrapped in flour and rolled together. It would be dipped in sauce made of bitter herbs and eaten.

Why did Jesus prepare a morsel and offer it to Judas? In the greatest act of servanthood ever, Jesus was offering Judas one more chance.

Jesus offered Judas a piece of the sacrificial lamb. Who was Jesus? The Lamb of God who would be sacrificed to take away the sins of the world. Jesus was offering Judas Himself. He was saying, "Judas, here I am. Do you want Me?" Judas took the morsel, but in his heart he said no to Jesus and Satan took over.

How far are we to go in selflessly serving others? As far as Jesus went. And how far did He go? He gave His life even for those who said no to Him.

We are back to the issue of sacrificial service to the point of death, so that we might truly live and offer life to others. Are you serving Christ with every ounce of your being? If not, you are missing out on real life!

CHAPTER TWENTY-THREE
NEEDING CHRIST

A man was eating dinner in a restaurant one evening when he noticed a couple at a nearby table eating dessert. Each time the woman took a bite of her dessert, a look of delight and satisfaction came over her face. It was obvious she was thoroughly enjoying her chosen dessert. But as the man ate his dessert, his face reflected disgust with each bite he took.

The man at the other table who was watching this little scene unfold was preparing to order dessert himself. He decided he had better find out what the man he was watching was eating so he could be sure to avoid it, and what the woman was enjoying because he might want to order the same thing.

So he called the waiter over and said, "Can you tell me what desserts the man and woman at that table ordered? I want to order the same dessert she has."

The waiter looked at the man with surprise and said, "But, sir, they're both having the same dessert."

This illustrates the way many of us approach the Christian life. Every believer has the same dessert, so to speak. All of us have the good things of Christ before us.

Some Christians plunge into these spiritual delicacies with delight and gusto. In the terminology of Scripture, they are pursuing Christ with all of their hearts, souls, minds, and strength. You can see their joy on their faces. But other believers aren't getting much out of their walk with the Lord. They're sort of scowling their way through the Christian life.

The problem, of course, is internal, because there is nothing wrong with the fare Jesus Christ has for us.

My desire throughout this book has been to stimulate your appetite for Christ, so that you leave these pages with a good taste in your mouth and a new smile on your face—not because of my words, but because God the Holy Spirit used His Word to open your life to the sweetness of knowing and following Christ.

That is my goal in this chapter too. And given the opening illustration about eating, it is appropriate that we are going to look at a familiar passage that deals with the subject of bearing sweet, ripe spiritual fruit . . . and the extent to which we need Jesus Christ to produce that harvest.

THE TOTALITY OF
OUR NEED FOR JESUS CHRIST

I'm talking about John 15, in which Jesus Christ states a profound truth:

> I am the true vine, and My Father is the vinedresser. Every branch in Me that does not bear fruit, He takes away; and every branch that bears fruit, He prunes it, that it may bear more fruit. You are already clean because of the word which I have spoken to you. Abide in Me, and I in you. As the branch cannot bear fruit of itself, unless it abides in the vine, so neither can you, unless you abide in Me. I am the vine, you are the branches; he who abides in Me, and I in him, he bears much fruit; *for apart from Me you can do nothing.* (John 15:1–5, italics added)

John 15:5 is one of the "Mount Everest" statements in the Bible. In the same sentence, Jesus both established the totality of our inability to do anything in our own power and offered us all the provision we will ever need to do anything.

Paul put it this way in Philippians 4:13: "I can do all things through Him who strengthens me."

Believing Jesus' Words

It's one thing to read the words, "Apart from Me you can do nothing." But it's another thing to believe them and live as if you believe them.

Plainly stated, a lot of Christians do not believe they can accomplish nothing apart from Jesus Christ. They may nod in agreement when they hear this passage read in church, but then they go back home and continue their "do-it-yourself" brand of Christianity.

They may believe that *some* Christians can do nothing without Christ, or that this may be true of other Christians. But in their deepest hearts they don't believe attachment to Christ is absolutely necessary for them. They don't see the extent of their need for Christ.

And judging by some of the substitutes that even Christians sometimes turn to for help, such as alcohol or drugs or material goods, it seems even more obvious that not everyone who claims to follow Jesus really believes His statement that we are utterly powerless without Him.

If you want a visible demonstration of what Jesus meant, and if you want to see firsthand the impact of His statement in John 15:5, try this experiment. Clip a healthy branch from a fruit tree or a grapevine, and lay it on your back porch or patio. Make sure that branch gets plenty of sunshine. Water it regularly as it lies there. Then watch to see whether it produces sweet, mature fruit when the season arrives, or whether it withers and dies. We both know what will happen.

Our Attachment to the Vine

That's a pretty simple experiment. But it will show you exactly how much you need Jesus Christ. You and I will get nowhere in our Christian lives unless we "abide" in the vine. That means staying attached to Jesus.

When we see an apple tree loaded with ripe fruit ready for harvest, we understand that what is visible to us is not the whole story. The explanation for the apple tree's productivity lies below the ground in a root system that, while it may be invisible to us, is supporting the tree and supplying it with the nutrients it needs. Without this invisible connection, the visible tree is of no value.

It's the same with other parts of nature. Our rivers are full of water because of snowcapped mountains many miles away that melt in the spring. We may not see where the water is coming from, but without it the rivers will dry up.

Similarly, our greatest need in life is not what we can see, but what we cannot see—our vital attachment to Jesus Christ. Unless we abide in Him, unless our invisible relationship with Christ is as solid and growing as branches attached to a vine, our visible life will be a mess.

But detachment is not what Jesus wants for us. He used the illustration of the vine and branches to describe our life in Him because He wants us to bear fruit. He wants us to live productive Christian lives.

THE NECESSITY OF
ABIDING IN CHRIST

For the most part, people in the world don't want to hear about their inability to do anything. They want to move out, not abide. That's why those self-help and take-charge and get-rich "infomercials" on TV are so popular. The world defines success in life in terms of power and wealth and status.

But for us as Christians, the key to success—what the Bible calls fruitfulness—is not in achieving, but in abiding. Jesus said in John 15:6, "If anyone does not abide in Me, he is thrown away as a branch, and dries up." That's what happens to a believer who is severed from intimate fellowship with Christ.

Have you ever felt dry in your walk with Christ? Has your heart ever felt dusty and distant from the Lord? If you are dry, it may be because you have forgotten how much you need Christ and, as a result, you are not really abiding in Him.

The Key to Fruitfulness

It won't surprise you to learn that the Greek word for *abide* means to remain or stay. The concept of abiding is to have and maintain an intimate relationship with Christ.

Let's not forget that Jesus is the One who said we need to abide in Him to do anything. In other words, He is inviting us to abide in Him. He is seeking intimate fellowship with us.

It is my observation that Christians find it harder to abide than they do to perform. A lot of us are performance-driven. We like to get stuff done. But performance without intimacy doesn't work in settings that are designed for relationship, such as marriage. A relationship in which the intimacy, the connectedness, has gone out the window can be a very cold relationship. Just as in marriage, it is possible to perform for Christ and yet not really know Him.

This was the situation that took place with the older brother in Jesus' famous story of the prodigal son (Luke 15:11–32). The prodigal definitely failed to abide in his father's house and his father's love. He went to a "distant country" and wasted his money on "loose living" (v. 13).

When the prodigal got sick of himself, he came home and reconnected to the father. But his older brother got very upset that the father had welcomed his younger brother and restored him to intimate fellowship.

The older brother said to his father, "For so many years I have been serving you, and I have never neglected a command of yours; and yet you have never given me a kid, that I might be merry with my friends" (v. 29).

But his father said, "My child, you have always been with me, and all that is mine is yours. But we had to be merry and rejoice, for this brother of yours was dead and has begun to live, and was lost and has been found" (vv. 31–32).

This father, who represents God, was saying, "Son, you could have had a party with me anytime, but you never wanted it. You've been around here all these years and have taken our relationship for granted. I've been waiting for you to need me, but you never have. But your brother needs me, and he realizes he needs me. He wants an intimate relationship with me."

Now don't misunderstand. As I said in an earlier chapter, there are things we must do in our relationship with Christ. There is room for performance and service, but not at the sacrifice of our abiding in Him.

In fact, Christ has so arranged things that abiding in Him is not simply a nice option. It is an absolute necessity. We can't do anything when we are severed from Him.

A Real-Life Example of Abiding

Every once in a while it's good to step outside the borders of our comfortable world and see how Christians in other cultures and other lands live out their faith in Christ.

I have made a number of trips overseas, and I want to tell you briefly about a trip to Nigeria I made not too long ago. I was deeply affected by the example I saw of people who know what it means to need Christ and abide in Him.

I ministered in several churches in Nigeria, large fellow-ships of six to ten thousand people. I remember one day in Lagos, Nigeria's capital. No gasoline was available in the city that day for whatever reason. And then it began to storm, with terrible thunder and lightning.

I was due to speak at a church that day, but I just assumed that no gas and bad weather would equal an empty church. (Obviously, I was thinking like an American!) But when we got to the service, ten thousand people were there.

The pastor, whom the people there call "Daddy," told me some of the people had walked two and three hours to get here. Sunday school started at 7:30 A.M., with the worship ser-vice beginning at 8:30. At 1:00 P.M., we were still going strong.

It was an incredible atmosphere of worship and celebra-tion. The people would celebrate and praise God for a while, enter into prayer, and then celebrate and dance before the Lord again. I was able to practice my "praise jam"!

While all of this was happening, the ushers walked up and down the aisles with sticks, looking for people who were nodding off. No sleeping was allowed in God's presence, so they poked anyone who was sleeping. And even after about five hours of worship and two sermons, they could hardly get the people to go.

Later, the pastor and I talked about this phenomenon. He said, "Things are a lot different here than in the States. We need God. If God does not show up, we are a devastated people.

"You see, our people are relying on God for their daily bread. Most of them don't have refrigerators. They live one day at a time. There is such a desperate need for God here that every time there is an opportunity to come face-to-face with Him in His presence, our people take advantage of it.

"Our church doesn't have to compete with television and sports and all the other things you have to compete with in America. We need God here, and we see one miracle after another. We see Him intervene supernaturally, because we need Him."

I saw authentic Christianity in action in Nigeria. A baby had been left on the doorstep of this church, presumably by a mother who could not care for her child. That baby imme-diately had a father and a mother, because the family of God took over. There was such a passion for God that this life was held precious.

At one of the churches, the pastor said they were trying to decide whether to build a larger facility. They purchased the land for it, but in Nigeria there is no such thing as a bank loan to build a church. The people have to build out of their own resources. I asked the pastor where the money was going to come from.

He told me, "Pastor Evans, it will not be difficult. We don't have to beg or pull the money out of our people. We need God so much here that building Him a house is no problem. All we have to do is ask the people to give."

Reflecting the Glory of God

"Our people need God," that pastor in Nigeria had said. That's the difference between what I saw in Nigeria and what is so often the case in Christianity here in the West.

Our problem is we don't sense our desperate need for the Lord because we have so many things to distract us. And because we don't understand the totality of our need for Christ, abiding in Him every moment is not that big of a deal to us. Why trust Christ when you have American Express?

I'm speaking in general terms, but the observation holds true. If we were honest, many of us would have to admit that deep at heart, we have gotten used to living without daily dependence on Jesus Christ. We are independent Christians.

It's not that we don't do "maintenance" on the relationship. Many people give a "nod to God" every week at church and say a prayer a day to keep the devil away. But that's a far cry from needing Christ so desperately that we *have* to abide in Him.

How can we explain the fact that Christians such as those in Nigeria, who don't have a fraction of the things we have, are enjoying intimacy with the Lord and seeing Him provide in ways many of us only dream about? Why does one person walk two hours to church to worship the Lord, while another person can't seem to make it with two cars in the garage?

Needing Christ, abiding in Him, is the difference. To put it in biblical terms, those Nigerian Christians are people who are "beholding as in a mirror the glory of the Lord, [and] are being transformed into the same image from glory to glory" (2 Corinthians 3:18). Their faces reflected the glory of God.

Some Probing Questions

We need to ask ourselves some probing questions in light of what Jesus said about the necessity of abiding in Him. The first question is whether we really believe we are helpless and cut off apart from Christ. If we do, it will make a difference, starting today, in how we live.

Let's also ask ourselves why we do the Christian things we do. Are they done from a sense of duty, or because we want to be in the Lord's presence beholding His face, realizing that without Him we can do nothing? When we start abiding in Christ, things start happening.

THE BENEFITS OF ABIDING IN CHRIST

We've been talking about how needy we are, and in the world's view being needy and weak is not a good thing. But for the Christian, learning how needy we are and where the true power of the Christian life is found brings powerful results.

Answered Prayer

Look at the promise Jesus made to those who abide in Him. "If you abide in Me, and My words abide in you, ask whatever you wish, and it shall be done for you" (John 15:7).

The power of the abider is the power of answered prayer. No greater power is available to us in this life than the ability to take our requests to God and see Him work. Without Christ we can do nothing. But remember the other side of the equation: We can do all things through Christ, because He has promised to strengthen us.

Christ's Guidance

Another benefit of abiding in Christ is that you experience His supernatural guidance in a way you may never have experienced it before.

Use your imagination for a moment. Suppose you were an explorer, hacking your way through a thick jungle looking for a particular road that led to an ancient city you wanted to investigate.

You are cutting your way through the thick foliage when you come upon a small campsite. The man sitting by his tent asks where you are going, and you explain your mission. Then he says, "I have traveled through this jungle many times. I know the way to the road you are talking about, and I am heading in that same direction. I will be happy to lead the way for you."

But you, being a self-reliant explorer and traveler, say, "No thanks. I can find the way by myself." And so you set off, with him following behind you on the trail.

After a while you get a little off track, so you turn around and ask this man for his help in getting back on the right trail. He shows you, but then you go off alone again trying to clear your own path.

As you travel you keep running into this man, and the two of you start to get acquainted. You realize by now that he really does know the right trail, and he knows it a lot better than you do. You've gotten lost several times, so finally you turn around and say to him, "This really would be a much smoother trip if you took over and guided me." So he moves from behind you to in front of you, and he leads you flawlessly despite all the dense underbrush.

Many of us are trying to clear our own path in the Christian life, but we keep getting lost because we've never been this way before. And all the time Jesus Christ is behind us saying, "If you will abide in Me and let Me lead, I will show you the way."

That's exactly what we need to do.

Christ's Provision

I had one other experience in Nigeria that I want to tell you about, because it illustrates so well the way Jesus Christ provides for us when we acknowledge our need of Him and thus make it a priority to abide in Him.

One of the pastors at our church in Dallas, Dr. Sonny Acho, is from Nigeria. He was with us on the trip, and we were visiting the country village where he was born.

We had to leave the village in time to get back to the capital of Lagos so we could board our flight home. But the car we were in came up with a flat tire—and the spare tire was flat too. So we were stuck.

We found out that farther up the road lived a man who

could fix flat tires. We made it to his place and got the tire fixed, knowing we were going to be late for our flight.

But as we prepared to leave the village, a young woman came to see Pastor Acho. She was his niece, and she needed to talk to him about something very important. She had walked to his family's house, not knowing if he was still there or had left. She was praying that she would get to see him before he went back to America.

So the flat tire, which to us was merely an aggravation and an inconvenience, was for this young woman an answer to prayer, since we would not have been there otherwise. But God was not finished providing.

We got to the airport in Lagos five minutes before our flight was scheduled to leave. The airport people were willing to help us get on the plane, but we had an additional problem. Another vehicle carrying three members of our group had not arrived yet. We didn't know what to do except to keep moving, so we ran to the gate and boarded the plane. The other three people finally arrived, but by now the door of the plane was closed and they were preparing for departure. We were really desperate now.

One of our church members who was on the trip, a flight attendant for Delta Airlines, went to the pilot and interceded for the three people left at the gate. Three seats were available, but the pilot told this woman that once the door of the airplane was closed, it couldn't be reopened.

She continued to intercede, however, and he changed his mind. The plane circled back, the door was opened, and our three friends were taken on board. But even that isn't the end of the story. The three available seats were up front, in first class!

Do you get my point? If we ever get connected with Christ, if we can ever learn to abide in Him, He will be happy to turn things around and open doors to get us on board. And when He gets us on board, He will seat us up front, near Himself!

My prayer for you and for myself is that we might learn to abide in Christ. How can we do that? By making time to be in His presence so He can speak to us and we can hear and understand what He is saying to us.

This kind of abiding doesn't happen just once. It has to become a day-by-day habit. Once you and I grasp how total our need for Christ is, the desire and the commitment to abide in Him will be there.

CHAPTER TWENTY-FOUR
TRUSTING CHRIST

One Christmas when I was a boy my father bought me one of those punching bags that bounce back up when you hit them. You probably know the kind of toy I'm talking about. No matter how hard I hit that punching bag, even if I knocked it all the way to the floor, that thing would always bounce back up ready for the next blow. If I hit it one hundred times, it bounced back up one hundred times. Even if I knocked it across the room, it always came back up.

The secret to the punching bag's resilience, of course, was the weight in the bottom of the inflated balloon. The weight stabilized and controlled the bag no matter what kind of blows landed against it.

That child's punching bag is a good parable of life. Reality hits pretty hard sometimes. Family problems can knock us to the floor. Financial woes stagger us, and we lean hard to one side. Discouragement comes along and knocks us halfway across the room.

These things happen to everyone, Christians included. The difference between the believer who bounces back up after a blow and the one who stays flat on the floor is not that one person is stronger, smarter, or richer than the other. And the difference is certainly not that God favors the "bounce back" Christian over the flattened Christian. He loves all of His children equally.

Instead, I want to suggest that the difference between the

believer who comes back and the one who doesn't is the size of the "weight" that is anchoring their lives.

Jesus Christ is the only person strong enough and "heavy" enough to anchor your life. Since every Christian has equal access to the power and authority of Christ, I want to go a step further. The difference between a Christian who isn't held down by anything and a Christian who is held down by everything is found in the answer to a simple question. In fact, let me ask you that question right now: How fully are you trusting Christ?

My prayer and hope is that in this final chapter of the book I can help you grasp some biblical principles that will help you learn to trust Christ in a fuller, deeper, and more dynamic way than you ever have before. I want to help you add a new stability to your life so that no matter what kinds of circumstances hit you, you can bounce back up and keep going. Let's talk about what it means to trust Jesus.

TRUST JESUS TO KEEP YOU FOCUSED

Your focus in life is all-important. I know that's not a new concept to you, but I want to say it one more time precisely because it *is* so crucial. The author of Hebrews had something to tell us about our focus:

> Therefore, since we have so great a cloud of witnesses surrounding us, let us also lay aside every encumbrance, and the sin which so easily entangles us, and let us run with endurance the race that is set before us, fixing our eyes on Jesus, the author and perfecter of faith, who for the joy set before Him endured the cross, despising the shame, and has sat down at the right hand of the throne of God. For consider Him who has endured such hostility by sinners against Himself, so that you may not grow weary and lose heart. (Hebrews 12:1–3)

You may remember that the book of Hebrews was written to a group of Jewish Christians who were getting punched from every side and were thinking about staying on the floor instead of getting up again. They were thinking about throwing in the towel on their faith because of persecution and suffering. They were considering going back to Judaism.

But the author wrote to tell them not to quit, but to look to Jesus and trust Him for the strength they needed to continue.

Thank Jesus for His Witnesses

One way the Hebrews could strengthen their faith was to look around them and see the special "cheering section" God had given them to urge them on to victory. These are the witnesses referred to in Hebrews 12:1.

This chapter begins with the word "Therefore," which points us back to what has just been said. What is this "therefore" there for?

It's there to remind the readers that they had just been given a tour of God's "Hall of Faith." Hebrews 11 is a roll call of great men and women of faith who did not quit, but hung in there and gained the victory.

These people took the hardest blows the world, the flesh, and the devil could deliver, and they bounced back. They are there for us now, ready to testify in the pages of Scripture that if they could make it by the power of God, so can we.

Thank the Lord for witnesses like Abraham and Sarah and Moses and Rahab. We need to hear from them regularly. We need to be reminded we are not the first believers to be punched around a little bit.

When a preacher asks, "Can I get a witness?" he wants to know if there is anybody out there who knows what he is talking about, who can say, "I've been there, and I can tell you that if you trust Christ, He will see you through."

The author of Hebrews was saying, "I am about to state a major truth right now. Can I get a witness?" He wanted his readers to hear from people who had been where they were going.

Whenever I read this passage I picture a title bout in professional boxing. Before the match between the champion and the challenger begins, any number of special guests are introduced.

These are usually former boxing champions like Joe Frazier, Sugar Ray Leonard, and maybe Muhammad Ali—men who have been where the two boxers now stand. The announcer will introduce champion after champion, and each one will come into the ring, acknowledge the applause, and shake hands with each boxer.

These men are witnesses. By their presence they are saying to the two boxers, "I've been here. I fought the fight. I was battered and bruised and bloody, but I came out of the contest with the winner's belt around my waist. Don't get discouraged and quit when the fight gets tough, because you can win too."

When we are discouraged and want to quit, we need to hear from the Bible's witnesses, such as Abel (Hebrews 11:4), who took life's ultimate blow. He was murdered by his brother Cain, but because Abel was a righteous man God Himself still testified about his life after he was dead.

In Abel we have a witness that when we are faithful to the program of God, even death doesn't silence our testimony, because God keeps talking about us. So don't be afraid, because whether in life or death you are still on the winning side.

Here's another witness coming into the ring. Enoch was the only person in his generation who stayed so faithful to God that he did not "see death" (Hebrews 11:5). A little boy explained that Enoch and God were out walking one day and God said, "Enoch, we are closer to My house than to your house, so why don't you just come home with Me?"

The faithful deacon Stephen is not mentioned in Hebrews 11, but he gave a witness that's important here. Just before he was stoned to death, Stephen looked up into heaven and saw Jesus standing at the right hand of God as his welcoming committee into heaven (Acts 7:55–56). When you trust Christ with your life, you get to see Him before you die. That's why you don't have to be afraid of death.

How about the witness of Noah (Hebrews 11:7)? Noah had to build a boat on dry land and preach for 120 years to a congregation that wasn't listening. He only had one sermon: "It is going to rain."

It had never rained before. Noah didn't know what rain looked like. All he knew was that God told him to build a boat the length of three football fields on dry land. Noah worked during the day, he preached at night, and God delivered him and his family while the whole world was destroyed. I have a witness in Noah who says faithfulness to God will produce safety, even in the midst of a storm.

The writer of Hebrews went on to tell us about Abraham and Sarah (Hebrews 11:8–12). Even though they did not have the physical capability to produce a son, God did for them what they could never do for themselves. I have a witness that God can do miracles.

Then there was Moses (Hebrews 11:24–26), who was tempted by the luxuries of Egypt but decided to suffer with the people of God rather than to enjoy sin for a season. Moses is a witness that if you will live to please the Lord, it will be worth it all after all.

I could go on, just like the writer of Hebrews said he could keep going. But you get the point. Put your faith in Christ and stay true to Him. Look at His witnesses, and listen to their witness. Hang out with people who have run the race and won, not those who quit in the middle.

God has a hall of fame of witnesses, and everyone there earned his or her spot. Thank the Lord for His witnesses, and imitate their example.

Trust Jesus to Set You Free

As you learn what it means to trust Jesus Christ with every area of your life, you need to look at something else besides the witnesses around you. You need to trust Him to fix what needs fixing within yourself. You need to allow Christ to free you from the things that entangle you.

We read in Hebrews 12:1, "Let us also lay aside every encumbrance, and the sin which so easily entangles us."

The writer was using the metaphor of a runner here. No runner competes in the race with heavy weights tied around his ankles or with a heavy warm-up suit on. He strips down to the essentials of his running outfit, so he will carry no more weight than is absolutely necessary. Track uniforms are so thin and light that members of a track team used to be referred to as "thinclads."

We need to trust Christ to help us get rid of the things that can weigh us down in our Christian race. The Greek word for "entangles" means to ambush. That's a good picture of what happens when we try to run a race with all this stuff dragging us down. Let me suggest three entanglements or weights that can slow us down.

One weight is people who are negative and defeatist about everything, people who drag on us and discourage us. I'm not saying we can just shun people who have problems or need help. Not at all. I'm talking about the people we choose to spend time with and allow to influence us. We need to surround ourselves with people who are going to help us fulfill the calling God has given us.

Another thing that can entangle us and hold us back in the race is our past. The problem is that all of us have a past, even the most godly among us. And Satan knows where to find the stuff we buried and discarded yesterday.

Don't misunderstand. I'm not talking about sins or illegal things we did and tried to hide. I'm referring to choices we have all made that we wish we had not made or words we wish we had not said. The past can entangle us. We can spend so much time looking back at yesterday and regretting past mistakes that we become paralyzed today and unable to move on to tomorrow. We can spend so much time fretting over old failures that we never achieve any new successes.

My favorite analogy for Christians who let the past dominate them is the rearview mirror in a car. You can't drive while looking behind you all the time. You are going to hit another car or run over the curb or get in some kind of mess. You need to look through another piece of glass if you are going to drive successfully. It's called the windshield.

There's a reason your car's rearview mirror is very small while the windshield is very large. You need to glance quickly behind you on occasion, but you need to focus ahead of you on where you're going. Otherwise, you will get entangled in a traffic problem of your own making.

Here's a third potential entanglement: playthings. By that I mean the fun and games of life, the toys that can rob your faith of its vitality if you let them get out of hand. For many Christians the problem is too much television. It can be too much golf or too much time and energy invested in some other hobby. These things aren't wrong in themselves, but when the fun and games keep your Bible closed and keep you off your knees, those things become sin.

In fact, you'll notice that Hebrews 12:1 refers to "the sin" that entangles us. The sin is singular, not plural. Why?

Because everybody who is entangled is entangled by the same sin—which is unbelief. Notice that the chapter before this one focuses on what it takes to please God—which is faith. So here are the results for those who lack faith.

The sin of unbelief is the failure to trust Jesus Christ enough to act upon His Word. The failure to trust Him is at the root of every other failure we experience.

The sin of unbelief is like the college student who went to wash his clothes and tied all his clothes up in a sheet. He put the whole ball in the washing machine without untying the sheet and separating the clothes. So when he was done all he had was a big ball of wet, dirty clothes, because they were all bound up in the sheet.

In the final analysis, everything that's wrong in our lives is wrapped up in unbelief. Until we deal with that sin, we won't be able to get rid of the other sins that are bound up in it.

Your belief system is your willingness to obey Jesus Christ even when obeying Him is the last thing you want to do. The essence of trusting Christ is to obey Him, to take Him at His Word. That's why James 2:26 says, "Faith without works is dead."

We need to trust Jesus to deal with the sin of unbelief and set us free from its entanglement.

KEEP YOUR EYES ON JESUS

The writer of Hebrews had another excellent piece of advice for us when it comes to trusting Christ. We need to fix our eyes on Jesus (Hebrews 12:2).

The idea is to glance up in the bleachers once in a while, look at the witnesses, and draw strength from their testimony. Then glance at yourself as you seek to avoid entanglements. But don't fixate on yourself. That will give you a neurosis.

Our focus is to be fixed in one direction and one direction only: on Jesus. How do we know when we are keeping our life focused on Jesus and not the other stuff?

Keep Him in First Place

You know you're trusting Christ the way He wants you to trust Him when you keep Him in first place. That means not letting anyone or anything else supplant Him as the center of your worship, your service, and your love.

Several chapters ago we looked at the story of Jesus' visit to the home of Martha and Mary (Luke 10:38–42). Martha became so distracted and frustrated trying to prepare a big meal for Jesus and the disciples that her preparations became more important than sitting at Jesus' feet. But Mary chose to do this.

Martha's failure to put Jesus first that day caused a disruption in her horizontal relationships. She was ticked at Mary for leaving her in the kitchen to do all the work by herself.

But Martha also allowed her misplaced priorities to mess up her vertical relationship with Jesus. She accused Him of not caring about her and her problem.

Why should we keep our eyes on Jesus? Because He is "the author and perfecter of faith" (Hebrews 12:2). He is the Originator and the Completer of our faith.

That's like saying Jesus is the Alpha and the Omega, the first and last letters of the Greek alphabet. When the Bible says that, it includes everything in between. Jesus is the whole alphabet of our faith, everything we will ever need.

The English language only contains twenty-six letters. But if you were to go to the Library of Congress and peruse the millions of pages in its collection, you would find that all the English words in that library are made up of those twenty-six letters. They are all you need to tell a story, compose a love song, or write a multivolume encyclopedia.

Let Him Set the Pace

Since Jesus Christ is the beginning and end of our faith, and everything in between, the wisest thing we can do is trust Him to lead the way, to set the pace for our lives.

Over the past few years I have become interested in the Olympic sport of rowing. If you have ever watched a race, you have noticed something interesting. The crew members doing the rowing are sitting with their backs to the finish line.

What are the rowers looking at? Where are they directing their focus? To a person sitting in the back of the boat, called a shell. This person is the coxswain, who directs the rowers by calling out a cadence and thus setting the pace.

The responsibility of the rowers is to move in sync with the coxswain's cadence. They don't turn around and look at the finish line themselves. If they do that, they will break the rhythm and throw everyone else off.

In a rowing match, the coxswain is saying, "Look at me, listen to me. I have my eye on the finish line. I can see where we need to go to win. Let me set the pace for you."

We need to let Christ set the pace in our lives, because He knows where the finish line is. We need to trust Christ because He can direct us and get us to the finish line as winners. And He can make the race joyful while we're still in the thick of it.

THE JOY OF TRUSTING JESUS

Jesus Christ knows something about joy. The author of Hebrews said Jesus went to the Cross "for the joy set before Him" (Hebrews 12:2).

What joy was there for Jesus at Calvary as He hung suspended between heaven and earth for the sins of the world? The joy wasn't in the Cross itself. He "endured the cross." The joy was what He was accomplishing on the cross by providing redemption for the world.

I also believe the joy Jesus saw beyond the Cross was the joy of knowing that after His suffering, humiliation, and death, there awaited Him exaltation at the right hand of His Father in heaven, an exaltation above any honor anyone has ever received or will ever receive. That exaltation will someday be acknowledged and confessed by every human being on earth and every angelic being under the earth (Philippians 2:9–11). One day, all of creation will bow to Jesus Christ as King of kings and Lord of lords.

Jesus looked beyond the Cross and saw the throne. He looked beyond the pain to His resurrection and ascension and to the Father's welcome in heaven. Jesus joyfully accepted the Cross because it was the only way to get the crown.

But the joy the writer of Hebrews was talking about was not just for Jesus. As those who are learning to focus on Him and trust Him, we have a joy set before us too. It's the joy of taking up our cross daily and following Him no matter the temporary pain or suffering involved.

In other words, our joy is waiting for us beyond the cross too. That's why we don't want to focus on the people or the problems or the pain, but on Jesus. That's why we are to have the same attitude that He had (Philippians 2:5). When we look beyond the cross the way Jesus did, we will see the crown He has ready for those who are faithful to Him. With Jesus, the suffering leads to glory!

I'm a fan of the Olympic Games, as you can probably tell. I remember so well the way the U.S. gymnast Kerri Strug performed in the 1996 Summer Olympics held in Atlanta. You may have seen her incredible performance.

Kerri stood at the mark, waiting to make one of her runs and do a vault on the horse. She had to make a certain score to bring the U.S. women's team the gold medal. She ran and executed her vault, but she landed wrong and severely injured her ankle. As a result, her score was low, and she needed to do a better vault and bring her score up.

It seemed there was no way Kerri could make her last attempt. She could barely hobble. She had to be helped off the mat in obvious pain. But she still had another attempt to make if the team hoped to win the gold medal. No one could make the next vault for her. The tension was tremendous. I was on the edge of my seat at home. Would Kerri be able to perform?

Then something began to happen. The crowd started cheering and clapping for Kerri. Suddenly, there was a cloud of witnesses. People in the stands were waving American flags, cheering and yelling and chanting for Kerri to do it. Kerri had a cloud of witnesses saying, "You can do it!"

Kerri looked at the witnesses. But then she had to look at herself. She was in pain. She could barely walk on her ankle. She had made a mistake on her landing, and now she had to go back out there and put that mistake behind her. She couldn't allow herself to focus either on the pain in her ankle or the mistake she had made. She had to make her final attempt.

Was the crowd by itself enough to sustain Kerri? No. Was focusing on herself enough to overcome the pain and try again? No. In an interview afterward, Kerri said the key was when she focused on her coach.

When she saw him, she shut out the crowd and forgot

about the pain in her ankle, because her coach was telling her, "You can do it, Kerri. Do it for me." She decided to try again, not for the crowd or for herself, but for her coach.

If you saw what happened next, you know that Kerri Strug went back out to the floor, bad ankle and all. She stared at the horse, took off running as hard as she could, made her vault, and nailed a solid landing.

The crowd held its breath for a split second as the reality of what Kerri had accomplished sank in. She held her landing position just long enough to satisfy the judges, then she collapsed as the place went crazy. Kerri had won the Olympic gold medal for her team. She had endured the pain and gained the crown.

You can do that too! Never mind your past mistakes or your limitations. Just look to your Coach, Jesus Christ, who is telling you you can make it. He is saying, "Do it for Me." If you will obey Him and run the race, He will see that you receive the victor's crown. Keep your eyes on Jesus, and you'll make it!

CONCLUSION

Over the years, many celebrities have knelt on the sidewalk outside the Grummans Chinese restaurant in Los Angeles to leave their hand- and footprints in the cement on the Hollywood walk of fame.

Fans always gather to applaud their favorite stars as they leave their imprints. Those who qualify for a place on the walk of fame must have made a name for themselves—one that is recognized, respected, and even revered.

If that is the criterion, Jesus Christ would win hands down as deserving the top spot not just on some sidewalk, but the top spot in the universe. After all, when it comes to making a name, "God highly exalted Him, and bestowed on Him the name which is above every name, that at the name of Jesus every knee should bow . . . and that every tongue should confess that Jesus Christ is Lord, to the glory of God the Father" (Philippians 2:9–11).

The honor that Jesus Christ has gained for Himself will last for eternity. It includes not only human beings but angelic beings as well. Every person who has ever lived will bow in honor of Jesus Christ—either voluntarily in worship and submission, or involuntarily at the final judgment. But every knee will bow before the King of Glory. His position as Sovereign of the universe demands it.

Jesus Christ invites us to bow our knees and our hearts before Him as Savior and then follow Him as Lord over all of life. And then one day when we meet Him in heaven, we will walk down heaven's "walk of fame." But there will only be one set of hand- and footprints there, and they belong to the Lord Jesus Christ.

Those prints will bear the marks of nails, because He was nailed to the cross for our sins. As we see those nail-scarred hands and feet throughout eternity, we will be reminded that Jesus and Jesus alone is worthy of all praise, honor, and glory. We will pay eternal homage to Jesus Christ—the Celebrity of the universe, the mighty King of Glory, the Son of the living God. Amen and amen!

SUBJECT INDEX

Scripture Index

Moody Press, a ministry of Moody Bible Institute,
is designed for education, evangelization, and edification.
If we may assist you in knowing more about Christ
and the Christian life, please write us without obligation:
Moody Press, c/o MLM, Chicago, Illinois 60610.